The Yale Indian

NEW AMERICANISTS ❡ A SERIES EDITED BY DONALD E. PEASE

THE YALE INDIAN

The Education of Henry Roe Cloud

JOEL PFISTER

DUKE UNIVERSITY PRESS ❦ DURHAM & LONDON 2009

© 2009 Duke University Press

All rights reserved ❧ Printed in the United States of America on acid-free paper ∞

Designed by Jennifer Hill ❧ Typeset in Quadraat by Keystone Typesetting, Inc.

Library of Congress Cataloging-in-Publication Data appear

on the last printed page of this book.

For those waging the good fight.

The dead can sing and be with us.

JIMMIE DURHAM (Cherokee),
"Tarascan Guitars," in *Columbus Day* (1983)

CONTENTS

The Yale Indian explores the historical significance of some key chapters in the life of Henry Roe Cloud. He was a remarkable American Indian who migrated from a reservation to Yale and became a major Indian educator and leader in the early twentieth century. Before offering my introduction, I should tell the story of why I wanted to write this book and how it evolved.

The approach I take, as in my other books, is that of an American studies cultural historian and cultural critic. I have spent the past couple of decades investigating the historical shaping of family life, individuality, emotional investments, and the modern psychological self, structuring categories that many biographers leave unexamined. So while *The Yale Indian* invites readers to learn about episodes in the life of a fascinating and complex person, it is not a standard biographical effort that reconstructs a life from beginning to end. In the foreground of this book are important historical and theoretical matters that Roe Cloud's experience illuminates.

In its earliest incarnation, this project was one third of another book I wrote, *Individuality Incorporated: Indians and the Multicultural Modern* (2004). Some connections between the two books are worth mentioning, for neither would have been quite the same without the other. Both introduce conversations between Indian-white history and the history of the shaping of individuality and incentive. And both share the assumption that Indian-white history can make the American history of selfhood formation more complex and vice versa. In recent years some astute Native American studies scholars, including Gerald Vizenor (Anishinaabe), Arnold Krupat, Jace Weaver (Cherokee), Louis Owens (Choctaw and Cherokee), and Philip J. Deloria (Dakota Sioux) have advanced this conceptual and historical project in their own ways.

In September 1995, I commenced work in the Yale libraries and archives on the book that became *Individuality Incorporated*, resuming and expanding exploratory archival research I had begun as a graduate student in 1981. My 1981 foray into these archives on Indian-white history inspired my early interest in situating personal life in history. The delay in returning to this subject, 1981 to 1995, turned out to be fortunate because my initial books on the history of personal life, which did not focus on Indian-white history, had a profound influence on the concerns, problems, and questions I brought to *Individuality Incorporated* and *The Yale Indian*.

Part One of *Individuality Incorporated* revisits what first aroused my curiosity in 1981. It investigates what the Carlisle Industrial School for Indians (1879–1918) meant when it defined its mission, in the school's exact language, not just as "civilizing," "Americanizing," and "citizenizing" Indian students, but, even more extraordinary, as "individualizing" them. What, I wondered in the early 1980s, could *individualizing* possibly mean here? Weren't Indians already individuals? Aren't we all?

Carlisle didn't think so. It exhorted students to kill the tribal "Indian" within them so that they could be resurrected as "individuals" who would yearn to work, own private property, accumulate wealth, and lead a sentimental family life. Like many Americans, I had been educated in school and popular culture to believe that society influences, and often constrains, a precious inner essence sanctified as individuality. Movies, advertisements, literature, and politicians preached the gospel of individuality: Americans are mavericks who crave elbow room, make up their own minds, and are too unique to be standardized. But the more I delved into the history of individuality, the more I came to realize that modern corporations and advertisers invest heavily in persuading consumers to think about themselves as "individuals" and supply commodities that intensify and then address the need to be "individual." In one form or another, American social reproduction has long relied on mass-individualizing. The verb *individualize*, employed often by late-nineteenth- and early-twentieth-century white Indian reformers, dates back to the seventeenth century. This word names a socializing process and implies that individuality is not universal.

Carlisle imposed two identities on students—"Indian" and "individual" —that were in stark opposition to one another. It defined "Indian" as being lazy, dirty, conformist, and tribal. "Indianize," like individualize, also surfaced in the colonial period as a verb that described a socialization of identity (seventeenth-century colonizers feared being Indianized). The school Indianized students (imposing "Indian" stereotypes) to justify individualizing students (imposing "individuality" stereotypes) as the civilized solution. It expected "individuals" to be compliant skilled and semi-skilled workers who would blame themselves, not the system, when they failed.[1] Carlisle helped me better understand America as an individuality system, incentive system, worker-socialization system, and race-stratified class system.

In September 1993, I was only beginning to comprehend fragments of what I have just outlined. Still, when I met with the curator of Yale's Western Americana Collection in Beinecke Rare Book and Manuscripts Library that month to discuss the scope of my research interests, the cluster of critical concerns and questions I brought with me included Indians and the making of class identity. What, I mused, would a class history of Indians look like? I asked if Yale had other archives that could shed historical light on Indians who had entered universities and received different class trainings as professionalized "individuals." How would elite "individualizing" compare to what students encountered at Carlisle? The curator told me about an under-researched collection housed in another Yale library, Manuscripts and Archives. That other library contained extensive correspondence detailing aspects of the undergraduate experience of Henry Roe Cloud, the first American Indian who graduated from Yale, class of 1910. Judith Schiff, the Manuscripts and Archives chief research archivist, knew the archive in which Roe Cloud's materials were located (and later published a brief piece on them in the Yale Alumni Magazine 67 [Nov.–Dec. 2003]: 108). She had even had conversations with one of Roe Cloud's daughters in the late 1980s, when she visited Manuscripts and Archives to read her father's correspondence during his college and graduate-student years.

I undertook to study these letters, related writings, and photographs—thousands of pages in numerous boxes—with the idea that my research would become part of Individuality Incorporated, a chapter that would analyze how an elite university's efforts to individualize an Indian compared to what Indian students experienced in their industrial and grade-school training at Carlisle. I completed my first rough draft of a chapter on these

letters in 1996. As I kept working on the letters and other germane material, however, the chapter took on its own life, sometimes apart from the
themes that propelled Individuality Incorporated. So several years ago, as my
drafts of Individuality Incorporated continued to grow in scale, I excerpted
the chapter and began to transform it into what it deserved to be: a separate book. The dialogue between the kind of theoretical and historical
analyses I had done earlier in my career on the history of personal life with
the material in this archive turned out to be richer than I could ever have
imagined it would be.[2] It helped clarify ways in which "America" can be
analyzed not only as an economic and political system, but as interconnected reproductive processes of emotion making, race making, class
making, gender making, family making, and incentive making. The further exploration of these interconnected socializing processes is my main
conceptual goal in this book.

Henry Roe Cloud, however, became for me more than a historically
significant and complicated combination of social roles—Yale student,
member of a social class dominated by whites rulers, Indian educator,
white-collar Indian activist and bureaucrat. At the same time, I developed
an admiration for the man whose letters and writings opened up these
historical and theoretical issues in such illuminating ways. The letters I
studied were part of Roe Cloud's history and the history of those he loved.
Although his letters had been collected in folders with call numbers and
filed in boxes with call numbers, readily available to Yale students and
professional scholars—letters almost a century old, letters made public—
they were also letters connected to families back then and right now.

I first contacted two of Roe Cloud's descendants about my book in
March 2003, and eventually asked the descendants—there are many—for
permission to quote from Roe Cloud's letters. In 2005 and 2006, some
descendants read a couple of versions of the book manuscript, and the
responses I received have benefited my work on the book. In March 2006,
one descendant wrote an e-mail to other descendants that she also copied
to me and, based on her reading, offered some comments that I found
encouraging. However, a little over a month later, in April 2006, I received
an e-mail addressed to me from another descendant and copied to several
other descendants that declined to give me permission to quote from Roe
Cloud's letters. In this book I have respected that decision. Thus, in my

revisions I removed quotations from unpublished letters. Instead, I have described in my own words the statements made by Roe Cloud and the beliefs that they revealed without quoting the language he used except in rare instances where a term that he employed is necessary to accurately convey his perception of a relationship or the like. In a few instances, I have described photographs from the Roe family archive that I do not reproduce. I do include brief quotations from some of Roe Cloud's published work, and I have attempted overall to impart, both through those quotations and through my own descriptions, his eloquence, sensitivity, and humor. In addition, in my endnotes I have excised full citations of the letters and indicate only the date of composition.

The Roe family papers have been open for use at Yale since the early 1980s, and when I began work on this book a few Yale students had perused Roe Cloud's letters for research projects.[3] As I mentioned, Roe Cloud's daughter, the late Anne Woesha Cloud North, a professor of Native American studies, visited Manuscripts and Archives in 1989, read her father's letters, and was interviewed in the *Yale Bulletin*. Hence, at least one descendant became aware of the contents of this archive two decades ago. The descendants with whom I have communicated could contribute a volume of their own on Roe Cloud and his talented family.

Jason M. Tetzloff's dissertation on Roe Cloud, submitted in 1996, is a biography. His study, unlike mine, is a more standard Native American studies biographical approach to Roe Cloud and has some different emphases. Both projects advance the historical study of Roe Cloud, though they do not have identical premises about the scope of history that merits analysis.[4] His dissertation includes a half-dozen or so pages in sequence on Roe Cloud's experience at Yale and a paragraph on the complex sentimental relationship between Roe Cloud and Mary Wickham Roe (my work on these topics makes up about two-thirds of this book). The vast majority of the thousands of pages of Roe Cloud–related correspondence in the Roe family archive are Roe Cloud's exchanges with a white missionary couple, Dr. Walter Clark Roe and Mary Wickham Roe.

The Yale Indian takes as its concern a wide range of issues uncircumscribed by field: not only Indian reservations, Indian boarding schools, tribal cultures, the rise of pan-Indian groups such as the Society of American Indians, the Bureau of Indian Affairs, the shift from Protestant-assimilationist reformism to Indian New Deal bureaucratic-pluralism, and changing styles of Indian activism, but also the literature of the cult of domesticity, the ascendancy of sentimental discourses, the gospel of self making, literary critiques of Manifest Destiny imperialism, the history of the white middle-class family, the emergence of pop psychological discourse, the transformation of elite universities, and the development of the professional and managerial class. To formulate my questions and arguments, I had to consider not just writings by Indians such as Zitkala-Ša, Charles Eastman, Henry Roe Cloud, Luther Standing Bear, and John Joseph Mathews, but works by Helen Hunt Jackson, Henry Adams, William James, W. E. B. Du Bois, and Booker T. Washington. In *The Yale Indian*, Native American studies and American studies join forces.[5] It is Henry Roe Cloud's life and higher educations, boundary-crossing in so many ways, that led me to connect the history of Indians to the history of class and to the history of family life. His evolving lesson plan challenges us to study what he was obliged to learn.

ACKNOWLEDGMENTS

In 2000, the Rockefeller Foundation awarded me a fellowship that enabled me to work on the project that evolved into *Individuality Incorporated* and *The Yale Indian* at the beautiful Villa Serbelloni on Lake Como in Bellagio, Italy. I am thankful for having had this magical experience. Wesleyan University granted me several sabbaticals and leaves during the years I have researched and written this book. I have benefited a great deal from Wesleyan's continuing commitment to fostering interdisciplinary research. As usual, the reference librarians at Wesleyan and Yale have been incomparable. It was the inimitable George Miles, the William Robertson Coe Curator of the Western Americana Collection at Yale's Beinecke Rare Book Library, who in September 1995 told me about the Henry Roe Cloud letters in Yale's Manuscripts and Archives. When I migrated to Manuscripts and Archives, directly after my long talk with George, my old friend, Judith Schiff, the chief research archivist, welcomed me, and, as usual, was magnanimous and even lent me some relevant material that she had collected. Judy, an expert on Yale history as well as the Roe family papers, pointed me in important directions throughout my research.

My primary debt is to Lisa Wyant, love of my life. She is an extraordinary writer. Over the past few years she has read and made better several complete versions of *The Yale Indian*. I value her love, intelligence, creativity, and humor. My mom, Elizabeth Pfister, read and improved a draft in 2000. Sarah Winter read the first draft of the chapter that grew into this book in 1996 and has perused numerous drafts since then. Yet again, I have relied on and learned from her perspicuous editing and critical perspectives. Richard Slotkin and Indira Karamcheti, two Wesleyan colleagues, read early drafts and shared their wisdom with me. I had some superb conversations about the project with my former colleague Dorothy Wang in 1999.

Arnold Krupat and Bryan Wolf were smart and helpful readers of one of this book's earlier incarnations. Christina Berndt, who taught Native American Studies at Wesleyan's Center for the Americas, lent me material on early films about American Indians that I have found useful. Ande Diaz sent me some information about the history of Indians at Harvard. Laura Wexler and Werner Sollors directed me to additional readings about W. E. B. Du Bois and other African Americans at Harvard. Lisa Wyant put me in touch with her Stanford friend, Janeen Antoine, who gave me helpful feedback. Tom Hampson, Woesha Hampson, and Colin Hampson have offered me insights that have been useful. Exchanges with Chris McNeil and Melissa Butterfield have influenced the project in productive ways.

Reynolds Smith is not only a great executive editor at Duke University Press, he is an absolutely fabulous person. It has been my great fortune to have worked with him again. I am honored to see this book published in Donald Pease's pathbreaking New Americanists series. I thank Don for his patience and steadfast commitment to expanding the range of American studies. And I thank the entire Duke staff for their expert production of this book. Mark A. Mastromarino, assistant managing editor, served as an exemplary copyeditor. The royalties of *The Yale Indian*, like those of *Individuality Incorporated*, go to the American Indian College Fund.

CHAPTERS IN THE EDUCATION OF HENRY ROE CLOUD

Indians have no easy choices.

LEONARD PELTIER
(Ojibway and Dakota Sioux), *Prison Writings:
My Life Is My Own Dance* (2000)

We are red men still, even though we have plucked the feathers
from our war bonnets and are using them for pens. The battle scene
has shifted and the contest becomes one of brains and wit.

ARTHUR PARKER
(Iroquois-Seneca), 1913

HENRY ROE CLOUD (c. 1884–1950) is not honored in Indian museums
or dramatized in films as is the intrepid Sioux hero Crazy Horse. Yet both
were holy men of enduring courage, integrity, dignity, and spirit. In different eras and different ways, each inspired and empowered Indians who
knew them. Roe Cloud belonged to the Winnebago Bear Clan, whose
clansmen, among other things, "guard[ed] the village" and the sacred
warbundles and "took charge of the whole tribe when it was on the warpath." The great anthropologist Paul Radin, who first studied the Winnebago when Roe Cloud attended college and graduate school, singles out
the preeminent traditional value for males: "To be a successful warrior
was the highest ideal of a Winnebago."[1] Roe Cloud's battles, more modern than the kind Crazy Horse fought, were cultural, ideological, educational, and bureaucratic. He challenged entrenched conventions and
stereotypes that often passed for knowledge in his efforts to help resignify
"Indian"—what Indians could want to be, know, and do for the good of
their people. The cultural and bureaucratic forces mounted against his
efforts, like the land-grabbing armies faced by Crazy Horse, were legion.[2]

For in the late nineteenth century and early twentieth, the vast majority of Indians who entered, or were forced to enter, the federal educational system received no more than a few years of instruction evenly divided between grade-school study and "industrial" training in manual labor. Bearing such constraints in mind, one might think that historians would have been more curious about a Winnebago who migrated from his reservation to shine at one of the most elite universities in the country, who distinguished himself as the most vocal and compelling advocate of Indian higher education, and who won considerable eminence among Indians and non-Indians across the continent. If historians of Indians and the West so much as mention Roe Cloud, it is typically while discussing the influential Meriam Report, *The Problem of Indian Administration* (1928), a catalyst for the government's major reform of Indian affairs in the Indian New Deal. The report's ten co-authors, which included Roe Cloud, criticized the economic, social, and cultural effects of the division of reservation land into privately owned allotments, the substandard state education of Indian children, the government's impoverishment of Indian families, inadequate reservation health care, and related matters. Historians cite Roe Cloud's Winnebago identity, as if the report automatically gains enhanced legitimacy because of it. This pious nod, however, does not pause to take notice of Roe Cloud's remarkable life.[3] The other thing historians tend to say in scholarly sound bites about Roe Cloud is that he went to Yale. "A Yale graduate," one historian notes in passing, "his main concern was Indian education."[4]

In brief, in 1910 Roe Cloud earned distinction as the first full-blood Indian to graduate from Yale College. He had moved from the Winnebago reservation to Indian schools to Mount Hermon and then to Yale at a time when this transit was all but unimaginable. After graduating from Yale, Roe Cloud spent a year at Oberlin Seminary College and then transferred to the prestigious Auburn Theological Seminary (later absorbed by Union Theological Seminary) where he received his Bachelor of Divinity degree. He also completed his Yale master's degree in anthropology in 1914, thus making him the first full-blood Indian to receive a graduate degree from Yale. The following year Roe Cloud became a founder of the American Indian Institute, a private college preparatory school for Indians. Then in the 1930s and 1940s he worked in several capacities for the Bureau of

Indian Affairs. In that momentous Indian New Deal phase, which ushered in so many progressive reforms in educational policies as well as in other areas, he served as superintendent of Haskell Indian School for two years. His national reputation grew during the 1930s. In 1932 he was awarded an honorary Doctor of Divinity degree by the College of Emporia. And in 1935 the Indian Council Fire, based in Chicago, bestowed on him its third annual Indian Achievement medal—the prolific autobiographer Dr. Charles Eastman (Santee Sioux) was the first to receive this honor; the world-renowned potter Marie Martinez (Pueblo) the second; and the ethnologist and museum director Arthur C. Parker (Iroquois and Seneca) the fourth. In 1939 Roe Cloud returned to a reservation as superintendent of the Umatilla Agency in Oregon. Nine years later he accepted a post as regional representative in Portland. In 1950, while assisting Indians who had won a $16,000,000 court claim involving a land dispute, he died of heart failure.[5]

Roe Cloud endeavored to put higher education for Indians first on the philanthropists' and later on the government's agenda. He voiced a good measure of the Meriam Report's late-1920s outrage about the disgraceful state of the under-education of Indians while he was still at Yale and shortly after. In 1914 he protested that while census figures estimated that one in every three hundred Americans attends college, only a minute fraction of the Indian population was college bound. Many of the few who made it to and through the university, he suggested, had to *overcome* the ill effects of government boarding schools.[6] Roe Cloud's campaign resonates with that of W. E. B. Du Bois, who even in 1940 debunked the idea that "higher Negro education" actually existed, "[for] not more than three Negro institutions in the South deserve the name of 'college' at all." Du Bois had studied at Harvard College and graduate school, and, like Roe Cloud, recognized the racist premise underlying this strangulation of opportunity: "Why encourage a young colored man toward such higher training?"[7]

To resist this injustice, Du Bois insisted that African Americans would have to nurture a "Talented Tenth" comprised of "the best and most capable of their youth" who were "schooled in the colleges and universities of the land." Members of the "Talented Tenth" would have to commit themselves to regenerating not just themselves but the African American community by training teachers, educating leaders, and teaching students about the possibilities of "life," not just labor. This elite core could help uplift the race not simply by schooling young people in skilled and semi-skilled jobs—Booker T. Washington's strategy—but by educating many more to enter a higher "social class" and gain access to elevated levels of social power.[8] Roe Cloud was a major contributor to efforts to form an Indian "Talented Tenth" and spoke eloquently about the need to open colleges to Indians.

In 1944 a full-page newspaper profile paid homage to what Roe Cloud accomplished with his elite "higher training." The *Sunday Oregonian* featured Margaret Thompson's "From Wigwam to Mr. Bigwig," which played on the title of an autobiographical essay that Roe Cloud wrote a few years after he left Yale, "From Wigwam to Pulpit." Roe Cloud's self-ironic, big-hearted humor no doubt savored the mock-pompous appellation, Mr. Bigwig.

The article's Indianized Horatio Alger headline, printed in bold, made his life and struggles sound easy: "Dr. Henry Roe Cloud Lifted Himself by Moccasin Strings to Acquire Education and Become Spokesman for All Indians." Paradoxically, Roe Cloud's sparklingly dignified professional manner made him appear, to Thompson and in her mind to others, manifestly qualified to speak for "All Indians" because he did not seem stereotypically "Indian": "Broad shoulders with twinkling brown eyes and gray hair, the doctor is a fine-looking man, a man of quiet assurance and undeniable charm, and casual acquaintance with him would cause most people to assume that his success followed the well-defined pattern of most business and professional men."

Perhaps the most curious aspect of this biographical sketch is that in several instances it depicts Roe Cloud, not John Collier, President Franklin Delano Roosevelt's controversial and innovative Commissioner of Indian Affairs, as the driving intellectual force behind the conceptualization of the Indian New Deal. From 1931 to 1933 Roe Cloud, it states, prepared "a plan for Indian rehabilitation, a plan which under the official title of Indian Reorganization act, was passed by congress in 1934." The praise flows on: "In all probability, [Roe Cloud] is personally responsible for greater improvement in the immediate conditions affecting the American Indian than any other individual." This hosanna concludes on an unexplained elegiac note that seems to excuse Roe Cloud from not having been even more of a "Roe Cloud success story": "His has been a large dream. There may be times when he feels he should be doing more to make it a reality. It is possible, however, that his dream was too far-reaching for any one man to accomplish, too wide-spread for any life to span."[9]

Roe Cloud may have felt that he should have done more, or felt that he was prevented from doing more. His life surely was a "success story" in many ways.[10] Roe Cloud was not only preeminent in the history of Indian education and in the history of Indians in the Bureau of Indian Affairs, he was a key contributor to the formation of an Indian professional and managerial class (what Thompson termed "business and professional" men and women).[11] He was one of the founders of the Society of American Indians, a group of Indians who tried to assign social, cultural, and in some degree class distinction to Indianness. The very existence of the Society of American Indians testifies to some of the ways in which tribes were dealing with internal social divisions indicative of class and economic hierarchies in the larger society.

Class is too often ignored in a mass-mediated America whose myths frequently depict the nation as classless. And class is a social division and production of identity that is even more frequently unobserved—unanalyzed—in the history of American Indians. Some historians, such as Hazel Hertzberg, Devon Mihesuah (Choctaw), and K. Tsianina Lomawaima (Creek), have sought to correct this tendency. Class must be understood as more than an economic category. As Eugene Genovese wrote long ago, "social classes" should be "considered not only as representative of specific material interests but as complexes of goals, cultural assumptions, and social and psychological relationships." One of the presentations that Roe Cloud made to the Society of American Indians alluded to economically based social divisions emerging among Indians. His example was of an Indian who refuses to shop at a new store owned by a fellow Indian and instead prefers to patronize a white "grafter['s]" establishment because he feels that the Indian businessman "is trying to set himself above me." Thinking about the ideological and emotional as well as economic ramifications of such social changes among Indians, he voices the need to "overcome this prejudice among our own people."[12]

Often impressive histories of Indians relegate the study of Indian class formations to the background, sometimes by using terms other than class

—Indian leaders, Indian intellectuals—to describe what is partly class development or class identity construction. In his "Introduction: Twentieth-Century Warriors" to the illuminating volume of essays he edited, *The New Warriors: Native American Leaders since 1900* (2001), R. David Edmunds (Eastern Cherokee) sets the scene for contributors' essays on Charles Curtis (Kaw), D'Arcy McNickle (Metis-Flathead), Ben Nighthorse Campbell (Northern Cheyenne), and others, though he does not reflect explicitly on how some of these leaders belonged to an emerging class of activists who relied partly on class networking in their labors for Indians.[13] Two excellent books that follow up on and expand Hertzberg's pathbreaking 1971 study, Lucy Maddox's *Citizen Indian: Native American Intellectuals, Race, and Reform* (2005) and Joy Porter's *To Be Indian: The Life of Iroquois-Seneca Arthur Caswell Parker* (2001), observe that Arthur Parker and other members of the Society of American Indians were middle class and that there were tensions between these elite Indians and more traditionalist Indians on reservations (who cannot be described as middle class). While neither Maddox nor Porter highlights Indian class formation as their main object of study (neither includes "class" or "middle class" as entries in the index), both offer rich evidence and insights that make it clear that for many prominent early twentieth-century Indians the battle to be respected as intellectuals was also often the struggle to be seen as belonging to a class.

One can appreciate the pragmatism of this early-twentieth-century class-access tactic when considering the functional role that white-Indian warfare had long played in the stabilization and obfuscation of class conflict in the United States. Analyzing the various ways in which military and ideological wars against Indians (involving land theft) operated as a "symbolic surrogate" or safety valve for other "social and political conflicts," Richard Slotkin concludes: "By projecting the 'fury' of class resentment outward against the Indian, the American expands his nation's resources and thereby renders class struggle unnecessary. All the antipathies that make for Revolutionary Terror and/or dictatorial oppression in Europe are projected onto the American savage, who becomes the only obstacle to the creation of a perfect republic." The displacement of class antagonism onto Indians, however, became more complicated after the Indian wars ended. Frederick Jackson Turner declared in 1893 that the "frontier" had closed.[14] Gilded Age and Progressive Era Indians were increasingly utilized for other class purposes. Government boarding schools tried to funnel Indian youth into the class system as skilled and semi-skilled workers and christened this "Americanization." Grasping the ways in which the American power structure that ruled Indians was indeed a class structure, Roe Cloud and other college-trained Indians struggled to gain a foothold in the dominant classes to more effectively advocate for Indians. They endeavored to turn the very class system that had positioned Natives as scapegoats to Indian advantage on modern legal, political, cultural, and educational battlefields. Rather than relinquishing their Indian identity, many acquired class status to expand their range of social agency as Indians.

As Roe Cloud's career makes apparent, Indians' associations with academic institutions helped authorize their inventions of a twentieth-century white-collar Indian activism. They sought to confer social distinction not only on themselves but on the reforms they backed. Roe Cloud met with President Taft on behalf of the Winnebago in between his undergraduate and graduate study at Yale. Parker and other society members met with President Wilson a few years later. Cultural activism, political activism, intellectual activism, and class activism were symbiotic in their white-collar efforts.

At the same time, if Parker enjoyed networking with successful white academics and bureaucrats, he also traveled to reservations at his own expense to learn about the condition of Indians (and he wondered whether this would "bankrupt" him). As editor of the Society of American Indians' *Quarterly Journal* he estimated that he had helped send "50,000 pieces of mail" and "12,000 personal letters" to resolve "many thousand dollars worth of claims for Indians, without charging a single penny." The Society of American Indians sent its journal not just to libraries but to reservations. Numerous Indians like Roe Cloud and Parker tried to gain access to the halls of power to use power not just for themselves or members of their elite group-in-the-making but to help Indians who had no such access.[15]

White-collar Indian activists, such as Roe Cloud and Parker, had to grasp class dynamics, class feelings, class self-images, class sentiments, class prestige, and other class ideologies to battle effectively. If Roe Cloud and some of his contemporaries made it their business to understand how the formation of class identity might relate to Indians, *so must we*. To ignore this is to fail to learn from and appreciate the range of strategies that early-twentieth-century Indians implemented. Roe Cloud's Yale correspondence contains valuable and fascinating historical evidence about one Indian's reflections, written to privileged whites, about an elite university education that provided him not only with knowledge, but with entrée, or what seemed like entrance, into a class.[16]

Many of his letters, speeches, and articles exhibit what appears to be a class outlook. As a young man Roe Cloud's stated interest in transforming Indians into perseverant workers—a concern common among many white Indian reformers, missionaries, government school employees, and Bureau of Indian Affairs administrators—bears the marks not only of his immersion in popular self-help doctrines but of his professional and managerial class training. Roe Cloud sometimes made this case strategically to wealthy whites who would be likely to respond favorably to this Indian employment rationale and thus support Indian-run Indian education. It is important always, when reading Roe Cloud's letters and publications, to keep in mind the specific groups of readers—philanthropists, white upper-middle-class Protestant advocates of Indian assimilation, Yale students and alumni, his Indian students—to whom his words were directed.

At the same time, it is also crucial to appreciate that Roe Cloud rose through educational and bureaucratic systems in which he distinguished himself as a performer, not just intellectually, but socially. By performer I mean someone who, without undermining his characteristic sincerity, could understand numerous cultural languages and play several cultural roles. Maddox has emphasized that the manifold Indian performances for whites that recycled stereotypes—most obviously in venues such as Wild West shows, civic fairs, and Indian lectures—remain performances "by Indians," often to whites "who were ill equipped to recognize Indianness as anything but a performative role." She has productively extended the notion of Indian performances to the "multiple forms of address . . . including the address of Indian intellectuals to white elites." Indian intellectuals, she argues, sometimes "co-opted" these imposed roles, "working to take the control of performance away from the white managers." Therefore, Luther Standing Bear (Lakota Sioux), and one could say the same of Charles Eastman, wrote his books recognizing that most white readers were "incapable of fully understanding Native ideologies, individual Indian subjectivities, or the centrality of Indian histories and cultures to the formation of the country."[17]

To change metaphors, Roe Cloud could see through and act within what Philip J. Deloria terms "complex set[s] of cultural frames." Deloria's comments about his grandfather, Vine Deloria Sr., also could apply to Roe Cloud: "Each context—Indian and non-Indian—required a slightly different cultural strategy." Roe Cloud was as effective in speaking in the Sioux or Winnebago language to tribal councils in the 1930s as he was regaling Yale students with quotations from Goethe or white middle-class Protestant reformers with Biblical references. He had to be strategic about controlling not only what he said but how he was perceived so as to gain some power from those who held power over Indians. Roe Cloud mastered a range of class-based cultural styles and emotional rules.[18] If Roe Cloud sometimes tactically, not so unlike Carlisle's students, performed individuality and performed assimilation, he may also have performed upper-middle-class identity and performed reformer, espousing eloquently what Maddox terms the "language of reform."[19]

Thus, the "Roe Cloud success story" raises many questions about class —and the Indian uses of class identity, prestige, and ideology on behalf of Indians in their dealings with dominant white groups. To what extent is the formation of upper classes within racial groups, sometimes over-simply classified as "leadership" development, able to ameliorate racial discrimination? And in what ways do such class formations risk reproducing aspects of the very power structures that are invested in racialized socioeconomic, political, and cultural division? These are vital considerations in the history of Indian power and status acquisition. Roe Cloud's lifelong commitments to Indian welfare, education, and dignity contribute to understanding Indian class mobility as a means to a larger end: service to his people. His life highlights aspects of an Indian revision of professional and managerial class identity. For, as I will elaborate below, Roe Cloud, before becoming the Yale Indian, was and remained the Winnebago Indian.

Most studies of Indian education have focused on government boarding schools, and for good reason. Such institutions too rarely equipped or encouraged Indian students to go on to study at other schools—principally set up to teach white students—that would prepare them for college.[20]

The most celebrated government boarding school was the Carlisle Industrial School for Indians, located in western Pennsylvania. Captain Richard Henry Pratt founded the school in 1879 and served as its superintendent from its inception to 1904.[21]

Occasionally I will compare Roe Cloud's instruction in social class at Yale to the kind of training in social class that students negotiated at Carlisle. Yale groomed Roe Cloud to be a certain kind of cultural and emotional "individual" and a worker who would envision himself as a manager of men. Yale and Carlisle, notwithstanding some similarity in self-help rhetoric, sponsored very different constructions of incentive and subjective power. As late-nineteenth-century observers might have said, the two institutions *individualized* their students differently.

Roe Cloud knew Carlisle and was quite critical of it, partly because Pratt had subordinated religion as a central component of his industrial training program. As mentioned, early in his career Roe Cloud, like Pratt, dedicated himself, not least of all when soliciting white backing, to considering how Indians might best be transformed into motivated workers whose steady labor would make them less dependent administratively and financially on the state (though more drawn into the economy's labor-and-consumption system). But he regarded religion as far more effective at producing incentive, and cultural agency, than anything Carlisle had tried. As a young man Roe Cloud saw the utility of spiritualizing Indians, who struggled to survive often in brutal conditions, and, putting an economic slant on spiritualizing, tactically made it part of his sales pitches to supporters of the high school he ran, the American Indian Institute. In his own Indian and evangelical way, Roe Cloud reflected on the "connection[s]" between what Karl Marx termed "spiritual production and material production." His success story invites reconsiderations of the roles that spiritualizing played in shaping consciousness, ambition, and the work ethic—links that the great social theorist Max Weber posited, just before Roe Cloud entered Yale, between the Protestant ethos and the infusion of spiritual energy into capitalist incentive.[22]

In a few instances Roe Cloud's story brings up some differences between the Indian and African American social experience, especially in higher education. Early-twentieth-century ethnologists ascribed different evolutionary status to Indians and African Americans, favoring the former. It is understandable why some Indians saw themselves as better cultural prospects than African Americans for class mobility and roles as leaders.[23] Roe Cloud's education introduced him to anthropology's assumptions and debates about racial groups and their intellectual potential. In at least one case, which I shall discuss, he was discriminated against as if he were black—and resented it. Two prestigious Indian organizations to which Roe Cloud belonged, the Society of American Indians and the Indian Council Fire, had members who sought to exclude Indians who were part African American, though not those who were part white. (Arthur Parker, one of Roe Cloud's distinguished Indian contemporaries, disapproved of Indian intermarriage with blacks.)[24]

Sometimes I have found it useful to compare what Roe Cloud wrote about his experience at Yale to what Du Bois recalled about his schooling at Harvard, which took place more than a decade earlier. In doing so I am in no way suggesting that the historical forces that shaped them were identical. Du Bois's commentaries on his training at Harvard open illuminating perspectives on and questions about some of what is present in and absent from Roe Cloud's archived accounts of his Yale years. On occasion I also turn to Frantz Fanon, a black Antillean anticolonialist who studied psychiatry in Paris and practiced in Algiers, and Albert Memmi, a white Tunisian Jewish anticolonialist who also studied in Paris, for some insights.[25] Here too I do not wish to suggest that these authors, both of whom published the critical works I draw on not too long after Roe Cloud died, are responding to a uniform colonialism identical to what Roe Cloud and other Indians confronted in various locations and circumstances during the late-nineteenth century and early twentieth. Rather, some of their reflections, like some of Du Bois's observations, though shaped by some different conditions, help clarify aspects of Roe Cloud's predicaments, challenges, and achievements.

Roe Cloud's career—from Yale to the American Indian Institute to Bureau of Indian Affairs administration—spans the uneven transformation of American capitalism from what historians term an industrial producer culture, the work ethos and character-building precepts of which were evident in Roe Cloud's self-help reading, to a corporate consumer culture, which deemed some expressions of ethnoracial diversity profitable. This complex and often contradictory shift involved some back-and-forth movement from melting-pot ideologies that defined Americanizing as assimilation to more pluralist protomulticultural ideologies that sought to "modernize" Indians more effectively by acknowledging their diverse cultural identities. I employ the word protomulticultural to place emphasis on the fact that the government's changing strategies of managing Indians starting in the early 1930s was not simply pluralist in attitude; these New Deal policies institutionalized values, identities, economic supports, and educational reforms commonly associated with the multiculturalism of the 1960s and later.[26]

Roe Cloud's developing philosophy and strategies as an educator were informed by this shift in assimilation tactics and policies. While the Indian New Deal to which Roe Cloud contributed helped pioneer protomulticultural education, work, and bureaucracy, it remained a form of the government's control, sometimes the overt domination, of Indians.[27] Even before the New Deal, Roe Cloud distinguished himself as a pluralist and supported the teaching of some Indian cultural traditions in school. But like many other cosmopolitan Indians in his class, he evinced no willingness to enact what some whites stereotyped as traditional Indianness—in some of its manifestations, tourist-industry Indianness. Roe Cloud could have said what Parker wrote: "If the educated Indian or persons of Indian blood have no more stamina than to continue to play the carved wooden 'cigar store Indian' to sell tobacco for another man's profit—he is poorly educated indeed."[28] Consequently, this dignified and good-humored Winnebago Yalie tried to reimagine what contemporary Indian identity could be as he struggled both to win cultural respect for some Indian traditions and to establish opportunities for some Indians to go to college.

For all these reasons, Roe Cloud's strategic efforts merit not just much more historical recognition but more historical analysis than they have received. Roe Cloud's correspondence is worthy of historical analysis for another reason. In autumn 1906, the first term of Roe Cloud's freshman year in college, Mary Wickham Roe (1863–1941), a white, upper-middle-class missionary who worked principally with the Cheyenne, Arapaho, and Apache in Oklahoma Territory, lectured at Yale on her and her husband's evangelical work. She was an inspiring speaker. After the talk Roe Cloud's exchange with her was so engaging that he wound up devoting his summers to working with Mary and her husband, Dr. Walter Clark Roe (1859–

1913), in Oklahoma and on the Winnebago reservation.[29] She was then in her mid-forties, while Roe Cloud was in his mid-twenties. Roe Cloud continued to work with the Roes and in affectionate acknowledgment of his informal adoption by them changed his middle name from Clarence to Roe during his Yale years.

Although some prominent, highly educated middle- and upper-middle-class Indians endeavored to serve their people as cross-cultural "brokers," as Hazel Hertzberg observed, this often brought with it not just "prestige" but "difficult inner conflicts."[30] The Roe Cloud–Roe correspondence records much more than Roe Cloud's responses to his undergraduate setting. For during his college years and for several years after he graduated, the mother and son letters suggest that they developed a deep, cross-culturally complex, highly sentimentalized, melodramatic affection for one another. In some instances their epistolary dialogues took on a romantic-sentimentalism that I will analyze in chapter 2. Because of their intimate relationship, occasionally I will refer to Roe Cloud as Henry, Mrs. Roe as Mary, and Dr. Roe as Walter. What makes the Roe Cloud–Roe tie historically significant is not just the racial, class, gender, and religious power dynamics, but the informal mother-son power dynamic that contoured it. Yet their bond was touching and loving, more life-enhancing than the sentimentalized infiltration of power. Till the end of her life Henry called his dear friend and supporter his mother.

History involves more than educational institutions, government bureaucracies, investigative surveys, and fundraising, all of which make up the more obvious historical elements of the "Roe Cloud success story." In addition, history includes the social structures of the familial and emotional relations that sometimes consciously, sometimes unconsciously, help make us who we are and want to be. History pulses through the head and the heart and shapes "inner conflicts."[31] The Roe Cloud–Roe correspondence has complex historical value because it offers insights into a gifted Winnebago's interactions not only with Yale, but with an early twentieth-century white upper-middle-class sentimental and psychological family that, along with Yale, influenced his emotional bearing, incentive, self-monitoring, and self-image, and, not always by design, partly educated him in how to perform affectively as well as intellectually in the social class he entered, navigated, and needed to use. That is, the cultural codes, the racial and class codes, imprinted in the social behavior that surrounded Roe Cloud communicated not just intellectual issues or codes of conduct but sentimental systems of emotions. Such racial, class, and emotional codes provided him with access to power and a chance to educate, and perhaps even heal, not simply Indians but members of dominant groups that oppressed Indians. "A basic absence of archival evidence," one historian of Indian-white relations acknowledges, makes it challenging to recover this intimate dimension of history.[32] This general scarcity of archival evidence is one of several reasons why the extensive Roe Cloud–Roe correspondence is precious.

My goal in this book, as well as in my other books, is to understand history and social forces so that we can better comprehend how we have been situated and reassess our capacities to make a better world. As noted in the preface, for several decades now one of my contributions has been to trace the workings of history, culture, and ideology not only in the public sphere but in the so-called private sphere, in socially rooted systems of emotions, in cultural constructions of a self experienced as "inner." Cultural forms of family life and emotional investments must be fathomed if one is to discern some of the more subtle ways in which power structures have reproduced themselves and have been resisted.

I have divided the biographical, historical, and theoretical reflections that follow into three chapters, each of which focuses on some, not all, of the key experiences in Roe Cloud's life. Chapter 1, "Yale Education," explores his archived Yale correspondence and the formation of his ambition. It also considers Roe Cloud's role in the Society of American Indians and its class-influenced resignification of Indianness. Chapter 2, "Sentimentalized Education," examines the historical importance of Roe Cloud's relationship with the Roes, especially Mary Roe, who attempted to channel his emotional investments. This chapter extends the theoretical as well as historical scope of the cross-cultural American history of emotional life. Chapter 3, "Cultural Incentive-and-Activism Education," surveys some developments in Roe Cloud's career as an educator and Bureau of Indian Affairs administrator. It moves from a study of his somewhat pluralistic self-help approach in the American Indian Institute to his involvement in the reform of the government's Indian policy and finally to his service as a more critical protomulticultural superintendent of Haskell Indian School.

It was at Haskell that Roe Cloud tried to sponsor some training not just in industrial vocations, the standard state emphasis, but in cultural activism.[33] I also examine some of the tensions between Roe Cloud and John Collier, the head of the Indian New Deal. Collier's many critiques of Indian policy helped clear the way for Roe Cloud's criticisms. Yet some evidence of friction between them suggests part of what Roe Cloud's advocacy of higher education was up against, even when dealing with some "liberal" white Indianists.

Long before Roe Cloud underwent a Yale education, a sentimentalized education with the Roes, and a protracted bureaucratic education in the limitations of the Presbyterian church's and federal government's support for Indians and Indian education, he received a Winnebago education.[34] Before developing this point, I will note again that the archives covering aspects of Roe Cloud's Yale years are invaluable because of the paucity of scholarship on Indians at elite universities in the early twentieth century. Yale's class and intellectual status helped Roe Cloud gain access to powerful Americans in religious circles, white reform groups, the Bureau of Indian Affairs, and Indian organizations such as the Society of American Indians and the Indian Council Fire. As I said above, in 1912 Roe Cloud headed a Winnebago delegation to the White House, where he conferred with President William Howard Taft, a Yale alumnus, whose son Robert had been Roe Cloud's Yale classmate. Such access, Roe Cloud knew, was not generally available to Indians who never left the reservation. Roe-Cloud-the-reformer was a class activist unafraid to involve himself with Yale's power elite, the Protestant power elite, and the bureaucratic power elite to try to get the job done.[35] He wanted more Indians to venture into the white world of power and assume power to aid their people (for that power had a huge impact on reservation life). His association with Yale offered him not just class legitimacy but cultural and political visibility. More than this, Roe Cloud was intellectually curious: he clearly treasured much of what he learned at Yale and in the white world. He did not suppress his Indian identity; rather he developed and manifested it in relation to his twentieth-century cross-cultural interactions. The Yale Indian puts these under-researched concerns high on the scholarly agenda.

Of course, the Yale years, crucial years, were not the only formative years in Roe Cloud's life. The impressive charmer whom Thompson nomi-

nated Mr. Bigwig was first a Winnebago Indian. Roe Cloud had a Winnebago family and upbringing. Furthermore, he spent considerable time
on the Winnebago reservation after his boyhood. It is easier to assert this
than it is to grasp the details of its causal and lifelong significance, for Roe
Cloud chose to publish fairly little about his Winnebago experience other
than "From Wigwam to Pulpit." Even this autobiographical essay, which
circulated in Presbyterian and missionary circles in the mid-1910s, concen-
trates much attention on his boyhood conversion to Christianity. Nor does
Roe Cloud's correspondence with the Roes dwell on his foundational
Winnebago education—his tribal intellectual, emotional, cultural, ethical,
and spiritual education. Chapters 1 and 2 examine historical aspects of the
Winnebago context. But Roe Cloud's decision not to ruminate on his
Winnebago formation at length in his archived writing and publications
do make it challenging to specify how this socialization affected his cross-
cultural negotiations.

In thinking about Roe Cloud's Winnebago origins, it is useful to ponder one of the many illuminating points that Eastman makes in *Indian
Heroes and Great Chieftains* (1918): tribes have diverse members. "I am conscious that many readers may think that I have idealized the Indian. Therefore I will confess now that we have too many weak and unprincipled men
among us." Among Sioux leaders, Spotted Tail exhibited the "desire to
accumulate property"; Little Crow "was intensely ambitious"; American
Horse was not humble and loved "notoriety"; Sitting Bull was "affable and
genial" to his tribe and "boastful and domineering" toward white Americans; Crazy Horse was "reserved and modest," though assumed leadership when danger threatened; Rain-in-the-Face "remained silent" and
stoical in defeat. Some Sioux were transformed by historical pressures
and became possessive and self-interested in response to a predicament
against which resistance seemed futile.[36] "Winnebago," like "Sioux," was
not a timeless essence unaffected by historical change (indeed, in 1994 the
Winnebago officially altered their name to Ho-Chunk Nation; however, I
shall use the term Roe Cloud employed to describe his tribe).

The early-twentieth-century Winnebago, like Eastman's Sioux, were
not uniform. Radin realized this when he studied the Winnebago between
1908 and 1913. As he saw it, the tribe was a "compound of three distinct
elements: an old basic culture, going back to at least A. D. 1000 and

possibly much earlier, which has repeatedly reorganized to meet new situations and new challenges; a considerable number of borrowings from Central Algonquian tribes after A. D. 1400; and a few borrowings from the whites and from Christianity beginning with the middle of the seventeenth century but not becoming of any real importance until a century later." The tribe responded to the pressures of modern history in multiple, sometimes competing, ways. Factions in flux made it difficult to define "typically Winnebago."

For instance, some Winnebago were traditionalists, others were Christians, and still others were peyote eaters who practiced Christianity and objected to, or subscribed to, traditional values. Albert Hensley (Winnebago), who, like Roe Cloud, had short hair, dressed well, attended a government boarding school for Indians (in Hensley's case, Carlisle), and converted to Christianity, practiced the peyote faith and strove to maintain its legal status, whereas Roe Cloud abhorred the practice and wanted to outlaw it.[37] John Rave (Winnebago), who served as one of Radin's main informants, introduced peyote eating to his fellow Winnebago in 1901. Rave favored traditionalist practices as well as peyote eating, but then developed an antipathy for traditionalism. Hensley, a few years after Rave started the cult, conjoined Christianity, Bible reading, and peyote eating so successfully that the popularity of peyote evangelism alarmed missionaries. The peyote eaters split into two groups for a time: one led by Rave (who began baptizing his flock, although he was illiterate), and the other by Hensley (who eventually lost this power struggle).[38]

Also, during these turbulent early years of the century, alcoholism had spread among the Winnebago. Oliver Lamere (Winnebago), a follower of the Peyote Cult, lamented that both Rave and Hensley had been "heavy drinker[s]" before converting. Crashing Thunder's (Winnebago) autobiography, published in 1920 and then revised and added to in 1926, offers a portrait of how poverty, alcoholism, and the peyote faith affected traditional ways and values (more on this in chapter 1). In this context of shifting identities, Crashing Thunder's Americanized names were Sam Blowsnake and Sam Carley. Lamere, who was educated, assisted Radin as an interpreter (Radin studiously learned Winnebago) and helped the anthropologist translate Crashing Thunder's/Sam Blowsnake's/Sam Carley's story from the Winnebago syllabic alphabet (which actually originated with the Sauk and Fox).[39] He, like Roe Cloud and Hensley, belonged to the Society of American Indians. In 1913, writing in the Society's *Quarterly Journal*, Lamere argued that Americanization did not ineluctably make "American elements and Indian elements" so "intertwined that it will be impossible to separate one from the other." Rather, Indian "elements" and American "elements," some of which were in opposition to one another, could be kept "side by side."[40] Whether they were "side by side," "intertwined," or in historical flux, combinations of such elements were legion. Neither Hensley, nor Rave, nor Lamere, nor Roe Cloud was unambiguously representative of this diverse tribe.

However, in the 1930s Roe Cloud made a generalization, which I discuss in chapter 3, that articulates an Indian way of being, an Indian characteristic, manifest in so many of his published and unpublished writings, a posture that he must have witnessed first among the Winnebago. He generalized that Indians tend to be more composed and in command of themselves than whites. One cannot say for sure that Roe Cloud's emotional poise, humor, and warmth are wholly attributable to his Winnebago education, but these characteristics vivify his writing. Roe Cloud kept much that could have shaken him—the ethnocentrism and racism he surely encountered in Nebraska, Massachusetts, New Jersey, Connecticut, Oklahoma, Kansas, Oregon, and elsewhere—at a rhetorical and perhaps emotional distance. His writings are neither acrimonious nor caustic. I review some of the lessons, the wisdom, one might learn from this relative steadiness and resilience in each chapter.

Another enduring characteristic, one that I infer has tribal origins, is Roe Cloud's heightened sense of responsibility to Indians. Each chapter, and especially the coda, considers how Roe Cloud contributed to the Indian reinvention and deployment of class status and power. Roe Cloud consistently used elite access to serve the Indian cause. His relative calm partly derives from his unswerving sense of mission. Roe Cloud's focus on service may be rooted in the traditional Indian ethos of giving, which is also an ethos of redistribution.[41] As the coda makes plain, this orientation and commitment among Indians, the Indian ethos of service, remains strong today.

This ethos of service is also grounded in traditional Indian kinship epistemologies, kinship values, and kinship understandings of selfhood and its powers. By this I mean the traditional Indian sense of kindred and tribal relationship to all other humans and nonhumans (intertribal, tribal-animal, tribal-bird, tribal-tree, tribal-river, and so on). This is in opposition to European colonial ideologies that imagined humans as different from and superior to what was objectified as "nature." Such binary assumptions helped sanction the conquest of "nature" and "other" humans. Kinship forms of selfhood differ from dominant European and American cultural formations of "individuality." Anthropologist Clifford Geertz explains that "individuality"—the premise that "the person as a bounded, unique, more or less integrated motivational and cognitive universe, a dynamic center of awareness, emotion, judgment, and action organized into a distinctive whole and set contrastively both against other such wholes and against its social and natural background"—is not all that common if one surveys "the world's cultures."[42] Hence one not easily answered Winnebago question to consider is: How did Yale's ideologies of Christianity and "individuality" (as I will show, the latter were in flux) interact with Roe Cloud's tribal education in a kinship self-conception that emphasized interconnectedness and reciprocity rather than hierarchy, dominance, or egoistic self-monitoring? It would be intriguing to read how Roe Cloud, with his Winnebago education and master's degree in anthropology from Yale, would have reflected on such questions.[43]

Yet another consideration to weigh, when thinking about Roe Cloud's origins, is that when he converted to Christianity as a boy on the reservation and matriculated at Yale as a young man and used the category of *individual* to describe himself, he entertained a range of new ways of being, thinking, feeling, and identifying himself without eradicating his Winnebago development of self. Historians are just starting to appreciate the elastic capacity of Indians—products of kinship systems—to engage simultaneous, seemingly contradictory beliefs. What Philip J. Deloria calls "Indian Christianity" often exhibited this. Many white reformers, missionaries, and educators were baffled when they learned that boarding-school students or converts never really expunged their native beliefs, values, and lifeways as they accumulated new ones called "civilized." Pratt, for example, once complained about an Osage chief who, educated by the "Romish church," stubbornly remained Indian. Even though the chief understood English, he persisted in using interpreters. Pratt did not grasp this seemingly regressive practice as one shaped by what the chief had learned not only in his tribe, but in the "Romish" school. Historians as well as reformers have long underestimated Indian pragmatism and artfulness by assuming that what looks like Indian assimilation—say, as Christians and as individuals—amounts to a definitive intellectual, spiritual, and emotional conversion. Rather, many Indians have quietly transformed what was supposed to be their transformation.[44]

The reader of Roe Cloud's correspondence must exercise his or her critical imagination as a historian of silences, sometimes strategic silences. Doubtless, Roe Cloud had ideological crosscurrents swirling through him. The world of white power in which he circulated may have made him cautious about what he committed to paper, even in personal communications. Make no mistake: the Roes, Roe Cloud's loving correspondents, belonged to the white power structure. Even Roe Cloud's most intimate letters are on a certain plane public. If Roe Cloud learned gradually how to practice a repertoire of rhetorical and emotional styles, encompassing sentimental and melodramatic appeals, his range of exchanges with the Roes helped him do so. Roe Cloud had great integrity and sympathy: the Roes were his dear friends and allies. Still, the Roes were also his readers and auditors. This makes reading what he chose to write them a challenge. One cannot really know what he chose *not* to write them.[45]

My critical emphasis is on what Roe Cloud *did write* about his life. A major part of his relationship with the Roes took place in writing. Their tie had a distinctly literary quality: the form is epistolary; the genres are Christian sentimentalism and melodrama. Since Yale's Roe family papers archive and other resources I have examined focus on Roe Cloud's relationship with non-Indians, my chapters do so as well. Because of its Roe orientation, the archive does not expansively document the significance of Roe Cloud's many rich and loving bonds with Indians.[46]

It is important to keep three things in mind when taking stock of the Roe family archive and its focus. First, there is no Roe Cloud archive per se at Yale. Yale has some of his published and unpublished essays, quite a few issues of the American Indian Institute's school newspaper, The Indian Outlook, many pamphlets about the American Indian Institute, and newspaper clippings of his and his family's activities. Roe Cloud sent some letters to alumni representatives about alumni affairs (collected in his alumni file). But he did not give Yale reams of his private letters. Many of these, no doubt, would have been sent to and received from family members and Indian friends (Roe Cloud was often on the road, especially in the 1920s and 1930s). Second, Roe Cloud kept Roe as his middle name—as if it was the first name in a hyphenated last name—throughout his life, as he basked in the love of his family. People usually referred to him as Roe Cloud. The name Roe evidently continued to signify part of his sense of self and of his possibility, and he bestowed this sense, represented by this name, on his family (I elaborate on the significance of this in chapter 2). Third, the Roe family archive includes not only Roe Cloud's many letters to Mary and Walter Roe, but their letters to him. These letters make the Roe Cloud section of the Roe archive a real dialogue.

My study of Roe Cloud raises as well as answers some important historical questions. Philip J. Deloria expresses the spirit with which one should approach the correspondence, alumni files, records, published essays, school newspapers, and other resources I have found. In "Thinking about Self in a Family Way" (2002), Deloria underscores how challenging it has been for him to try to understand his own grandfather, Vine Deloria Sr. as well as the need to exercise critical humility. "If I am so confusing to myself, how can I begin to think I can know anything about the confusion of my subjects? The more I learn about my grandparents, the more I make sense to myself, but the farther my grandparents recede into the mysterious and the unknowable. I think—I hope—that this is a good thing, a sign that I am not simply appropriating their experience to my own (or vice versa) but honing the critical lever of humility so necessary to good history. But can I be sure?"[47]

The chapters that follow clarify why this book could not be subtitled: *The Oppression of Henry Roe Cloud, The Tragedy of Henry Roe Cloud,* or *The Vicitmization of Henry Roe Cloud.* I view his life as not just a struggle, but a triumph of fortitude and attitude. Surveying several spheres, I study some complex higher educations that Henry Roe Cloud received and tried to establish for others. Yet Roe Cloud's experience—at Yale, with the Roes, as head of the American Indian Institute and of Haskell—should not be thought of as implicitly representing Indians in various social circumstances who could not or would not attend institutions like Yale.[48] As the preface emphasizes, my book is as concerned with seminal theoretical and historical issues intertwined with certain chapters of Roe Cloud's life—the history of class identity formation; the class and racial history of sentimentalized intimacy; the history of cultural, educational, and bureaucratic resistance strategies—as it is with aspects of his exemplary life. I hope that my fusion of historical and theoretical as well as biographical concerns— my focus on *analysis*—will lead more people to contemplate a life that should be learned from and remembered.

one

YALE EDUCATION

HENRY ROE CLOUD was not culturally slated to wind up at Yale or any institution remotely like it. He was not supposed to acquire the knowledge, and the social uses of the knowledge, that Yale taught. Neither was he expected to meet, no less befriend, most of the men of social standing that Yale welcomed or the refined women who moved in Yale circles. Equally, he was not intended to receive anything resembling a Yale schooling in incentive, aspiration, taste, and feeling. At early twentieth-century Yale he also encountered the changing ways in which markers of American middle- and upper-class individuality were coming to assume conspicuously psychological forms. For the Yale he attended was beginning to assign class value to new cultural and literary forms of an elite psychological individuality. The Winnebago realized well before he matriculated that colleges like Yale (he had also visited Princeton and Wesleyan on his college tour) offered not just academic courses of study but a cultural authorization, an intellectual status, a social identity, a gilded stage for improvisations, an access to class power that he could use for himself and the Indians he served.[1]

At the same time, I do not think that he saw his education at institutions such as Mount Hermon, Yale, Oberlin, and Auburn purely as socially instrumental. The letters I have read convey Roe Cloud's love of learning and rhetorical play. Unafraid of intellectual challenges, he took social pleasure in oratory and debate. He was curious about exploring multiple ways of thinking, multiple ways of feeling, multiple ways of seeing and of seeing himself. Roe Cloud did not think that an Indian should be interested only in particular subjects or ideas. Charles Eastman rhapsodized that his education led him to dive "deep into a strange life from which I could not retreat. . . . I absorbed knowledge through every pore. . . . The more I got, the larger my capacity grew, and my appetite increased in proportion."[2] This also expresses the intellectual spirit of Henry Roe Cloud.

Below I situate Roe Cloud's letters in a phase of Yale's history and address key questions about this case study in the development of white-collar Indian activism. Did Roe Cloud enjoy Yale? Was his presence there significant? Did some campus groups, activities, publications, and faculty sponsor Indian stereotypes? If Roe Cloud performed the role of student, did he also enact the role of teacher? How did he use what he learned? Who did he try to influence?

COLLEGE INDIANS AND CLASS LITERACY

The writings of Indian Affairs Commissioner Thomas Jefferson Morgan help clarify some aspects of the systemic production of inequality Roe Cloud battled. In 1890, possibly thinking himself beneficently progressive, this well-educated commissioner advocated the formation of three five-year industrial high schools for Indians (Carlisle, Haskell, Chemawa) to form "character," adapt students to "modern civilization," accustom them to repetitive toil, and inculcate what was openly termed "treason to the tribe." He affirmed that "the Indian [has] the same diversity of endowment and the same high order of talent that the other races possess" and voiced parsimonious encouragement for those "very few" Indian students with "special aptitudes and lofty ambition" who wish to attend college. Although he acknowledged the "urgent need" among Indians "for a class of leaders of thought, lawyers, physicians, preachers, teachers, editors, statesmen, and men of letters," his interest in addressing this "need" was by no means "urgent."

Any Indians who aspired to attend college fared no better with Indian Affairs Commissioner William A. Jones. In 1900 he admitted that the state education of its "wards" in no way constituted "an elaborate preparation for a collegiate course." He used the gospel of self-help as his cover for the systemic under-education of an entire people: "Their future career should always be dependent upon their own exertions and not at the expense of the General Government." Then in 1905 Commissioner Francis E. Leupp, a graduate of Williams College and Columbia Law School, enthusiastically supported teaching Indians "handy tinkering" (such as mending harnesses and wagon wheels), elementary letter writing, and basic literacy skills (for reading bills and newspapers), while he confidently assured whites that only a tiny proportion of Indians possess the talent and "individuality" (his term) to attend college. He believed that Indians' evolutionary racial characteristics as well as their cultural environments handicapped them. A year later Roe Cloud commenced "tinkering" at Yale. Only in the late 1920s did the Bureau of Indian Affairs, in response to lobbying on the parts of Indians and reform groups, which included Roe Cloud, offer some Indian youth a high school education that, in Morgan's words, was readily available—and available not in a five-year half-academic and half-vocational training industrial program—to "the great mass of youth of every race and condition except the Indian."[3]

In the early 1910s, Robert Yellowtail (Crow), who later became superintendent of his reservation, and Thomas Sloan (Omaha), a Hampton Institute valedictorian who had been accepted at Yale Law School and chose instead to apprentice to become an attorney, published articles in Carlisle's *Red Man*, in which they argued that young Indians now needed college educations to fight new sorts of battles in American courts, legislatures, and bureaucracies.[4] Similarly, in 1913 the Society of American Indians decried systemic efforts to reproduce Indians as a "grammar school race" ill-equipped to "compete with a [white] college bred race."[5] Some Indians who had not been able, or permitted, to take this educational route identified its importance. Thus in the 1930s Luther Standing Bear, the great Sioux autobiographer and cultural critic who had attended Carlisle, but not high school or college, told the ridiculous tale of his brother Henry's request to the Indian Affairs commissioner for funds to study in a Chicago college. His brother had just returned from Carlisle, where he had only a few years of half-academic and half-vocational education. The commissioner turned him down because other Indians "who crave[d] a higher education" would expect the same backing if he granted it to his brother. "That is the most exalted opinion I ever heard an Indian Commissioner express on the educational aspirations of the Indian youth of the land, and I think his compliment was unintentional," Standing Bear quipped. "Anyway, it was absurd, for in our Black Hills alone there was wealth enough not only to educate all the Lakota boys, but the boys of other tribes as well." He hoped that Indians would be trained not only as "doctors, lawyers, engineers, and architects," but also as students of "native dances, songs, music, poetry, languages and legends, as well as the native arts and crafts."[6]

In 1888 the white Women's National Indian Association formed a Special Education Committee that most famously sponsored Susan La Flesche's (Ponca and Omaha) training in medical school. Four years later the "Friends of the Indian" established the Lake Mohonk Fund to support Indians who pursued higher education.[7] Yet in the late nineteenth century and through at least the first half of the twentieth century, most Indians, like most African Americans, confronted the ideology that W. E. B. Du Bois condensed into his ironic rhetorical question: "What need of higher culture for half-men?"[8] In the colonial period Harvard and Dartmouth used Indians to raise funds to support Indian education, but did not follow through on these plans and promises for very long. During Carlisle's existence few Indians experienced the sort of education offered at colleges like Yale, Harvard, Princeton, and Dartmouth—sites that N. Scott Momday (Kiowa and Cherokee), a Stanford alumnus, once called "the enemy camp."[9] Carlisle's Howard Gansworth (Iroquois), for example, after graduating from Princeton in 1901 (M.A. 1906) and working at Carlisle, held several jobs in Rochester, New York, and finally owned his own company. William Jones (Sac and Fox), a cross-blood grandson of a Fox chief, was raised on his reservation, attended a Friends' boarding school in Indiana, enrolled in Hampton Normal and Industrial Institute, moved on to Philips Academy at Andover, and finally entered Harvard (B.A. 1900, M.A. 1901). Later he took his doctorate at Columbia under the tutelage of Franz Boas and prepared for his career as an anthropologist in the Philippines. There the Ilongots killed him with a spear in 1909.[10]

Charles Eastman, perhaps the most illustrious Indian college man, graduated from Dartmouth (class of 1887, with honors). Harvard had tried to woo him away. He enjoyed the patronage of the Boston elite when he matriculated at Boston University Medical School. Because of racial prejudice he was unable to find steady work as a physician. Instead he devoted himself to what was called Indian "uplift."[11]

Eastman was not uncritical of the system he partly infiltrated. He noted that the Continental Congress had granted Dartmouth five hundred dollars to help educate Indians, but added: "This was . . . less an act of benevolence than of self-interest, since its avowed object was to conciliate the friendship of those Indians who might be inclined to ally themselves with the British during the struggle for independence." Eastman cited "the impression of many people who are not well informed on the Indian situation that book education is of little value to the race, particularly what is known as the higher education," and retorted emphatically: "The contrary is true." Notwithstanding his support for Carlisle, he characterized it as a "vocational school" whose "graduates must attend a higher preparatory school for several years before they can enter college." He outlined the difficulties Indians underwent to secure the language skills, education, and funds requisite to attend college as older students: "quite a feat." Much of his writing was directed at redefining "Indian" as a name that would reference the "deeper thoughts and higher possibilities" associated with potential college students. As examples of Indians who have succeeded, he heralded Dr. Carlos Montezuma (Yavapi-Apache), Dr. Susan La Flesche Picotte (Ponca and Omaha), Senator Charles Curtis (Kaw), Dr. William Jones, Gertrude Bonnin (who published her fiction under her Yankton Dakota Sioux name Zitkala-Ša), Howard Gansworth, Reverend Sherman Coolidge (Arapaho), and Reverend Henry Roe Cloud, whom he described as "one of our promising young ministers."[12]

Roe Cloud, as a full-blood Winnebago and a graduate of Yale, was a particularly visible member of this nascent professional and managerial group. He comprehended that policies such as those advocated by Morgan, Jones, and Leupp fostered the unequal distribution not just of knowledge but of cultural, linguistic, and class capital, and that it was imperative to place such resources in Indian hands.[13] His collegiate socialization—academic, emotional, and performative—highlights ways in which Yale's structuring of desire, ambition, self-image, and individuality contributed to class identity formation.

Some of Roe Cloud's undergraduate experiences resonate with John Joseph Mathews' (Osage) insights in *Sundown* (1934), his semi-autobiographical novel about the cross-blood Osage, Challenge Windzer, who for a time attends the University of Oklahoma. Mathews graduated Phi Beta Kappa from that university and later turned down a Rhodes Scholarship, instead electing to pay his way for his education at Merton College, Oxford. His novel understands partly assimilated Indian selfhood as being comprised of group identifications, often in conflict with more traditional Indian group identifications, that may stimulate a tenuous sense of belonging: "[Challenge] wanted to be identified with that vague something which everybody else seemed to have, and which he believed to be civilization."[14] Roe Cloud too seems to have felt the need to belong, though not always so simply to Yale or the professional and managerial class.

WINNEBAGO SURVIVAL AND CHRISTIANIZING

Some historical background on both the Winnebago and Yale will help set the scene for Roe Cloud's experience in college and later life. Roe Cloud's Winnebago name was Wo-Na-Xi-Lay-Hunka (Wonah'ilayhunka), meaning war chief.[15] He was a member of the Bear clan, traditionally the clan that, as he described it, "obstructed or permitted war."[16]

The anthropologist Paul Radin notes that the word "Winnebago" is of Algonquin origin, speculates that the Winnebago migrated to what is now Wisconsin from the East, and observes that the tribe "belong[s] to the far-flung Siouan-speaking peoples whose members at one time inhabited an area which extended from South Carolina and the lower Mississippi River northward and westward to the states of Wisconsin, North and South Dakota and Montana, and the provinces of Saskatchewan and Alberta in western Canada."[17] In 1634 the French became the first Europeans to encounter the Winnebago. They found a tribe passionate about self-defense (Nicolas Perrot alleged that the Winnebago were cannibals). Within a few decades the Winnebago were decimated by epidemics, war, and famine, and increased their numbers in the seventeenth and eighteenth centuries by intermarrying with neighboring tribes.[18] In the 1800s treaties claimed most of the Winnebago land and at midcentury the tribe was divided between Nebraska, where some consented to relocate, and Wisconsin, from which some scattered groups refused to leave.

Helen Hunt Jackson's hugely popular critique of the government's treatment of the Indians, A Century of Dishonor (1881), which galvanized the Protestant Indian reform movement in the 1880s and 1890s, devoted seven chapters to tribes that had endured egregious abuses. Her chapter on the Winnebago details treaties, broken treaties, forced land cessions, and coerced removals (paid for by the Winnebago) from 1816 through the 1870s. Her research documents how the Winnebago were pushed around and moved around starting in the early 1830s and, despite this, by the 1860s had become a success story as farmers. Their achievement, however, only made their land even more coveted by the government and land grabbers. Jackson closes her narrative of systemic injustice on a cautionary note sympathetic to Winnebago desperation with government alibis: "What its next chapter may be is saddening to think. It is said by those familiar with the Nebraska Indians that, civilized though they be, they will all make war to the knife if the attempt is made by the Government to rob them of their present lands on the plea again of offering them a 'permanent home.' "[19]

The Nebraska to which the Winnebago were moved changed rapidly as the region's white population tripled in the 1870s.[20] Because of allotment, fraud, land sales, and lack of Winnebago funds to farm, by 1913 the tribe lost about two-thirds of its property.[21] The administrator of Winnebago allotment in the late 1880s was the energetic assimilationist Alice Fletcher, whose mixture of sentimentalism and evolutionary theory convinced her not only that Winnebago lands should be "individualized" (divided into allotments), but that their family life should be uplifted.[22] Thus she championed monogamous marriage and literacy training. Not long after the remedial allotment was underway, the Winnebago Reservation agent had to call in federal troops to remove cohorts of white land-hungry squatters.[23]

Roe Cloud was raised on the Nebraska Winnebago Reservation in the midst of these tumultuous changes and pressures. Radin, who learned Winnebago, started his fieldwork on the reservation while Roe Cloud was at Yale and began publishing his findings in 1909 (by 1944 he had accumulated about 44,000 pages of Winnebago texts).[24] He observed that the economic and political assault on and transformation of Winnebago society had produced a situation in which religion, always important to the Winnebago, was more vital than ever as cultural nourishment—"religion,

rituals, music, mythology" flourished in traditional forms.[25] Radin found
that Winnebago religious societies and rituals, far from being rigid, contained a syncretic "clustering of the most multitudinous and shamanis-
tic ideas within them."[26] Many Winnebago religious rituals traditionally
served a pragmatic function for males—to invigorate warriors' confidence
and sense of collective purpose when going into battle.[27] In the early
twentieth century these rituals were indispensable in the cultural and bureaucratic war for tribal survival.[28] Radin asserted in 1909 that the Presbyterian missionaries "had in seventeen years succeeded in converting only
one family, and a family which then unkindly died without leaving issue."[29] He seems not to have been aware of a young Winnebago converted
by the Presbyterians in the 1890s, a boy who became Henry Roe Cloud.[30]

An autobiography by a Winnebago named Crashing Thunder (whose
Americanized names were Sam Blowsnake and Sam Carley), that was
sponsored and commented on by Radin and published first in 1920 and
later with additional material in 1926, is informative about late nineteenth-
and early twentieth-century Winnebago life-in-flux on the Nebraska reservation. Crashing Thunder was only a few years older than Roe Cloud. He
was educated in Winnebago religious beliefs, rituals, and cultural values such as being kind to one's wife, good to children, and appreciative
of imaginative, often instructive, storytelling. What is so striking about
Crashing Thunder is his unabashed, self-interested pragmatism: he simply pretended to believe in traditional Winnebago ways when he found it
in his favor to do so. This included exploiting the ethos of giving in his
role as gift recipient and consistently taking advantage of women, especially his several wives.[31] Dire economic conditions on the reservation may
have motivated his self-interested performances (at one point he joined a
Wild West Show). He converted to the Peyote Christian faith, confessed
his sins in the rituals, and reflected more critically on his behavior. Crashing Thunder was not keen on writing his story, but, low on money, Radin
paid him for it.[32]

Roe Cloud's motives were different from Crashing Thunder's, but his
writings suggest that he had a pragmatic view of his situation and that of
the Winnebago, one that kindled his interest in using the motivational
power of Christianity for Indians. His most famous essay is "From Wigwam to Pulpit: A Red Man's Story of His Progress from Darkness to Light"

(1916), by—take note—"A Winnebago Indian Graduate of Yale University." Here he recounts some of his early impressions of tribal life. His parents trapped for skins; his uncles taught him how to worship and disciplined him, harshly, he said; his grandmother tended him and counseled him to reject the missionaries' Christianizing efforts; the elders told him and his brother stories and didactic myths. His main focus is not on the wigwam, but on the schooling that led him to convert to Christianity. When he was seven, Indian police conscripted him to attend school. He became a student at a non-reservation school at Genoa, Nebraska, where half of his education consisted of manual training (operating a hand-turned washing machine). Having been permitted to speak English only, he lost his native tongue. A couple of weeks after Roe Cloud returned home two years later, he healed this institutional amputation: "I got back my native tongue and have never lost it since" (8).[33]

Roe Cloud's account of his Christianizing foregrounds his bold singularity and nonconformity. "When the day came that I was to be baptized, I stood up alone before all the Indians, and the preacher asked me whom we should obey first, Christ or parents and relatives, I answered, 'Christ.' . . . There were no other 'preaching Indians' in the whole school, and only one or two in the tribe" (10, 11). Shortly after his christening and renaming in the mid-1890s, he had to adjust to the death of his father. Roe Cloud's autobiographical essay would surely have inspired trust in the Presbyterians, missionaries, and white Indian reformers who read it. Notwithstanding the individualistic thrust of this standing-up-for-Jesus testimony, I read Roe Cloud's Winnebago commitment to Christianity as inseparable from his commitment to the Winnebago. "The Indian does not interpret life in terms of religion," Radin underscored, profiling the Winnebago, "but religion in terms of life."[34] Registering points of contact between Presbyterian missionary and traditional Indian beliefs, Michael Coleman observes that for both groups "the spiritual pervaded life."[35] Roe Cloud employed Christianity spiritually and emotionally to empower not just himself but his people. Furthermore, organized Christianity gave him access to education and ruling social groups.

Philip J. Deloria's historical perspective on his Dakota ancestors' interest in Christianity is worth bearing in mind when thinking about Roe Cloud. Dating back to the mid-nineteenth century, many Dakota and other Indians viewed religion as the route to leadership, especially in conditions that prevented them from exercising military leadership. The church, writes Deloria, was "a place of social power and opportunity." As the government's bureaucracy tried to dominate reservation life, Indian Christianity became an alternative—and permissible—form of social organization.[36]

The anti-colonialist Albert Memmi writes perceptively, as did Radin, about religion's colonial appeal. Religion's refuge, he suggests, can save "the colonized from the despair of total defeat." The colonized society can benefit by withdrawing its "present from the conquering invasion of colonization."[37] Perhaps Christianity preoccupied the young Roe Cloud partly because it simultaneously integrated him into the colonial present while holding out the hope of ameliorating and transcending that present in ways many whites would not only respect but value and uphold.

It was Roe Cloud's Presbyterian minister, William T. Findley, who persuaded him to enter the Santee Mission School in northeastern Nebraska, which Charles Eastman had attended in 1875–76. Dr. Alfred L. Riggs was the head of Santee. His pedagogical approach differed from that taken in schools like Carlisle, which he deprecated as "godless." Carlisle permitted only the speaking of English. Riggs used Indian languages to teach English and even encouraged some of his students to attend prep schools and then colleges. Roe Cloud took this path.[38] In the early 1900s, in his late teens, Roe Cloud was accepted at Mount Hermon School, which had been founded in 1881 by Dwight L. Moody, the prominent evangelist, in Northfield, Massachusetts. His years there prepared him for Yale, which he entered in 1906, in his early twenties.[39]

THE GOSPEL OF SELF-HELP

Roe Cloud's seeming conversion was not only to white mission authority, which was allied with the larger forces that ceaselessly engulfed the reservation; it was to the gospel of self-making. American capitalist and class ideologies have often been popularly transmuted into the language of self, self-making, and self-management. At Santee, Roe Cloud was inspired by Samuel Smiles's *Self-Help* (1859): "This book led me to resolve to earn my way through school, but to stay away from Government institutions" (12). Smiles's classic of the burgeoning incentive-building industry sold almost a quarter of a million copies around the world by 1900.[40] The Scottish author, an ex-radical journalist who began his career by studying medicine at Edinburgh University, framed liberal individuality as the test of a society's worth. As John Stuart Mill, whom Smiles quotes, writes so stirringly: "Even despotism does not produce its worst effects so long as individuality exists under it; and whatever crushes individuality is despotism by whatever name it be called." Young Roe Cloud may have been reassured by Smiles's love-thy-neighbor contention that the improvement of the individual leads to the improvement of the masses and the nation.

In Smiles's secular religion of self-help, the equivalent of sin was "ease and self-indulgence." While Smiles acknowledged that no one solely helps himself or herself without the aid of institutions and friends, the idea he made fascinating was unshakable confidence in individual power and agency. Many traditional Indians, who believed that their power emanated from the spirits, would have considered Smiles's secular theory of "inner" power spiritually wrongheaded.[41] Notwithstanding Smiles's sincere interest in motivating the working class to be what he termed "independent"— a project that Roe Cloud, thinking of his fellow Winnebago, considered— his pep talks about perseverance and social mobility downplayed the systemic structuring of inequality and, in the words of historian Asa Briggs, conveniently failed to "distinguish between work and drudgery."[42] Smiles held that the "school of experience" and the accumulation of character capital were more fundamental to the achievement of success than a college education, yet used his own university credentials to constitute his authority to say so.[43] Roe Cloud must have entertained doubts about this premise as he saw the links between university training and class access to social power grow stronger in the twentieth century.

YALE CAPITAL

Roe Cloud appreciated the institutional and cultural status Yale held in the battleground of "civilization." Because of his schooling in Protestantism and self-help, he would have been familiar with some of the notions of Christian individuality that circulated at college. At Yale these notions were given greater intellectual elaboration, cultural distinction, and class glamour. Yale's president, Arthur Twining Hadley, an expert on railroad economics (railroad expansion relied on the acquisition of Indian land), proselytized the idea of the Christian gentleman who possesses Christian character to what the historian George Wilson Pierson profiled as "the sons and heirs of the American ruling class."[44] Some of Hadley's sentiments would have reminded Roe Cloud of Smiles's *Self-Help*, much of which is comprised of quotations from leading intellectual and cultural figures, past and present. For Hadley, the Christian gentleman was one who manfully engaged in competition, not simply to profit from winning, but more unselfishly to better serve his society.[45] This fine patrician idea, perhaps for some an even finer alibi, lent spiritual legitimacy, moral authority, and character value to competitive individuality. Its invocation of service also resonated with Roe Cloud's Winnebago, and Christian, ethos of service to others.[46]

When Roe Cloud was in college, from 1906 to 1910, Yale was going through an important transitional and highly self-reflective phase: it was in the process of growing as a research university (expanding professional schools) and was beginning to take its intellectual mission more seriously than ever. A Yale education was coming to mean much more than training Christian gentlemen for enlightened, manly marketplace competition.[47] That said, during Roe Cloud's time at Yale, corporate campus life—secret societies, intellectual societies, sports teams, debate clubs—was considered at least as crucial in building the "Yale man" as academic excellence. Yale romanticized striving and bestowed samples of society's rewards and prestige on its students. Its sports captains would indeed go on to become captains of industry. Through its cultured atmosphere of exclusivity, the college bolstered its students' social self-confidence and sense of entitlement.[48]

During Roe Cloud's undergraduate years *The Yale Daily News* published articles on Yale's expansion as a university, the college's continued commitment to teaching, its growing interest in research (and the new form of national and international prestige this investment yielded), its increasing prosperity, its social life, and, mainly, its ongoing sports and debating competitions with other universities.[49] The *Daily* sometimes addressed the harsher realities of American life. Roe Cloud could have scanned articles on poverty, immigrants, child labor, and even the evils of capitalism (this piece by Dr. Lyman Abbott, the white Protestant Indian reformer, nonetheless reassuringly rejected socialism as an unreasonable measure that would violate the sanctity of American individualism).[50] To its credit, Yale awarded Jane Addams an honorary degree at Roe Cloud's commencement in 1910.[51] Reports on President Hadley's speeches and sentiments conveyed his Yale beliefs both in individual nonconformism ("[do not] follow the crowd on lines of least resistance") and in individual "intellectual" and "moral responsibility" ("do your own thinking, not just for self, but for God and country").[52]

The cascade of articles on sports and debates anointed competition as a cardinal virtue. This virtue was given an intellectual aura in articles such as one that quotes Professor Max Farrand's speech to the Phi Beta Kappa chapter in 1910: "From my own course, that of History, we learn that the American is supposed to go into life as into a game—and he plays the game to win. He picks out something and tries to follow it through—to succeed where others have failed."[53] One class historian affectionately characterized Roe Cloud's sophomore class as "harassed by incessant competition."[54] Articles often linked competition to business and business to management. The wealthy Henry Clews advised students to spend a couple of years working on Wall Street after college—advice that F. Scott Fitzgerald's Yalie narrator, Nick Carraway, took in The Great Gatsby (1925)— not only to learn about business, but more generally to discover how to manage life.[55] Another piece in 1910 encouraged Yale students to visit and work in the New Haven slums, not so much to ameliorate socioeconomic conditions, but to learn firsthand how to manage workers. The author termed this training in industrial "humanics."[56] The Daily's readers were groomed, implicitly and explicitly, in middle- and upper-class social values and in the value of competition so that they could more effectively graduate to, and feel confident about wanting to, manage others. Yale cultivated not simply industrious scholars, or responsible Christian gentlemen, but highly competitive managerial individuals.

Student biographies in the Yale classbook for Roe Cloud's class of 1910 indicate the social backgrounds of students (many had fathers who owned and managed their firms or factories), their educational pedigrees (many students attended prestigious prep schools), and their career objectives (most planned to study law, go into manufacturing or banking, or attend medical school). Few aspired to become teachers. Even fewer intended,

YALE   UNIVERSITY

Reproduction of a Photogravure 15 x 28 inches
Published by
W. T. LITTIG & CO., 15 William St., New York

1   1907 print (issued in 1910) of Richard Rummell's drawing based on aerial (hot air balloon) photograph of Yale campus. Manuscripts and Archives, Yale University Library.

like Roe Cloud, to enter the ministry, a major purpose for which Yale was founded.[57] Yale self-reliance was supplemented with extravagant institutional support, which lent the ideology considerable cultural, intellectual, and class authority (figure 1).

YALE INDIVIDUALITY

Notwithstanding the career success that was an expected consequence of this institutionally driven self-reliance, Roe Cloud matriculated at a moment when some Yalies were questioning whether the college was effectively designing individuals. The *Yale Lit.*, for instance, published J. Howland Auchincloss's highly critical "Yale and the Individual" (1907). Auchincloss identified the "typical Yale" man as one who "is practical, creative,—one who is bound to push his way along in life." But this Yale typicality was too often achieved, he contended, by the suppression of one's individuality, one's difference from the group.[58] Auchincloss then committed the unpardonable sin of praising Harvard's institutional sagacity in its tendency to give individuality freer rein than Yale did: "The life at Harvard is broader than here,—the individual has a better chance to follow his own salvation." This is why, he claimed, Harvard has produced many "great men," while Yale has suffered from a "dearth of genius . . . the lack of illustrious names."

The individuality Auchincloss had in mind—that Yale's preoccupation with corporate identity, team competition, and school spirit had allegedly muffled—had a literary and psychological cast, and was exemplified in its more dramatic form by Henrik Ibsen's plays: "One of his critics said, 'Ibsen believed that in every human being slumbered the germ of a mighty unconquerable soul, its human individuality. It is man's duty to develop that individuality to its full powers, for its own sake.' " What Auchincloss meant by soul is at once more romantic and more modern than conventional nineteenth-century theological concepts of soul. He added a notion that would be central to the rise of twentieth-century therapeutic individualism, especially to its appeal as compensatory affective insulation from the slings and arrows of outrageous fortune, or misfortune, in the American economy: "What we are is more important than what we do. . . . In the end it will always be [one's] individuality that counts."[59] He closed his piece with the hope that Yale may soon "silence all complaints" by graduating men who will be "illustrious" and possess "great personality."[60]

Auchincloss's enthusiasms sound as if they had been whipped up by the popular writings of Harvard's brilliant romanticist of elite university individualism, William James, who got his students and readers excited about hero worshipping, the superiority of "genius," the ineffably unique nature of the self, "subjective propensities," and "inward capital." Geniuses, according to James, were the real "wealth of a nation," and it was their "higher energy" that was capable of making a university great.[61] The greatest of all universities, James announced in 1903, to no one's astonishment, was Harvard: "The university most worthy of rational admiration is that one in which your lonely thinker can feel himself least lonely, most positively furthered, and most richly fed. . . . As a nursery for independent and lonely thinkers I do believe that Harvard still is in the van. Here they find the climate so propitious that they can be happy in their very solitude. The day when Harvard shall stamp a single hard and fast type of character upon her children will be that of her downfall."[62]

The Yale Daily News scoffed at Auchincloss's Jamesian conventions of what constitutes admirable subjective exclusivity and retaliated: "Are we all stamped with the same individuality?" The irate reporter invoked the seeming moral force of older, nineteenth-century producer culture terms of subjective value: "One wonders whether the somewhat unlovely doctrine of the individual has not been preached long enough. It is a pagan business at best. There is something finer than a picturesque personality. . . . Character is more than personality, service than self-development, and by a strange paradox he that seeks the former gets the latter too."[63] His character-centered Christian critique of the individual-as-personality, a personality that he deemed pagan, in no way disparaged the drive to compete and succeed. In effect, the Daily commentator defended Yale's elite version of republican civic individualism against a newly prestigious literary and psychological reworking of liberal individualism. The matter was enduring enough to be alluded to obliquely in a cartoon in The Yale Book for 1910 that depicts two Yale students mocking Harvard students after a Yale-Harvard competition. "How did the Harvard men get home?" one asks. His companion replies with a pun: "They followed the beaten track" (figure 2).

Issues in the debate about the modern form that Yale individuality— class individuality—should take are themes in Owen Johnson's classic novel of collegiate life, Stover at Yale (1910).[64] Johnson (Yale, class of 1900) depicts tensions between an older Yale civic individualism, associated with character and team playing, and a newer Yale liberal individualism, associated with psychological nonconformity, literary soul searching, and modernity. The hero, "Dink" Stover, football star from Lawrenceville, arrives at Yale to find his freshman "individuality" submerged (9) amid intense social-status structures, especially on the football team. He recoils from the "stamping out [of his] individuality" yet learns to appreciate the "discipline," "self-abnegation," and "sacrifice" that go into making the team an efficient, competitive "machine" (55). He is taken up by some student leaders who offer him campus distinction if he conforms to their norms of exclusivity and guidelines for Yale success. Another more "individual" literary student who rebels against such managerial cliques frames Yale not as a "school for character" (268), but as a "factory" (308) and "social clearinghouse" (268) for the ruling class.

Stover, increasingly influenced by a more nonconformist informal discussion group who wish to "call [their] souls [their] own" (172), under-

2 Cartoon of two Yale
students speaking
about Harvard stu-
dents, in *The Yale Book
for 1910*. Manuscripts
and Archives, Yale
University Library.

He –How did the Harvard men get home ?
Him –They followed the beaten track.

goes a new form of self-reflective institutional individualizing as he comes
to reject Yale's anachronistic status systems—and helps overthrow some of
them. But his newfound belief in real "democracy" threatens to become
too self-centered. "There's only one thing that counts," Stover muses,
"that's your own self" (210). In the end, Johnson recuperates the value of
Yale's older corporate individualism in need of some "modern" reform as
Stover, true-blue Yalie at heart, gets the spunky rich girl and is elected to
the most exclusive of all secret societies and the epitome of Yale success,
Skull and Bones. Paradoxically, what we are seeing at Yale and in American
history is the emergence of a more ostensibly progressive professional and
managerial class whose formation of self would increasingly incorporate

independence of "soul" and nonconformity as psychological "person-ality" values geared to reproduce its members. Chapter 2 discusses some of Roe Cloud's letters that display not just his university and domestic grooming as a manager but his class-based elaboration of psychological inwardness.

At Yale knowledge of English literature, a field Roe Cloud studied in several courses, was swiftly replacing familiarity with the classics as a marker of class in daily interaction.[65] Historian George Wilson Pierson notes that "the cultural expectations of the new business aristocracy had been changing." The psychological expectations of this class had also been changing.[66] Put another way, the "conspicuous consumption" and "conspicuous leisure" that the social theorist Thorstein Veblen examined as part of the new prestige system of the late nineteenth-century business class was also gradually conjoined with a valuing of *conspicuous individuality* and *conspicuous inwardness*.[67] The Ibsenesque trend toward literary individu-alism that Auchincloss thought existed at Harvard and that Pierson saw taking shape at Yale, amid some vituperative *Yale Daily News* protest, was allied to a more general trend toward a psychological individualism that should be analyzed historically not in any oversimple way as a deeper expression of "self," but as a professional and managerial class perfor-mance of identity represented as "self."[68] Roe Cloud's college education barely predated the rise of the New Psychology and pop psychoanalysis in America. But in chapter 2 we will see that some of his emotional bonds (which at times had Ibsenesque intensity), rather than any exposure to published psychological discourses, contributed to his partial class indi-vidualizing, not solely as a Christian character or gentleman, the type of individual that Smiles and Hadley hoped to shape, but as a modern "psy-chological" individual.

YALE, DOMESTICITY, AND SELF-MANAGEMENT

During his Yale years Roe Cloud received instruction well beyond that which was available to government Indian school students. These stu-dents, as was Roe Cloud, were educated in the work ethic, were taught to blame themselves if they failed, and were inculcated with ideologies of self-restraint. Yet the sophistication of Roe Cloud's controlled and em-

ployable individualism went far past Indian school instructions in how to
say "Yes, sir," wear clean clothes, and not slouch when searching for a
job. Roe Cloud studied the Yale banter, the Yale ambition, the Yale English,
the Yale Greek, the Yale German, and the Yale canon from Homer to
Goethe. This cultured individualism was essential to a class style of
self-monitoring intended to groom him as a manager of men. His Protestantism, Yale culture, and Yale lessons in class identity, and his tactical enactments of all this, had a political slant. He wrote in 1909 that a
Yale professor indicted socialism for opposing organized religion. Roe
Cloud's response was unambiguous: he endorsed the professor's critique
and embraced individualism rather than socialism. And he believed that
substantive social change came about when individuals first experienced
the need for transformation deep within the self, as in evangelical conversion, not simply as a consequence of altered conditions external to
the self.[69]

Most of Roe Cloud's letters collected at Yale are to Mary Roe, though he
also wrote numerous letters to her husband, Dr. Walter Roe. Roe Cloud's
archived correspondence with Mary was heaviest until about five years
after he graduated from college (1907–15). As noted, the Roes were based
mainly at Colony, Oklahoma Territory, and served as Reformed missionaries to the Arapaho and Cheyenne. Their mission was not far from the
Fort Sill Chiricahua Apache Reservation. Geronimo was incarcerated at
Fort Sill and died in 1909. Part of Geronimo's band had been exiled to
Florida and then Alabama, and after that denied allotments in Oklahoma.
Walter Roe and later Roe Cloud lobbied on their behalf, even taking their
cause to Washington.[70]

Walter Roe pursued his Indian missionary work under the auspices of
the Reformed Church in 1897 and was appointed the Superintendent of
Indian Missions by that church in 1908. He became a Presbyterian minister
in 1882. Roe Cloud's involvement with the Presbyterians was longstanding. His pastor on the Winnebago Reservation, the Santee Indian Mission
School, Auburn seminary, and the American Indian Institute in the late
1920s were affiliated with the Presbyterians. Roe Cloud was ordained as a
Presbyterian minister in 1913. The historian Michael Coleman characterizes nineteenth-century Presbyterian missionaries as an "army," a "people
possessed, possessed, in their own minds, of the most precious of truths,

the ultimate answer to all life's problems." By and large, Coleman argues, Presbyterian missionaries were "unremittingly ethnocentric," but not racist, in their refusal to value traditional Indian spiritual beliefs, cultures, and lifeways. Generally, they viewed Indians not as racially inferior but as capable of learning anything that dominant white Americans had learned. Because they believed in Indian potential, Presbyterian missionaries—themselves mostly a middle-class elite—stressed not just a good range of schooling but instruction that would encourage some Indians to become professionals.[71]

The Roes, like good Presbyterians, prized Indian education and potential. Yet in some important respects this gentle couple deviated from Coleman's Presbyterian portrait. In 1902 the novelist Hamlin Garland published a scathing appraisal of the government's Indian policy and included a critique of the hypocrisy, cultural narrowness, and sometimes even the avarice of many of the missionaries he had encountered on reservations. He cites two exceptions to his criticisms, two missionaries who serve as sterling examples of what missionaries can be. "Mr. and Mrs. Roe, of Seger's Colony, Oklahoma, are examples of missionaries with larger aims than merely making converts. Mr. Roe's influence is not due to his preaching of dogma, but to his kindliness and helpfulness as a man and brother." The historian Hazel Hertzberg also praised the Roes for being "among the most respected and dedicated workers in the Indian field." The Roes were not unremittingly ethnocentric. They aimed to preserve Indian arts and crafts and to stimulate their production. Hence they employed "seventy men and women making bead-work, tepees, bows and arrows, moccasins, and ornamental pouches."[72]

The Roes' letters and other related letters in the archive outline the kind of managerial individual that Yale, the Roes, and their family ties were nurturing. In December of his senior year, Mary addressed the supernumerary racial challenges Henry might have to face as a manager. To lead effectively he would need not simply ambition or a strong work ethic but unflappable self-management skills. She foresaw the time when Roe Cloud would manage not only Indians but well-educated whites who might resent his power. Therefore his formidable character, control, skill, and determination would have to inspire them to obey. Her sentimentalism infused affective power into her managerial counsel. She saw herself as equipping him emotionally to qualify for acceptance within an American white, upper-middle class comprised mostly of university-educated professionals.[73] Dr. Roe pitched in as well. He advised Henry—using the German translation of his first name as an endearment, Heinrich—to handle his college expenses more carefully not just to save money but to develop prudent financial habits that would serve him well in his later career as leader and administrator.[74]

The Roe Cloud–Roe letters show multiple dimensions of Roe Cloud's sentimental and psychological positioning within a white upper-middle-class family. Here I will begin to show how Yale, not just the Roes, influenced Roe Cloud's reimagining of his emotional investments and of his class presentation of self. When Roe Cloud's daughter, Ann Woesha Cloud North, visited Yale in 1989 to peruse her father's correspondence, she commented in a university publication that he had told her and her sisters little about his undergraduate days. Roe Cloud did tell his daughters that he used to place crushed ice on his forehead in order to stay alert while studying late. The letters suggest that some complex educative experiences occurred during his Yale and postgraduate phase.[75]

PRIMITIVISM AND ANTHROPOLOGY

The correspondence suggests that Roe Cloud loved Yale and that Yale reciprocated. Nevertheless, ideologies of "primitive" and "civilized" were recycled at Yale and sometimes given class distinction. They were very much "in the air." For example, in the spring of his senior year the *Yale Daily News* published remarks that William Lyon Phelps, Lampson Professor of English, had made about the value of engaging literature. An appreciation of literature, he maintained, provided students with references that had become essential signals of social class and "civilized," as opposed to primitive, talk: "A large staple of conversation consists of books and reading; the exchange of views on poets and novelists is one of the great clearing-houses of human intercourse. A man with no taste in reading and with no knowledge of English literature, has no real place in modern civilization. He is just as grotesque—just as much out of his element in modern life as a South Sea Islander would be in a Fifth Avenue drawing-room."[76] From his letters to the Roes it is not possible to guess if many analogies such as the one Phelps offered—comparing the "grotesque" student unschooled in literature to a South Sea Islander in a Fifth Avenue drawing room—entered Roe Cloud's orbit either in print or conversation.[77] And the letters do not suggest that Roe Cloud, who was charming, polished, and humble, ever identified in any way with Phelps' rendition of a South Sea Islander in his Yale interactions.

Roe Cloud, however, probably would not have been surprised that such a comment had been made by even one of Yale's most popular young professors. Nor is it likely that he would have been particularly taken aback had any of his classmates, his friends, made similar remarks. The years he spent at Yale were ones in which "primitive" Indianness—stylized in handicrafts, lore, drawings, clothing—was becoming more quaint, picturesque, fashionable, and commodifiable within the dominant American culture, and in which evolutionary theory was writing off Indians as intellectually suited only for manual labor, with some exceptions to the rule, like Roe Cloud, sanctimoniously acknowledged.

Indeed, this latter ideological development took on the status of official government pronouncements. Roe Cloud made fairly frequent visits to Hampton Institute to lecture and may well have been aware that when President Theodore Roosevelt, a Harvard man, addressed Hampton's black and Indian student body in 1906, he assured them that their character, not their intellect, was worth cultivating: "No race, no nationality ever really raises itself by the exhibition of genius in a few. . . . What counts is the character of the average man and average woman." And before he became president, Roosevelt opined: "To train the average Indian as a lawyer or a doctor is in most cases simply to spoil him."[78] When William Howard Taft, a Yale man, was elected president in 1908, the event was a special one for Roe Cloud's class because Taft's son, Robert Alonso Taft—later a U.S. Senator and coauthor of the arch-conservative Taft-Hartley Labor Act—was one of Roe Cloud's most accomplished classmates (a Skull and Bones man and captain of the debate team). Two years after he graduated from Yale, Roe Cloud visited President Taft in the White House as head of a Winnebago delegation.[79] At Hampton in 1909 Taft advised the students to focus on their training in "manual dexterity" and praised the life of the farmer. Three years later, speaking at Haskell Institute, Taft omitted the virtue of intellectual development when encouraging the young Indians to cleave to the virtues of industry, patriotism, character, and morality.[80]

That Roe Cloud would choose to write a master's thesis focusing on anthropology in 1914 is intriguing because had he believed early-twentieth-century American anthropological taxonomic pronouncements about race, many of them would have made him feel like a freak of evolution: a highly intelligent North American "aborigine" who against all evolutionary—not social—odds made it to Yale.[81] While still at college he could have been aware of ethnologists such as W. J. McGee and Lindley Keasby and widely read race theorists such as Daniel Garrison Brinton and Madison Grant, who argued that evolutionary racial hierarchies existed and that they determined cultural and intellectual potential. Indians were usually ranked above Africans and just below or equal to "Mongoloids."[82]

Well-published Indian culture enthusiasts like George Bird Grinnell (a Yalie who published Indian lore), Charles Lummis (an editor and author who embraced Indian culture, in part to spur southwestern tourism), and Hamlin Garland (the famous novelist and observer of Indian lifeways) often patronizingly subscribed to the pseudo-benevolent premise that Indians had cultural and mental race-bound limitations: "Our red brethren," Garland decided, "cannot be transmuted into something other than they are by any fervor or religious experience, or by any attempts to acquire a higher education."[83] As these presuppositions were gaining converts outside and inside the Bureau of Indian Affairs, then ruled by Francis Leupp, the allotment program was selling much Indian land to whites. And politicians were scheming to reclassify Indian lands as belonging to the public domain.[84]

On the other hand, by 1914 alternative anthropological perspectives were beginning to appear. During and just after his college years, Roe Cloud was likely aware of the work of the Ohio State University sociologist Fayette McKenzie, who contended that the Indian's mind, like anyone's mind, is a social mind—culturally shaped, not racially programmed. McKenzie, a white scholar, was instrumental, along with Roe Cloud and others, in helping build up the Society of American Indians during the years following its founding in 1911. He linked the Indian cause to new developments in the social sciences.[85] In addition, the pathbreaking writings of Columbia University anthropologist Franz Boas and those of his students were gaining wider circulation while Roe Cloud was writing his Yale thesis. Although Boas retained the colonial language of "primitive" and "civilized" in his work, he argued for cultural determinism and against notions of evolutionary racial hierarchies. Boas trained a stellar group of anthropologists from the early 1890s to the 1930s (including the maverick Paul Radin, who received his Ph.D. in 1910). But his intellectual premises would only gain ascendancy in the academy in the 1920s.[86] The dominant anthropological common sense with which Roe Cloud would have had to contend when he was a Yale undergraduate stuck him, like Phelps's Fifth Avenue South Sea Islander, on a low rung of the evolutionary and social ladder.

In choosing to complete a Yale M.A. in anthropology after his seminary training, Roe Cloud combined his knowledge of the Christianity that infused so many Indian reform initiatives from the 1880s through the 1910s with an education in the social sciences that would emerge powerfully in the early twentieth century and become dominant in Indian management by the Indian New Deal. The new Indian management elites would be bureaucrats who usually referenced not the Bible but sociology, anthropology, psychology, and economics to formulate their policies. Roe Cloud equipped himself to take his place among both groups.

YALE INDIAN STEREOTYPES

John Joseph Mathews's novel Sundown narrates the experiences of Challenge (Chal) and two of his friends at the University of Oklahoma in the mid-1910s. The three Osages endured many racist and stereotypical comments. An inner "voice," whose origin clearly was external, "kept telling [Chal] that he was out of step; that this was the University, and that these men were the representatives of civilization." Chal "didn't want to call attention to the fact that most of his blood was of an uncivilized race like the Osages." He responded ambivalently when his two friends dropped out soon after the beginning of term because they refused to let white fraternity brothers paddle them as part of their initiation: "Their going would relieve him of much responsibility, and the fear which seemed to be with him always; the fear that they would do something wrong. He had enough to do to adjust himself." When he returned to the reservation for recess he was "disappointed in his friends [who dropped out] because it seemed they didn't have any ambition." Yet he himself resigned from the football team and was not committed to earning good grades. Chal often made his conflicted adjustment through "deception": "His people had practiced deception in exactly the same way all life of the earth practiced deception; in order to survive, either in war with enemies or for the purpose of food-getting. . . . Outwardly at least he attempted to live the life of an undergraduate to the full, but these attempts only made him more aware of his uniqueness."[87] It would not be surprising if Roe Cloud sometimes felt similar pressures and had to negotiate clashes of codes at Yale.

Roe Cloud's letters, however, do not explicitly indicate that he was discouraged, deterred, or incensed by stereotypes of Indians while studying at Yale.[88] He tried to make his Indian as well as his Yale identity work to his advantage. In 1910 the New Haven Journal-Courier, intrigued by his Winnebago background as well as his standing with his peers, hailed Roe Cloud as the most notable student in his class.[89] He played baseball and tennis, and sailed with his classmates. The All-Hermon baseball and football athlete seems not to have invested energy in competing on Yale's teams—except, perhaps, for a time on the track team—in a period when Indian schools' athletic reputations, especially Carlisle's, were soaring. Whites, even when appreciative, often saw Indian athletes as primitive. Roe Cloud may have been cautiously selective about what kind of "Indianness" he projected. An excellent speaker, Roe Cloud debated, along with Robert Taft, though, it seems, not on one of the official debating teams.[90] The Indian tradition of oratory—inspired by leaders such as Pontiac (Odawa, Ojibwa) and Red Jacket (Seneca)—more than that of athletics was the cultural heritage Roe Cloud chose mainly to identify with and practice in college. In taking this tack he was not alone. Several years before, in the Atlantic Monthly, Zitkala-Ša, later famous as the political lobbyist and organizer Gertrude Bonnin, published an autobiographical story about a female student who triumphs over white students and racial prejudice in an oratory contest.[91]

Eastman gave a similar impression of his experience. Although Eastman found it too difficult to find satisfactory employment as a physician, even with elite Dartmouth and Boston University degrees, he held that the "intelligent and educated Indian has no social prejudice to contend with. . . . He is received cordially and upon equal terms in school, college, and society." The Sioux author attributed this acceptance to the American class and racial structure, noting that Indians are "member[s] of the oldest American aristocracy."[92] It should be remembered that Eastman and Roe Cloud, unlike Mathews's Oklahoma Indian Territory protagonist Chal, attended colleges in the East and hence in some ways stood out as special.

In the Introduction I suggested that the reader of Roe Cloud's letters must learn how to be an imaginative historian of silences, often a historian of strategic silences. One cannot know all that Roe Cloud discussed with the Roes when he saw them. But his extant letters certainly could have commented on some curious aspects of life at Yale that his archived correspondence, the letters I have read, did not mention.

For instance, in Roe Cloud's freshman year, 1906, some undergraduates started the Mohican Club, an organization that remained active till 1940. (Dean Acheson, who became the U.S. secretary of state [1949–52], joined the club around the time Roe Cloud completed his M.A. in anthropology.) They dressed up on campus as "Indians"—feathers, face paint— and reveled at the exclusive Yale-centered restaurant Mory's. A 1912 photograph shows them with the owner of Mory's, Louis Linder, and members of the singing group, the Whiffenpoofs, who are cross-dressed as women (perhaps the Mohicans indulged in *Indian drag*) (figure 3). Their president had the title Big Chief, their vice-president was Chief, and the members were Braves (figure 4). One of the intramural debate teams was named The Wigwams (Robert Taft belonged to this group).[93]

A cartoon in *The Yale Book for* 1910 demonstrates that some Yalies enjoyed complicating Indian stereotypes (or replacing them with newer Indian stereotypes). It is premised on the awareness that increasing numbers of Indians were acquiring educations that could protect them from whites who treated them as curiosities or exploited them. The white "Stude" (perhaps a Yale student) asks a traditionally outfitted Indian in a stage-Indian idiom: "Say chief, I'll trade you heap much beads and fire water for blankets and buffalo robes." And the "Chief" retorts: "Beat it, kid! Beat it! I'm Carlisle 1904" (figure 5). Many sports fans assumed that Carlisle, which played some historic games against Yale and Harvard, was a college, whereas most of its students received only a few years of schooling.[94]

Roe Cloud's *History of the Class of* 1910 yearbook photograph shows a handsome, confident-looking, tastefully dressed, clean-cut Yalie, short hair parted on the left—no sign of the conspicuously ill-fitting whiteness

3 Mohican Club, Whiffenpoofs, and Louis Linder in center (owner of Mory's), 1912. Manuscripts and Archives, Yale University Library.

R. K. RICHARDS . . . . Big Chief
J. F. JOHNSON, JR., ... Chief

Braves

D. S. Boynton   J. L. G. Hall

R. Clement   A. P. Howard

  T. C. Coffin   J. W. Lewis, Jr.

    W. L. Eyre   T.Lilley

      W. H. Parsons

      A. Gardner

      G. S. Patterson

      G. A. Richardson

      R. Roome

4 Mohican Club, in *The Yale Banner and Potpourri*, 1910. Manuscripts and Archives, Yale University Library.

Stude—(out w e s t)—
Say chief, I'll trade you
heap much beads and
fire water for blankets
and buffalo robes.

Chief—Beat i t, Kid !
Beat it! I'm Carlisle
1904.

5 Cartoon of an Indian and a white man in a hat (perhaps a Yale student),
in *The Yale Book for 1910*. Manuscripts and Archives, Yale University Library.

6 The young collegiate
Henry Roe Cloud,
in *History of the Class
of 1910* (1910), 95.
Manuscripts and
Archives, Yale
University Library.

that Luther Standing Bear's autobiography relates that he loved to perform, parody, and parrot at Carlisle (playfully utilizing squeaky boots, ties
without collars, over-large clothes to dramatize his point) (figure 6). In
1908 Roe Cloud joined the fraternity Beta Theta Pi, whose members, he
felt, bonded closely to one another.[95] Despite Roe Cloud's lack of funds—
most of his money came from his allotment lease and from waiting
tables—he mused, like other new Yale graduates, about traveling.[96] Roe
Cloud was a member of the Cosmopolitan Club, many of whose members
had come from around the world (China, Japan, Europe). He appears to
have had good times socially and seems to have courted some women
eager to know him.

Chapter 2 will consider some of the more melodramatic letters surrounding Mary Roe's efforts to influence Henry's romantic ventures with
white women. While Roe Cloud was at Yale, avidly taking his English
courses, the doomed courtship narrative of an Indian male's attraction to
and tragic though inevitable rejection by a white woman was becoming a
literary cliché that piqued the curiosity of some Yalies. The *Yale Lit.* of May
1907, published at the close of Roe Cloud's first year, includes an anonymous review of Marah Ellis Ryan's *Indian Love Letters* (1907). This sentimental novel may well have drawn the freshman's notice and his classmates'
attention in part because of the Winnebago's presence on campus. Sé-
téwa, the melancholic protagonist, is a Hopi, misspelled by the *Yale Lit.*
reviewer as Hapi, who has been educated in an eastern university. Having returned to his reservation in the West, he corresponds with a white
woman whose affections, he gradually learns, are being lavished on one
of his white classmates. The reviewer observes that Ryan portrays the
broken-hearted Hopi as a tragic cultural hybrid, more victim than benefi-
ciary of higher education and romantic longings: "The terrible realization
comes over him that though she is everything to him, he can never be
anything to her. . . . He can never become as one of his own tribe again;
touched by the East and its ideas, he is forever different." By attending college, Indians risk being homeless as well as loveless. His rejection—
integration goes only so far when romance is the issue—is suffused with an
aura of inevitability: "In these letters we read it all,—the beauty, the pathos,
the despair,—and the conviction that it could not have been otherwise."

The novel's ideological significance goes beyond what the review describes. Sé-téwa's declension from Christian belief is the consequence of his rejection by the white woman who inspired his missionary zeal: "In the light of your faith I saw things radiantly. I was to be their own apostle of your religion,—and yours was mine,—blindly and without question!" (7). Interestingly, *Indian Love Letters* invests white femininity with greater transformative, or colonizing, power than Christianity, education, or the government. It suggests that if an Indian man falls in love with a white woman he will be willing to overlook a multitude of oppressions and contradictions afflicting his people. While Sé-téwa can develop considerable critical distance from the authority of the U.S. government and Christianity, his melodramatic fixation on the unattainable white woman he worships remains primary, determinative, and ultimately destructive. He gives her the Indian name Hoetska. She has no voice in the novel. Nevertheless, Ryan grants Hoetska the devastating romantic and sentimental power, whether she exercises this power consciously or not, to implant in the Hopi a sense of cultural and racial inadequacy and hopelessness he cannot counteract: "My new Hogan—but to you, O Dream Beloved!—that thought sounds nothing to you." An Indian woman tries desperately to revive Sé-téwa, but, lacking class respectability and refinement, she has no such power. The plot fulfills Lyman Abbott's prediction that educated Indian men will spurn unschooled Indian women on the reservation with "natural disgust." So the novel's college Indian, quite unlike Roe Cloud, loses his will and dies.[97] The Yale review and the novel circulated increasingly popular college Indian stereotypes and rejection narratives that Roe Cloud may well have had to negotiate.

At least in hindsight, Du Bois viewed racial rejection at Harvard as a source of his critical strength because it made visible the unfair power relations structuring "Fair Harvard" and Fair America. Yet he also viewed this defensive posture as "something of a certain inferiority complex . . . I was desperately afraid of not being wanted; of intruding without invitation; of appearing to desire the company of those who had no desire for me." At Harvard the well-armored Du Bois made few white friends and tactically "cultivated a certain brusquerie." This was not Roe Cloud's style or strategy. He had no wish to appear defensive. On occasion Du Bois showed interest in joining "student organizations, but was not greatly disappointed when the expected refusals came." Instead Du Bois "found

7 "In Freshman Year," in *History of the Class of 1910* (1910), 8. Manuscripts and Archives, Yale University Library. The figure sitting cross legged in the first row, sixth from left, may be Roe Cloud.

friends and most interesting and inspiring friends among the colored folk of Boston and surrounding places." This included dancing, partying, and escorting "colored girls and as pretty ones as I could find, to vesper exercises and the class day and commencement social functions."[98]

Not only were there no other Indians at Yale, Roe Cloud's correspondence does not mention any in New Haven.[99] A yearbook photograph of the Class of 1910 in their freshman year exhibits the wall of white faces that dominated (figure 7). In this way too Roe Cloud's student life differed significantly from that of Chal at the University of Oklahoma. Whatever discrimination or slights Roe Cloud encountered on or off the reservation before entering Yale, he seems to have made the most of his interactions with his fellow Yale students.

In this endeavor he was not so unusual, for some of Du Bois's African American contemporaries at Harvard had experiences more like Roe Cloud's at Yale. Clement Morgan, who graduated from Harvard's college in 1890 and law school in 1893, was, like Roe Cloud, popular with his classmates and startled the nation by being elected Class Orator. He won by one vote over a student dubbed a Harvard "aristocrat" by the *New York World*. Du Bois registered the event's racial and class significance: "There were editorials in the leading newspapers, and the South especially raged and sneered at the audience of 'black washer-women' who would replace Boston society at the next Harvard commencement." Just as Roe Cloud received his preparatory training at Mount Hermon (matriculating at Yale around age 22), Morgan worked his way to the prestigious Boston Latin School (matriculating at Harvard at age 27), so both were accustomed to the social set they found in college. W. Monroe Trotter, like Morgan, combined academic and social achievement. He consistently ranked near the top of his Harvard college class, graduating magna cum laude in 1895 and taking his Harvard M.A. in 1896. Trotter insisted on integrating with white students. Du Bois acknowledged that he would have enjoyed getting to know the "curiously aloof" Trotter better, but Trotter believed that "colored students must not herd together, just because they were colored." Du Bois portrayed himself not as "arrogant" toward white students, just "not obsequious." But his Harvard classmates, he said, read this as a sign that he "was trying to be more than a Negro." Hence Du Bois, who wrote a fair amount about his Harvard experiences, claimed: "I was in Harvard, but not of it."[100] Roe Cloud was not only in Yale, he appeared to be of it.

Du Bois's "brusquerie" strengthened his resolve. It could be an effective strategy. When Du Bois sought financing for European study from the Slater Fund, he had every reason to be pessimistic. The fund was set up in 1882 to provide assistance for intellectually deserving African Americans who sought to advance their educations. For more than a decade the fund, rather suspiciously, found it difficult to discover applicants truly worthy of its support. Rutherford B. Hayes, former President of the United States, directed the fund and in November 1890—the year Morgan was elected Class Orator and two years after Morgan and Du Bois came in first and second respectively in Harvard's Boylston oratory contest—quipped in the *Boston Herald* that only "orators" had applied. Du Bois had some tense correspondence with Hayes, who originally rejected him offhandedly, not expecting a rebuttal. However much Roe Cloud would have agreed with parts of what Du Bois wrote Hayes, it is unlikely that he would have considered this confrontational letter tactical: "I find men willing to help me thro' cheap theological schools, I find men willing to help me use my hands before I have got my brains in working order, I have an abundance of good wishes on hand, but I never found a man willing to help me get a Harvard Ph.D." Du Bois shamed Hayes. The funding came through, though half as grant and, "to salve their souls," "half as repayable loan with five percent interest."[101] While both Du Bois and Roe Cloud were interested in winning, Roe Cloud seems to have been more intent on winning people over.

When Du Bois pursued graduate work at the University of Berlin, he found in European culture, and in the much lower incidence of racial discrimination against African Americans there, some impression of "the possible beauty and elegance of life." He developed "a respect for manners" and took time to savor what Europe offered not only intellectually but also aesthetically. In America he had "wanted a world, hard, smooth and swift, and had no time for rounded corners and ornament, for unhurried thought and slow contemplation. Now at times I sat still." In some ways Roe Cloud's perception of Yale seems closer to Du Bois' perception of Europe than of Harvard. Roe Cloud's Indian racial encoding and singularity may have given him enough breathing space to form and maintain this response at Yale. Of course, Roe Cloud also invested his sense of Indian mission, especially after meeting the Roes, in Christianity. This helped sustain him. Du Bois, by contrast, was "critical of religion."[102]

I must emphasize again that Roe Cloud's archived letters are mostly to the Roes, and he may have censored some of what he thought would have been embarrassing or worrisome for them to read. When Vine Deloria Sr. (Yankton Dakota Sioux) attended St. Stephens College, later renamed Bard College, in Annandale-on-Hudson, New York, in the mid-1920s, he was a star athlete and popular with his classmates. Deloria, like Roe Cloud, was the only Indian in his college. His friends gave him clothing because stores in town refused to let him try on their garments. Yet when Deloria attended Kearney Military Academy, a "non-Indian Episcopal boarding school" in Nebraska, he "rarely confronted racial prejudice . . . and, indeed, taught his friends bits and pieces of the Dakota language while they in turn renamed him 'Pete,' a transformation he seems to have thoroughly appre-

ciated."[103] Perhaps it was a combination of Roe Cloud's Winnebago upbringing, his turn-the-other-cheek Christianity, and, not least of all, the
ongoing kindliness and moral support of the Roes that accounts for his
unwillingness to respond to whatever stereotypes, slights, or discrimination he encountered at Yale or elsewhere in this period with Du Boisian
"brusquerie" rather than poise, resilience, and compassion.

YALE AMBITIONS

Roe Cloud's 1906 application for a tuition scholarship indicates that he
aspired to be a medical missionary, and for that reason he felt that he must
incur the travel expenses necessary to remain in contact with the Winnebago and practice his native language.[104] The Roes dissuaded him from
attending medical school right away—he was interested in Johns Hopkins
—in favor of divinity school.[105] He went to two divinity schools, but eventually pursued a career in Indian education and later government service on behalf of Indians rather than in missionary evangelism. Du Bois
too had to contend with ministerial efforts to establish the character
and level of his education and career. He had yearned to attend Harvard
from the start, but needed financial help. His high school principal and
several ministers agreed to have their churches donate a hundred dollars
annually to support his college education. But one of these ministers, Rev.
Charles C. Painter, an agent of the Indian Rights Association who advised
the government to invalidate all treaties, insisted that Du Bois attend Fisk
rather than Harvard. Later the president of Fisk offered Du Bois a scholarship to attend Hartford Theological Seminary.[106] Du Bois pragmatically
accepted the churches' money, ignored their paternalism, and, after Fisk,
won a Price Greenleaf stipend to Harvard. His original intention was to go
to Harvard not to do another B.A., but to take his Ph.D., which he received
in 1898.[107]

One of Roe Cloud's two referees for his Yale application was Dr. Alfred
L. Riggs, the superintendent of his alma mater, Santee Mission School.
The novelist D'Arcy McNickle (Cree and Métis, enrolled as Salish), who
worked for the Collier Bureau of Indian Affairs, wrote for the commissioner a review essay that includes excerpts from an 1898 report on Indian
schools that quotes some of Riggs' views of Indians—notions in conflict

with those promoted by the Indian New Deal. Riggs decried the non-rational behavior of Indian youth, especially girls, and characterized the Indian as an unproductive mixture of individualism and socialism. He highlighted the importance, as Roe Cloud would at Yale and after, of reaching the souls of Indians to resocialize them.[108] In Roe Cloud's Mount Hermon and Yale phase, he had to leave at least one close family member: his 1909 financial aid application mentions that he had a twenty-eight year old brother, but does not name him or specify his whereabouts.[109]

Roe Cloud was academically ambitious. Amid a welter of competing commitments on and off campus the Mount Hermon salutatorian worked in the (vain) hope of being elected to Phi Beta Kappa. Different grading standards and modes of grading back then make his record difficult to assess. Graduating with a 289 average out of 400, he was awarded a "dissertation appointment," the third highest category.[110] Roe Cloud took more courses in English than in any other subject (six courses out of twenty-six) and usually did well, and he excelled in philosophy (four courses) and Greek (two). He signed some of his letters Heinrich, was fond of quoting Goethe, and included passages in German in his letters (especially to Dr. Roe, a Phi Beta Kappa graduate of Williams College, Class of 1881).

Roe Cloud was earnest about acquiring intellectual breadth, cultural polish, and social poise, while Du Bois seems to have had a fiercer intellectual drive and ego. "I do not doubt that I was voted a somewhat selfish and self-centered 'grind' with a chip on my shoulder and a sharp tongue," Du Bois boasted. Roe Cloud appears to have enjoyed and respected his professors, while Du Bois appears to have been even more intellectually consumed by his critical engagements with faculty such as William James, Josiah Royce, and George Santayana. He seems to have been closer to his teachers—whom he called his "salvation" at Harvard—than to his fellow students. "I was repeatedly a guest in the home of William James," he reminisced; "he was my friend and guide to clear thinking." And he "sat in an upper room and read Kant's *Critique* with Santayana."[111] After Yale, Roe Cloud left Oberlin for Auburn's seminary, partly, he said, because he felt it could offer him a more rigorous intellectual program.[112]

However much Yale may have given Roe Cloud and Harvard may have given Du Bois a need for class distinction, both institutions also gave these men a certain degree of intellectual and social confidence that helped embolden them to question the very precepts of the dominant society their powerful universities reproduced. Henry Adams, who had matriculated at Harvard about fifty years before Roe Cloud entered Yale, was almost comically blasé about what he learned there: "Education had not begun." But his detached attitude was as much a Harvard badge of upper-class membership as the "self-possession" he acknowledged as Harvard's "strongest" training. It may have been this racial and class security that both anchored and set loose the self-questioning and social questioning that made some of what Adams wrote as critical as some of Du Bois's and Roe Cloud's critical reflections.[113] Throughout his life Du Bois was as quick to associate himself with the name Harvard, even while criticizing it, as Roe Cloud was with the name Yale.[114] Both realized the strategic cultural value of associating themselves and their causes with such institutions—as did Adams, who eventually joined Harvard's faculty.

Roe Cloud's second most important Yale triumph was earning one of five second-place prizes in the 1909 Henry James Ten Eyck Prize speaking contest (Robert Taft also garnered this distinction).[115] Many of his supporters felt that he was the clear winner. Roe Cloud, somewhat like Booker T. Washington, appreciated how oratory and charming self-effacement could smooth the interracial way to middle- and upper-class acceptance—and influence.[116] Oratory gained him prestige at Yale. When Du Bois took second place in Harvard's Boylston speech contest, however, he was more interested in the prize money and in combatively demonstrating his oratorical superiority than in giving the impression that he belonged or wanted to belong.[117] Adams, a Boston Brahmin descendant of two American presidents and a string of Harvard men, felt none of the longing to belong or admiration that may have motivated Roe Cloud, for he took much of what he found at Harvard for granted. Turning on the electric self-irony that runs through so many of the Yale class books, Adams was surprised to have been elected Class Orator, given his lack of popularity, and responded to a relative's criticism that his class oration lacked verve by musing: "Was this absence of enthusiasm a defect or a merit, in either case, it was all that Harvard College taught, and all that the hundred young men whom he was trying to represent, expressed." It may be that Roe Cloud's popularity owed much to his spirited deviation from this type, while Adams's election partly reflected his talent, as he put it, for endowing his and his classmates' "commonplaces" with Harvard eloquence and distinction.[118]

Roe Cloud's most outstanding accomplishment at Yale was his election in 1909 to the socially prestigious, intellectually inclined, and recently established Elihu Club. Joseph Roe, an Instructor of Mechanical Engineering in Yale's Sheffield Scientific School, wrote beamingly to Mary Roe, his sister-in-law, that the Elihu Club operated on the same high level as the exclusive secret society Skull and Bones. He estimated that 300 students would have felt privileged to be elected. Although Roe Cloud had not been elected to leadership positions in his class, or starred in varsity sports, or come from a wealthy family, he had achieved this recognition. The young faculty member attributed Roe Cloud's success to his classmates' respect for his character.[119]

William Young Duncan, a classmate of Roe Cloud's at Mount Hermon and at Yale president of the Mount Hermon Club, was elected to the Elihu Club in his junior year. Roe Cloud had roomed with Duncan as a freshman and sophomore. Perhaps he played some role in advocating for Roe Cloud's election with three other classmates in November of their senior year. Roe Cloud would have been familiar with Winnebago secret societies that required their members to deliver eloquent speeches as part of their rituals.[120] The Elihu Club was founded in 1903 as a nonsecret club devoted to intellectual interaction and the refinement of forensic skills. Its members staged debates on social issues as well as Yale concerns; practiced giving after-dinner extemporaneous talks; wrote, presented, and criticized essays (members voted on which essays merited inclusion in the club library); invited distinguished faculty at Yale and other institutions to lecture at the club; and expanded the club library. Though none of this was available to nonmembers, the club's openness about its mission marked it as a modern Yale invention. It quickly established a large and powerful base of support by electing accomplished alumni as well as outstanding juniors and seniors. The administration and faculty applauded its intellectual and literary seriousness. As Joseph Roe testified, Roe Cloud's election indicated the esteem in which he was held.

Its minutes show that from 1903 till Roe Cloud's election club members often debated issues about race, ethnicity, and prejudice, such as should negroes be admitted to Yale (the majority voted yes in 1905, no in 1907 and 1909); should "the present social ostracism of the Jews be tolerated" (the majority voted yes in 1905); should the Chinese Exclusion Act be supported (the majority voted yes in 1906); should Japanese laborers be excluded legally from the U.S. (the majority voted yes in 1906 and 1908); and should the United States sell the Philippines (the majority voted no in 1907). Members wrote, presented, and criticized essays not only on Edith Wharton (1906) and Henrik Ibsen (1908) but on "Captain John Smith and Pocahontas" (1905), "Marriage Customs and Means of Attraction Which Primitive People Used" (1906), "A Few Remarks on New Haven Tenements" (1909), "Child Labor" (1905), and "The Old-fashioned Negro" (1909). During Roe Cloud's senior year the club debated neither race nor imperialism (one member wrote a paper, however, on the history of Haiti). Members voted that Roe Cloud's essay, "The Elihu Club and Its Relation to the Sheff.[ield Engineering School] Question" (1909), be kept in the club's collection, but did not elect to retain another essay, perhaps by Roe Cloud, on "A Trip Through the Rose Bud Country" (1910). The club debated whether "employers [should] be held absolutely liable for injuries to their employees in the course of the business" ("won by the negative" in 1910).[121]

The Elihu Club's annual banquet in 1910 was held at the sumptuous University Club in New York City. Not long before this Roe Cloud had enjoyed a splendid Mount Hermon alumni banquet in which the menu was printed in Latin and translated into English; so he was accustomed to posh affairs. But the Elihu Club evening at the University Club, the understandably impressionable young man wrote Mary Roe, exceeded even his expectations and elicited his awe and wonder. He remarked on his dreamlike impression of the magnificent marble columns, the plush carpets that felt exquisitely comfortable to walk on, and the wealthy Yale alumni with their auras of business, professional, and cultural distinction. It was patent to him why the opulent University Club's social status was unparalleled. Yale's Elihu Club, he assumed, with touching humility, had been part of God's plan for him. He had begun his career under quite different circumstances.

Roe Cloud's representation of this ennobling banquet—to the Roes—is challenging to interpret. On the one hand, Roe Cloud, faced with power-ful, white Yalies, tailored in success, *appears* to have adopted some of their points of view. On the other hand, schooled in *how* these Yalies think and feel, Roe Cloud may well have worked his Elihu audience to win their sympathies. He performed impressively that evening, and perhaps for the Roes as well.

In addition to the marble, the carpets, and the mingling millionaires, there were three African American entertainers who supplied the guests with a gay scenery and harmonious soundtrack for their conversations. In his letter, perhaps echoing his fellow club members, he called them "dark-ies." One might wonder how the Roes responded to this label. During breaks in the orations they sang the lyric, "My love is like a river flowing." The Yalies chimed in at the chorus. Whatever Roe Cloud thought about this racial divide, it would not have appeared altogether singular to him. Yale's University Dining Hall (Commons) was staffed by legions of African American waiters uniformed in white aprons (figure 8). A cartoon in *The Yale Book for* 1910 suggests the casual, even playful characteristic of racist remarks among some undergraduates. It depicts two young men, presum-ably Yale students, eagerly conversing about a "game of nigger baby" (figure 9).

During that splendid night at the University Club, Roe Cloud seemed to accept Yale's codes of distinction—its lavish stage set and props (human and material) for Yale's corporate gathering. He chose to relate publicly to the university men as thinkers (which, doubtless, many of them were)—not as the *crème de la crème* of a well-educated power structure that with its armies, laws, broken treaties, and bureaucracies systematically stole In-dian land; not as a cultural elite that with its ideologies of religion, prog-ress, human evolution, reform, and sentimental family life tried to feel good about itself while bamboozling Indians; not as the holders of rail-road, telegraph, mining, lumber, and cattle stock who possessed the vision to see that so many unused tribal lands (unused by their companies) should be labeled *surplus land* by the government and sold. Roe Cloud gave the Roes the impression that he felt the surge of social self-confidence, experienced the reassurance of entitlement, and basked in the aura of the intellectual achievement that Yale's Elihu Club was capable of conferring on him. Yale offered many students more than an education, explicit and implicit, in

8 University Dining Hall (Commons), 1906, African American waiters in aprons. Manuscripts and Archives, Yale University Library.

9 Cartoon of two young men (presumably Yale students) walking, in *The Yale Book for 1910*. Manuscripts and Archives, Yale University Library.

Mr. Micawber, you know, was always waiting for something to turn up.

Why didn't he get into a game of nigger baby.

how to win—and in how to rationalize this winning intellectually, culturally, and ethically. The Yale men with whom Roe Cloud mingled had acquired markers of impeccably designed individuality. Schools like Carlisle,
and those that Roe Cloud attended in his early youth, did not offer the luxury of this liberal arts ideology of self-expression. At Carlisle, when Luther
Standing Bear informed Pratt that he had no desire to continue learning
tinsmithing for half a day daily and would prefer to receive full-time academic training, Pratt told him that he had no choice in the matter.[122]

Suddenly, Roe Cloud wrote, the African Americans' music making
stopped, and the toastmaster announced that he had something special in
store for the gathering and, to the Indian's surprise, started to introduce
him. He profiled Roe Cloud as exemplifying the characteristics of the
greatest Indians who were fast disappearing from the American land-
scape. Although the toastmaster punned lamely on his name in an effort to
be witty, Roe Cloud appeared energized by the introduction. The Indian's
hortatory remarks demonstrated that he had no interest in disappearing or
in having his race disappear.

Roe Cloud rose to the occasion, and with his well-honed nonchalance
and charm improvised and proved that he could belong, or strategically
stage class belonging. He could easily and entertainingly reproduce Yale's
upper-class rhetoric and allusions. The Winnebago's erudition, perhaps
more than that of his fellow club members, bespoke the civilizing and
individualizing power of Yale. Yet, like the African American musicians,
part of his entertainment value to the group was his racial otherness. Roe
Cloud, recognizing this, proud of this difference, and knowing his audience, elected not to discuss Goethe and instead regaled the Yale thinkers
with Indian stories and maxims. Iterating the moral of an Indian legend
with oratorical flourishes, he testified to the importance of exercising
courage and not turning away from a battle that needed to be waged. The
auditors soon learned that the smoky struggle Roe Cloud alluded to pertained to the current national situation of Indians. In some ways the
eloquent Roe Cloud fit the description of the intrepid Indian warrior in the
legend he narrated. Perhaps this smoky struggle was taking place right
then and there in the University Club with the Elihu Club in force.[123] Roe
Cloud underscored the importance of having an Indian lead Indians. Moving in the direction of Indian self-determination, he rhetorically posi-

tioned the Elihus as sympathetic rather than skeptical, as allies rather than self-interested antagonists, as part of the solution rather than part of the problem. At that point some of Roe Cloud's auditors may have mused: who better to manage 250,000 or so Indians, many of whom were camping out on unutilized surplus land, than an Elihu? The audience erupted with applause. The evening was, yet was not quite, Roe Cloud's.

Du Bois's acknowledgments of the institutionally and culturally produced limits of his not-so-critical thinking as a young man are worth keeping in mind when weighing the awesome power of what may have influenced Roe Cloud's thinking—or tactical improvisation of a certain type of thinking. Before entering Fisk and then Harvard, Du Bois, raised in western Massachusetts, and a superb student, had simply subscribed to his town's "patterns of economic thought"—essentially unadulterated self-help, private property, free enterprise ideology: "My general attitude toward property and income was that all who were willing to work could easily earn a living; that those who had property had earned it and deserved it and could use it as they wished; that poverty was the shadow of crime and connoted lack of thrift and shiftlessness." Young Du Bois, in words that surely would have ingratiated him to the Gilded Age's Robber Barons, supposed that "the foundations of present culture" and "progress" were "undoubted and inevitable": "There was room for argument concerning details and methods and possible detours in the onsweep of civilization; but the fundamental facts were clear, unquestioned and unquestionable." His "higher education" did not seem to provoke him to question the ostensibly unquestionable. In 1888, his final year at Fisk, Du Bois chose to write his thesis on his "hero" Bismarck, a selection which, he later realized with acute embarrassment, "showed the abyss between my education and the truth in the world": "I was blithely European and imperialist in outlook; democratic as democracy was conceived in America." While Fisk helped fortify his racial identity, it also supplied him with a class pose—what Manning Marable describes as "elitist tendencies and an aversion to the struggles of workers." He fared little better after Fisk. Du Bois entered Harvard as a junior, graduating in 1890 and taking his master's degree in history in 1891. At Harvard, which was "rich," "reactionary," and "contemptuous" of working-class movements, the "politics which we studied . . . were conventional." Du Bois pointed out that his professors rarely mentioned Karl Marx (Adams noted that his professors never cited Marx). When they did it was only to suggest that "his theories had long since been refuted." Two years of graduate work at the University of Berlin, from 1892 to 1894, enriched and globalized Du Bois's perspective on "the race problem" and the social contradictions entwined with it. But he had to wait until he "was long out of college" before he "began to see clearly the connection of economics and politics; the fundamental influence of man's efforts to earn a living upon all his other efforts." Therefore, while Du Bois's consciousness of racial oppression and his social exclusion as a black man was what consistently rescued him "from complete conformity with the thoughts and confusions of . . . current social trends," it was a long haul before his thinking gained critical distance from Harvard's reigning intellectual premises and preoccupations.[124]

Memmi's concerns, informed by his education at the Sorbonne in the post–Second World War years, also may throw light on some of Roe Cloud's inscribed responses to, or strategic articulation of particular responses to, his ideological climate. Writing in 1957, Memmi sketches the colonized's "ambition" to "disappear" in the "splendid model" of the colonizer. "How could [the colonized] hate the colonizers and yet admire them so passionately? (I too felt this admiration in spite of myself.)." Built into the colonized's admiration is at once an "approval of colonization" and a rejection of "the colonial situation." This rejection, however, encompasses a rejection of self that produces "feelings ranging from shame to self-hate"—and, sometimes ascendant in Roe Cloud's experience, insecurity. Such "self-doubt" is often allied to "the long maintained hope that the almighty power of the colonizer might bear the fruit of infinite goodness."[125] More critically, one may also use this admiration, and the colonizers' self-admiration, to redirect the "power of the colonizer" to ends that might bear new sorts of "fruit" for the colonized.

Notwithstanding the capacity of Yale, the Elihu Club, the opulent monumentality of the University Club, and the singing African Americans to bestow on the guests secure feelings of being meritorious, supremely individual Christian gentlemen, Henry confessed to Mary, in that effusive letter about his speech, that he, pilgrim from wigwam to University Club, still felt shaky about his destiny. He noted that Martin Luther and Jonathan Edwards questioned whether they deserved God's blessings. While he did not wish to compare himself to men of this religious stature, the pious Winnebago wondered self-effacingly if he warranted all that God had done for him.[126] Perhaps residually uneasy with his riveting extemporaneous performance and audience, he felt unsure of his role and power in that smoky fight.

One year earlier Roe Cloud observed how frequently he was asked to discuss missionary work among the Indians in the residences of professionals, managers, businessmen, and ministers, and how gratified he was by the pleasures of such recognition.[127] But he had to remind himself, with encouragement from the Roes, that religious service must be elevated above all. It was his Yale affiliation as well as his bond with the Roes that provided him with a passport into this tempting class, so that he might raise funds for missionary work. Just as Eastman moved in distinguished circles at Dartmouth, and eventually sent his daughter to Wellesley, Roe Cloud moved in Yale, Williams, Harvard, and Vassar circles. In the 1910s he attended Yale, Harvard, Princeton, and Carlisle football games. He did not despise luxury. At Auburn he fretted just a bit over not being able to resist buying, on his tight budget, new pens, stationary, and a camera.[128]

Perhaps his Winnebago tribe did not quite sound or dress like his sophisticated eastern set. He still had Winnebago friends, although the archived correspondence I have read does not include many of his communications with or extensive profiles of them. This does not mean he forgot them. In 1911 he gave the Roes the impression that he saw one of the more exuberant Winnebago dances only through his Yale-crafted and Roes-crafted lens. He compared the Buffalo dance to Homer's sketches of bees and waterfowl in the *Odyssey*. Roe Cloud associated these Homeric creatures with the drives that supercharged the dance.[129] Here he did not cast the Winnebago as distinct or distinctive individuals, at least not in the Yale sense. Although Carlisle's *Red Man* reported in 1916 that Indians had no interest in learning white dances and preferred their own, Yale social life influenced the formation of some of Roe Cloud's fascinations. His social involvements at Yale prompted him to consider taking dancing lessons.[130]

Of course, Roe Cloud's Winnebago charm in tandem with his Yale charm opened social opportunities. In 1907, shortly after he met the Roes, he wrote Mary, with obvious mock self-deprecation, that he could converse with her in Winnebago, as if this would be something requiring her toleration.[131] Some of their truly endearing names for one another were in Winnebago. Perhaps he hoped to teach Mary not just to appreciate, but to think in, the Winnebago tongue, even though her cultural language formed the basis of their friendship. At times his Indian and Yale identities, which frequently worked so well together, may have been in tension with one another. Yale certainly gave him class visibility as well as intellectual delight.[132] But this power sometimes made him anxious about preserving his Yale status—and class agency. He would later employ this status, this agency, to aid and expand his work with and for Indians.

MISSIONS TO THE YALIES

The greatest test of Roe Cloud's oratorical prowess at Yale was the Henry James Ten Eyck speech contest. He included part of the text of his speech, "Missions to the Indians," in his letters to the Roes and sought their editorial advice. In places his text mimics a Progressive Era inevitability-of-progress oration. He wrote of the cities and railroads that have come to line the country and link all parts of the nation. Mass production, too, he observed, has made commodities previously available only to the wealthy accessible to many Americans. But Roe Cloud knew that before this development laid down its laws the seemingly uninhabited lands had already been populated. Once there had been hundreds of thousands of not quite vanishing Indians and countless but increasingly vanishing buffalo that, perhaps strategically, Roe Cloud did not choose to mention to his Yale peers. Instead, the Indian student tactically fused Independence Day and Manifest Destiny rhetoric. He lauded the U.S. Constitution as the inspiration for many countries in the hemisphere. And he alluded to the Revolution as a sign of America's commitment to freedom. Throughout the draft of his speech Roe Cloud's plural pronouns convey the speaker's own patriotic identification with America's political, legal, industrial, and cultural achievements and expansion. He does not criticize the American colonizers who erected the cities and imposed the railroads, producing the wealth of the rich often out of the needs and labors of the poor, pushing and shoving American versions of improvement and culture westward.

Next he invoked the melting-pot metaphor, suggesting that the hegemonic powers that be has provided a dominant mold for the diverse multitudes that have undergone melting and await reshaping.[133]

The inevitability-of-progress theme with which he began concluded by describing the Indians' destination—the hegemonic melting pot. Yet melting was not the crux of his point. His principal criticism was that the Indian has never been enfranchised, what Carlisle and white reformers called "citizenized." The laws have not treated Indians justly as Americans. Here Roe Cloud reassociated the railroaded lands with the systemic abuse of Indians. At this phase of his speech Roe Cloud's plural pronouns signaled his identification with colonized Indians rather than colonizing Americans.[134] Curiously, he then enunciated what appears to be an evangelical strategy of affective and religious restructuring, seemingly based on prevalent evolutionary race theory. Indians, he implored, will not change happily in response to meager government support and coercive laws. Instead, Indians can be moved to join American culture in another, more subtle way. They must be reached, like youth, through their affective, spiritual, and ethical dispositions.[135] This was a sentimental, and sentimentalizing, tactic: Indian feelings were the key to winning Indian loyalty and identification. Such sentimental rhetoric was likely to win white backing. And yet, as made evident by his later writings that Christianize incentive building, what Roe Cloud had uppermost in mind was Indian support.

As the Yale Courant published a briefer version of Roe Cloud's speech in May 1909, it must have drawn widely favorable notice when it was delivered in the contest.[136] The essay both deploys popular romantic stereotypes—"I speak in behalf of a vanishing race"—and at times is staunchly critical and ironic: "Civilization, sure of its divine right, has extended the hand of fellowship to those outside its pale, only to let fall the mailed fist of the oppressor." But Roe Cloud softened, or redirected, his guilt-producing critique of "divine right" by turning it into a decidedly melodramatic supplication: "In the name of enlightened progress I say the strong peoples of the earth must bear the burdens of the weak" (520).

Interestingly, his essay underscored in print the central message of the speech about the possibilities of emotional restructuring—"reach[ing] the heart of the Indian" (520) and "implant[ing] the love of God" (523). Roe Cloud presented his overarching civic concern as: how can desire, incentive, drive, given the comprehensive destructive power of the "oppressor," best be implanted in Indians?[137] In an address delivered in 1914, Roe Cloud again sounded his strategic theme: Indians must be schooled to acquire manual, intellectual, and emotional skills that would enable them not just to survive but thrive.[138]

However, in thinking about the scope of this transformative schooling he had more than Indians in mind. While Roe Cloud was telling elite whites how to rearrange the emotional motivations of Indians, he was trying to reorient his powerful white audiences sentimentally and ideologically to motivate them to help rescue Indians from federal domination on and off reservations. He wanted his melodramatic appeal to activate white Christianized hearts. In effect, through his membership in the "club," the Winnebago undergraduate attempted to emotionally realign the Yalies. Roe Cloud was outnumbered, always outnumbered, by whites and by stereotypes. But the sentimental reconstruction of white perspective and value was part of his encompassing mission at Yale and after.

SENTIMENTAL AND MELODRAMATIC CHARISMA

The Roes realized quickly how expertly Roe Cloud made sentimental appeals to members of their class, and Roe Cloud recognized this too. It is significant that the authorial line for his "Missions to the American Indians" in The Yale Courant foregrounds his origins and thus his cultural and sentimental authority: "By H. Cloud, of the Winnebago Tribe, Nebraska." As early as 1907 Roe Cloud wrote of white women who cried during his talk in the home of a prosperous woman.[139] He was also much in demand as a teller of Indian tales at the Elihu Club.[140] A few years later President George B. Stewart of Auburn Theological Seminary suggested to Dr. Roe that Roe Cloud's exceptional popularity as a speaker did not redound to the benefit of his studies.[141] Roe Cloud, as an Indian and a Yalie, had a powerfully sentimental and melodramatic class cachet.

Members of this privileged social circle not only liked listening to a Yale Indian, they enjoyed buying things from him. Over the Christmas holiday in 1908–9, Roe Cloud sold $200 worth of goods to a Yale alumnus who was a millionaire stockbroker. He helped make Roe Cloud aware of how valuable Indianness was becoming as a collector's item or collector's prop, particularly a Crow scalp taken by a Winnebago warrior: Roe Cloud proposed ten dollars as a price and the stockbroker countered with fifty.[142] In the early 1900s it was becoming fashionable for the middle and upper classes to decorate their homes and sometimes their bodies with Indian souvenirs. Mary encouraged him to sell Indian belts not only to males but to females, for Bessie Page, Mary's niece, affirmed that her Vassar class-mates enthusiastically complimented her belt. Women, Mary assured him, appreciated her Indian clothes. (The Roe family archive houses a photo-graph of Mary as a young woman dressed in full Indian regalia.)[143] Bessie wrote Henry that she was so taken with her belts and her friendship with him that she wanted to be an Indian and live in nature.[144] In this period Dr. Charles Eastman and Elaine Goodale Eastman established a summer camp that taught "American girls" Indian ways. However much Roe Cloud was accepted as an upper-middle-class Yale man, he had to risk being stereotyped more romantically and faddishly as an "Indian," though this too, like his collegiate polish, often gained him access to ruling groups.[145]

Henry's charismatic salesmanship caused Mary some apprehension.[146] She distrusted the motives behind some of these cross-racial interests and felt that Roe Cloud's Yale-Winnebago magnetism had to be presented in the right manner. What stirred up Mary's anxiety especially was her niece's growing fascination with Henry, whom Bessie referred to as her cousin. Mary wrote him that affections from young white women such as Bessie should not be taken too seriously and that Henry should decorously deflect their youthful interest in him. She attributed his romantic charm to his racial novelty within her social circle. Mary suggested that Vassar women would be drawn to him as a Winnebago, not simply as a young man of good character. On the other hand, she recognized that this sort of interest could assist their religious mission. If his Indian appeal enabled him to evangelize for Christ more effectively, its understated expression could serve a noble purpose.[147]

If promoting Christ's—and Mary's—cause involved redirecting the sen-timental concerns and economic interests of the wealthy, then so be it. In his unsuccessful effort to persuade department-store millionaire Rodman Wanamaker to support the new Roe Indian Institute, then Roe Cloud equated what was then termed "Christian motive," which he said he hoped to inculcate in students, with his own ongoing endeavors to work hard and support himself. Christian motive, he suggested, makes more dedicated workers because of the type of character it can produce. It may be that here he had in mind the labor theory of race value that Booker T. Washington proselytized: "No race that has anything to contribute to the markets of the world," Washington predicted, "is long in any degree ostracized." Thus Washington trained students to adapt tactically to the reigning order, "to be able to do the thing which the world wants done."[148] Roe Cloud told Wanamaker that prominent federal Indian schools—Carlisle, Haskell, Chilocco—were unable to take practical advantage of soul-based motivation because they were prevented from teaching religion.[149] Such sales pitches spiritualized the management ethos to garner financial support for Indian-run Indian education. Henry confessed to Mary that he found fundraising for Christ a fascinating vocation.[150]

RACE AND CLASS

Roe Cloud's archived correspondence cites a few instances in which his racial anxieties or concerns crystallized beyond the sphere of the Roes. In 1913 a Miss Eikel prevented him from escorting her all the way to her residence. Roe Cloud inferred that it may have embarrassed her to be seen by people who recognized him.[151] Six years earlier he distinguished himself from a member of another racial group that had had perilous times pursuing happiness in America. On a railroad platform in the Potomac Valley, he saw an African American woman (here he used the same word, "darkey," that he selected to name the African American singers in the University Club). As dusk turned into nightfall, she seemed to him to vanish in the darkness.[152] Could she have said the same of him, might he have wondered? What this eerie scene of obfuscation, blacking out, provoked him to do was to ask Mary for assistance in fortifying his spiritual strength.

The most flagrant occurrence of racism that Roe Cloud recorded was when he and his female Chippewa companion entered a restaurant in Wisconsin in 1916 and were misread as African Americans. They were directed to the kitchen to eat and were expected to use a pail to wash. Roe Cloud and his companion refused and entered the dining room, where they joined the Harvard Club and had lunch. Both were disheartened by this overt discrimination.[153] Here they insisted on occupying the category of class and the Harvard Club supported their assertion of social identity. The story resonates with one told by Booker T. Washington who, when working at Hampton, supervised an Indian student on a trip to Washington, D.C. On entering the steamboat dining room he was "politely informed" that while his Indian charge could eat there, he could not. "I never could understand how he knew just where to draw the color line, since the Indian and I were about the same complexion."[154] In these few narrated instances—none took place at Yale—Roe Cloud's apprehension of racial prejudice seems to have jostled his self-image. Again, it must not be forgotten that Roe Cloud wrote many of his letters to a white woman whom he admired and whom he wanted to admire him, and thus may have excised or modified some of what he could have told her about his daily life. And the letters I have read do not cover all they discussed in person.

Such experiences may have influenced what appear to be Roe Cloud's own occasionally class-based racial representations of Indians. When he wrote, seemingly so disparagingly, even testily, of "mad" dancing Indians for the Yale Courant in 1909, it may have been because he felt that they threatened his faith, and the faith of others, in his own Yale distinctiveness and what he could do for Indians with that image: "With weird chants, swaying to the wild rhythm of that strange music, the long line takes up its barbaric march. . . . in one mad whirl [the Indians] encircle the hall until exhaustion ends in frenzy. Has twentieth-century civilization nothing better than this for the red man?" Did he mean to signal his Yale classmates that he could not imagine himself acting in such a ritual, apparently staged for white tourists of the "barbaric"? More certainly, he wanted to make his Yale readers, as representatives of "twentieth-century civilization," take moral responsibility for giving Indians opportunities that would relieve them from having to perform in such "barbaric" ways for white audiences. Roe Cloud did not note the remarkable resemblance between this "barbaric march" and the much-publicized "snake dance" through New Haven that crowds of Yale freshmen ritually performed, screaming like "Aristophanes' frogs," during their first glorious college days.[155] Notwithstanding Yale's debates about changing forms of elite individuality, Roe Cloud would surely have seen that Yale—sponsoring Skull and Bones, the

Elihu Club, Mohican Club, Wigwam debate team, and other societies—
was curiously tribal.[156]

MEMBER OF THE CLASS

The Yale class of 1910 volume for 1935 notes that Roe Cloud, prominent
Indian New Dealer, is a Republican, enjoys horseback riding and golf, and
has sent his oldest daughter to Wellesley.[157] This was the portrait of himself that he composed for the consumption of his Yale confrères. Roe
Cloud did not manage factories or become a partner in a wealthy law firm,
as did many of his classmates. Rather he served as founder of an Indian
prep school, head of a federal Indian boarding school, administrator in
the Indian Bureau, and manager of a reservation.

Roe Cloud seems to have stopped writing to Yale class of 1910 volumes
after 1935, the year he was transferred from his Indian Affairs post as
superintendent of Haskell. Carl Lohmann, the genial class secretary, wrote
Roe Cloud in 1926 for more information than he had provided on a questionnaire and alluded to a recent Class Dinner in New York City during
which his classmates had requested news of him.[158] Roe Cloud wrote back
a fairly long letter about the Institute, his daughters, and his new son
Henry, who later died in infancy. Lohmann responded gratefully for his
report about the American Indian Institute and acknowledged that there
were not many in their class who had shined as had Roe Cloud.[159] Almost a
decade later, in preparation for the twenty-fifth reunion, Lohmann again
wrote Roe Cloud graciously pleading for more information than he had
given on the questionnaire. And again he singled out Roe Cloud as one of
the most fascinating members of their class.[160] In 1935, the reunion year, a
representative of Yale, perhaps Lohmann, requested his article, "Future of
the Redmen in America," published in *Missionary Review*, and copies of the
American Indian Institute's *Indian Outlook* to be exhibited with the publications of other members of his class. He asked Roe Cloud to contribute
them permanently to the Yale library.[161] For whatever reason, these blan-
dishments did not successfully woo Roe Cloud to reinvolve himself with
Yale, if his alumni file is complete.

Roe Cloud, however, never ceased involving himself with Indians and
their struggles, a pattern repeated by many of his successors. He may have

been far too busy convincing Indian tribes around the nation to vote for John Collier's Indian New Deal legislation to keep up his alumni contacts in 1935. Roe Cloud's declining, sometimes embattled, position in the Bureau of Indian Affairs after the mid-1930s also may partly explain his apparent distance from Yale.

THE SOCIETY OF AMERICAN INDIANS
AND CLASS DIVISION

Along with the importance she attributed to Christian service and un-selfishness, Mary fueled Henry's ambition in her plans for his individual achievement—for a career as a leader of his people far above the status of the secular Dr. Carlos Montezuma and Dr. Charles Eastman. In one letter she chose the metaphor of a torch—perhaps, in her mind, a Pentecostal torch burning with the fire of the Holy Spirit—to symbolize what Christ had handed over to him.[162] Mary saw Henry as the Du Bois of the Indians, with herself playing a role as supporter, or even as intellectual collabora-tor. She had read Eastman's *The Soul of the Indian: An Interpretation* (1911) and wanted to read it again with Henry. She favored Du Bois's *The Souls of Black Folk* (1903) over Eastman's book and suggested that Henry, or that she and Henry, write their souls-of-Indian-folk version.[163]

Roe Cloud stepped onto the national stage with alacrity. In 1910 the Roes sponsored his appearance at the famed annual Lake Mohonk con-ference held at a beautiful mountain resort in New York. This conference convened white Protestant pro-assimilation Indian reform organizations and sought to shape Indian policy and newspaper representations of In-dians. These illustrious assimilation activists encountered an Indian who could speak their language, and their self-reliance rhetoric, eloquently.[164] A year later, Roe Cloud attended the first organizational meeting of the Society of American Indians. In his correspondence Roe Cloud had some harsh words for what he saw as the conceited, self-serving behavior of both Montezuma and Eastman. While still in his twenties, he was made one of the society's four vice-presidents and served as chairman of mem-bership. In both organizations his Yale degree distinguished him, just as Du Bois's Harvard background helped set him apart, as a young man on the move.[165]

The link between Roe Cloud and Du Bois is intriguing because Roe Cloud's American Indian Institute's promotional literature, which I consider in chapter 3, associates the late Dr. Roe and the school with the philosophy of Booker T. Washington, founder and head of the Tuskegee Institute. As pointed out, even while Roe Cloud was at Yale, he and Dr. Roe had tried to convince the university to start a prep school that would enroll Indians. But the Du Bois that Mary and Henry admired was not just an advocate of the "higher education of Negro youth," he was also a critic of Washington's "industrial education," political accommodations, and self-help rhetoric. "And so thoroughly did [Washington] learn the speech and thought of triumphant commercialism, and the ideals of material prosperity," Du Bois thundered, "that the picture of a lone black boy poring over a French grammar amid the weeds of dirt of a neglected home soon seemed to him the acme of absurdities. One wonders what Socrates and St. Francis of Assisi would say to this." Perhaps Henry and Mary identified with Du Bois's interest in "developing exceptional men" and feeding the "ambition of our brighter minds."[166] Du Bois reminded his readers that Tuskegee could not "remain open a day were it not for teachers trained in Negro colleges, or trained by their graduates." He excoriated Washington's self-making ideology as "a dangerous half-truth," in part because it allowed "whites, North and South, to shift the burden of the Negro problem to the Negro's shoulders and stand aside as critical and rather pessimistic spectators; when in fact the burden belongs to the nation." For Du Bois, Washington's philosophy was another expression of "the old attitude of adjustment and submission," an endorsement of "a gospel of work and money" that "overshadow[ed] the higher aims of life."[167]

Du Bois and Washington debated one another in The Negro Problem (1903). The former again made his case for a leadership and class education that would permit African Americans to improve their chances of acquiring social power that would change the living and working conditions of all members of the race. This was a top-down power model intended to ameliorate the conditions of bottom-up struggles. He readily agreed with Washington that the need to instruct "the Negro to work" was "paramount." Nevertheless he contended that academic and social distinctions would distinguish highly educated leaders not only in the eyes of African Americans but in the eyes of those who ruled and that such achievements could enable them to reform more effectively. By the same token, Washington acknowledged the importance of helping African Americans "secure all the mental strength, all the mental culture—whether gleaned from science, mathematics, history, language or literature that his circumstances would allow." However, he reiterated his bottom-up skepticism about "mere book education" and "mere abstract knowledge" because numerous African Americans who had received higher educations had been deterred from pursuing professional careers and actually making the social difference that Du Bois had envisioned. Washington held that the African American social predicament was too urgent for African Americans to expend such effort, time, and money on education and then be unuseful.[168]

Roe Cloud's early approaches to Indian education call to mind the writings of both Du Bois and Washington. *Souls of Black Folk* may well have inspirited Roe Cloud's early collegiate dreams of helping Indians gain access to universities. It is likely that he saw the Society of American Indians as an organization in which he could further this challenging project.

The Society of American Indians, established in 1911 and disbanded in the 1920s, constituted an Indian effort to become a force in an Indian reform movement dominated by white middle- and upper-class Protestants. Hazel Hertzberg profiles Roe Cloud, the society's youngest leader, as "serious and quietly self-assured," "one of the most balanced and temperate men in the organization," and "firm but not dogmatic" and well able to "sympathize with points of view other than his own." He held executive roles helping oversee the society's membership, educational mission, and magazine. Noting the great respect he garnered from both Indians and whites as a culture broker, she concludes: "Although he believed fully in its purposes and was active in its behalf, he did not commit to it as passionately as some of the other leaders."[169] Montezuma, whom Mary hoped Henry would supersede in influence, kept tabs on Roe Cloud's opinions as expressed in the society and faithfully reported his findings to General Pratt (an associate member—that is, a non-Indian and nonvoting member—of the society). The Yavapi physician struggled through Chicago Medical College, served as Carlisle's physician for awhile, and favored the idea that more Indians should have the opportunity to attend college.[170] His impression of Roe Cloud in 1915—perhaps colored by their mutual concern about education, a cause that the Winnebago found more pressing—was that Roe Cloud had the same outlook that he and Pratt shared.[171] This inference was only partly correct.

As Roe Cloud clarified his positions, Montezuma's perception of the up-and-coming Winnebago altered, and what he thought he saw was a Yale man interested in developing college-groomed Indian leaders who would assume respected roles within the professional and managerial class. Roe Cloud's priority, Montezuma believed, was to earmark young Indians with potential and equip them to enter universities. There they would learn the critical skills that would help them prevent their fellow Indians from being exploited. Roe Cloud's college Indians, he imagined, would also devote themselves to bringing more Indians into the cultural mainstream. Montezuma's language suggests that he detected a status division, perhaps something like a class division, in Roe Cloud's mind between university students of Indian descent and less capable Indians in need of protective guidance. Writing to Pratt, Montezuma expressed some disappointment that Roe Cloud had not adopted his and his mentor's violent antipathy toward the Bureau of Indian Affairs, but rather sought the reorganization—the term often used to describe the reform of the Bureau in the New Deal—of the existing Indian management structure.[172]

Pratt, who had only a grade-school education before working as a printer's devil and then an apprentice tinker, supported the notion that some exceptional Indian students should attend college. But he was mostly ardent about vocational training. Pratt's own antiracial critique of Carlisle —that whites and Indians should not be constituted as distinct groups for long, even for educational purposes—could not have made him unequivocally enthusiastic about the formation of a society of middle-class Indians, even if some members had attended Carlisle and seemed to advocate assimilation. Arthur Parker wrote to Fayette McKenzie, the white sociologist who originated the idea of the society, about the possibility of founding an Indian college or university in 1911 and 1912 and then published "The Real Value of Higher Education for the Indian" in 1913. Pratt opposed this train of thought. Years before, Pratt had rejected the idea that Carlisle expand into what so many of its sports fans thought it already was: an Indian college. Pratt's antipathy begs the question: could a grammar-school-educated military officer have continued as head of Carlisle University? Perhaps Pratt felt uncomfortable not simply with a society of Indians, but a society of elite Indians some of whom, like Roe Cloud, had far outclassed him academically.[173]

A letter sent by the noted Bureau of Ethnology ethnologist George Mooney to Parker offers perspectives on the significance of the society's membership, and helps contextualize why Montezuma read Roe Cloud as he did. Mooney had first become controversial, and infuriated Pratt, because he defended the religiosity and legitimacy of the ghost dance in the 1890s, and then became equally controversial for his defense of the religious peyote ceremony before a congressional committee in 1918. His peyote advocacy enraged some members of the Society of American Indians, who sent a delegation to observe the ceremony so that they could submit their findings to a House of Representatives committee hearing. They condemned the ritual. Mooney's letter to Parker, which claimed that the twenty members had actually failed to witness the ceremony, went on to question the representativeness of this Indian society. He argued that many society Indians were barely Indian and also had little grasp of the issues that absorbed Indian chiefs and Washington delegates.[174] Gertrude Bonnin also felt that the society, rather than functioning effectively as an educated Indian vanguard, was too distant from the problems of many Indians on reservations. Parker tried to reassure one reservation Indian who identified himself as "uneducated": "We will not forget the uneducated Indians or the backward tribes. . . . Some of them may not understand it because in our printing we try to appeal to the white man's intelligence so that he will be our friend." Yet in another letter Parker admitted: "The real value of the publication lie[s] in stimulating greater activity on the part of those who are educated up to a certain degree, in seeking to crystallize the sentiment of those with broader views and higher training."[175]

In 1913, before Mooney lodged his criticism, society member Joseph K. Griffis (Kiowa), who would soon publish his before-and-after autobiography, *Tahan: Out of Savagery, into Civilization* (1915), lamented: "The trouble is that so many of us go out in the world and pass as white men. At schools and college they are passing as white men until they try to forget they are a part of the Indian people."[176] Members of the society generally referred to themselves as progressives, alluding to the evolutionary ideology of progress.

In this context, progressive often served as a code for class. Historians of the Society of American Indians concur that its preferred public image was bourgeois, professional, and intellectual. This white-collared propriety risked being compromised by "backward" reservation Indians. There was something akin to a class gap between these groups. Parker wanted Indians to see membership in the society as a "badge of aristocracy." (In 1903 Du Bois envisioned the "Talented Tenth" as an African American "aristocracy of talent and character.") For some society members, their race pride was at least partly dependent on their class pride. The society's somewhat scholarly conferences and publications equated educational uplift with class status. In effect, the society sought to educate whites about the class potential of Indians. If the society tried to redefine "Indian," it also—understanding the racial exclusions built into "class"— attempted to redefine "class." In doing so, the society maintained one racial exclusion in shaping their class image. Some members were prejudiced against African Americans (although Parker asked Du Bois if he wished to be an associate member, an invitation to which Du Bois did not respond). Their refined class image, some members hoped, would enable them to network better with white Indian reform organizations whose concepts of Indian uplift too commonly assigned Indians roles within the skilled and semiskilled working class.[177]

Parts of Eastman's *Indian Heroes and Great Chieftains*, published seven years after the society was founded, may be read as veiled warnings about the Society of American Indians class-leadership project. Eastman originally left the society because of doubts about whom they represented.[178] Several chapters criticized Indians who sold out Indians. His profiles of Sioux leaders Spotted Tail, Little Crow, and American Horse, and also of Hole-in-the-Day (Ojibway), exposed an Indian elite that, feeling the pressures of what seemed like permanent defeat, succumbed to "the temptations of graft and self-aggrandizement." Notwithstanding their talents, they exchanged tribal interest for self-interest and accumulated money, houses, land, government prestige, and tribal power. Eastman characterized this as the transformation of "chiefs" into government- and company-bribed "politicians." These Gilded Age and early Progressive Era "politicians" had not formed a professional and managerial class in the way that the Society of American Indians had begun to do. They had not been "assimilated" in government boarding schools or universities. Nevertheless, Eastman's cautionary tales hammer home the thesis that some Indians were just as capable as whites of betraying Indians to satisfy what Sitting Bull derided as the "love of possessions."[179] At times the Society of American Indians Indian uplift looked more like a program of class uplift, an imposition of top-down power, and an experiment in class networking.

Dennison Wheelock (Oneida) wrote Pratt that some society members were indeed engaged in a battle to define Indianness, though in their social group's favor. Wheelock related the difficulties that some older, more traditional Indian delegates from Nebraska and Wisconsin endured in trying to secure the attention of the society. He intervened on their behalf and they presented their case.[180] Even Parker recognized that the society had a class perspective contoured by its members' active class involvements in modern America.[181] In letters to Pratt, Parker intimated that Montezuma, whose passion often got the best of him, lowered the middle-class tone of the organization.[182] Parker, adopting a somewhat paternalistic accent, hoped that the society would contribute to helping Indians learn how to look after their own welfare adequately.[183] Thus the Society of American Indians, the first would-be pan-Indian political group, sought to circumscribe what dignified, legitimate, and responsible Indianness meant and exert some control over how it would be perceived by Indians as well as whites.

Another influential member of the society who exhibited the refined sense of propriety evident in Roe Cloud and Parker was Howard Gansworth. Although Gansworth served on the society's Advisory Council, his major interest was as president of the New York Indian Welfare Society. He replaced Parker in this post. Two incidents he related in a letter to Pratt, on Princeton Club of Buffalo stationery, indicate his preference for something like a decorous *embourgeoisement* of Indian rights advocacy. When arranging to publicize a conference, Gansworth had a trying encounter with a well-meaning newspaper representative. Contemplating the best way to focus public attention on the event, she asked Gansworth to recruit some Indians costumed in traditional garb. The publicist admitted in advance that this was not the image of modern Indians that the reputable Gansworth hoped to convey, but contended that the paper's readers were much more interested in those sorts of Indians (by implication, more fascinated in them than in upper-middle-class Indians like Gansworth). The diplomatic Iroquois businessman got her to laugh about her request and she dropped it. Then when faced with white sympathizers who wanted to exploit the traditional Indian image for publicity at the grave of the great Seneca orator Red Jacket, Gansworth, in his best understated manner, again managed to revise the plan. He told Pratt that in order to make the Indian cause respectable he often had to negotiate Indian stereotypes, sometimes stereotypes recycled by white supporters he did not want to alienate. In lieu of Red Jacket theatrics, he sponsored a banquet, an orchestra, and addresses by the city's luminaries (a class act). The Princetonian had no intention of permitting his Indian organization to lose cultural and class capital by criticizing whites and white stereotypes of Indians.[184]

Although the society veered from traditionalist Indianism, it sponsored class conscious pro-assimilation brands of Indianization. Thus some of its members advocated the establishment of American Indian Day.[185] Some members even wondered how the society might benefit from the prominence of Indians and the West in popular culture. Thomas Sloan, the society's president in the early 1920s, saw the commercial success of *National Geographic* as an example of how his organization might effectively market its message. His interest was in gaining mass circulation and publicity for the society's newly titled and designed publication, *The American Indian Magazine* (which originally had the stuffier and more academic title, *Quarterly Journal*). To help do so he was keen to secure advertising from the Stetson Hat Company, famous for manufacturing cowboy hats, and the Colt and Winchester Arms Companies, instrumental in what Theodore Roosevelt termed the "winning of the West."[186] Indianness was becoming increasingly fashionable and commodifiable as part of Western style and, in Sloan's reasoning, was not to be rejected indiscriminately by Indians interested in commercial as well as social progress. So the society itself banked on images of Indians that differed from its own class profile.

Consequently, several divergent positions created cracks in the society's foundations. A key fissure was between the pro-peyote and anti-peyote factions. As stated, Roe Cloud, like the Roes, was diplomatically in the latter group. Mooney may not have been fully aware of the society's internal divisiveness. To make matters more challenging, the society was plagued by a dearth of funds.[187]

THE GOSPEL OF DESPERATION

Roe Cloud believed in the political possibilities of the Society of American Indians. Nonetheless, as his undergraduate comment about socialism versus individualism suggests, he was no orthodox radical then and regarded organized social reform as ancillary to personal spiritual regeneration. Community reorganization and influence, the Yale Winnebago philosophized in 1912, cannot deliver salvation. The reform that counts must occur inside oneself. Over time, however, Roe Cloud's activist thinking about how to best motivate Indians, and whites, developed in other conceptual directions.[188] There was at least one moment during his young manhood when the security of his individualistic stance was shaken. A couple of months after he surmised that communities do not save people, Roe Cloud was engaged in missionary work in Dulee, New Mexico, among starving Apaches. On the reservation a desperate Apache, invoking the Indian ethos of giving, asked the Yale graduate and seminary student for some of his clothes, prompting Roe Cloud to reflect that proselytizing the gospel of hard work is difficult if the Indians to whom he is preaching have no chance of finding employment (or even clothing).[189]

two

SENTIMENTALIZED EDUCATION

IT IS UNDERSTANDABLE that Henry Roe Cloud would gravitate toward white Protestant Indian reformers, not necessarily because he identified unreservedly with them and their pro-assimilation, often paternalist stances, but because they succeeded in putting Indian issues on the nation's political agenda. Involvement in Christian reform, among other things, was an educated Indian's route to people in power.[1] And many politically visible Protestant reformers—working in numerous organizations, such as the Lake Mohonk Conference of Friends of the Indian, the Indian Rights Association, and the Women's National Indian Association—advocated educating Indians (though often for reasons besides Indian intellectual development). The white campaign to instruct Indians to live in a white-dominated world must have given Roe Cloud hope that he could redirect reform enthusiasms to support Indians teaching themselves.

Roe Cloud was an Indian white-collar activist on behalf of Indians, an organizer who used his contacts with white movers-and-shakers to secure a foothold in reform, philanthropic, and government circles. In the process he learned reformers' premises, rhetoric, and structures of sympathy. His battleground was the pulpit, parlor, lecture circuit, and classroom.[2] Mary and Walter Roe played roles in paving Roe Cloud's way not just to the annual Lake Mohonk conference in the Catskills, where the most important white Protestant reformers gathered to discuss how Indians could be best "uplifted," but to the sentimentalized hearths, and sentimentalized hearts, of influential people.[3]

Thus the Roes did more than give the Yalie cultural access to a white Protestant reform elite and a status system. Their relationship schooled him in the sentimental and psychological workings of white middle- and upper-class Protestant selfhood, affection, and control. His bicultural understanding of this organization of selfhood and emotional attachment, so distinct from his Winnebago experience, was an understanding that would better equip him to reform the reformers and convert the converters. He learned not just how to organize, but to achieve sentimental and emotional conquest. Female missionaries were socialized to be sentimental, and sentiment, in the words of one historian, was their "central strategy of conversion."[4] In nineteenth-century America, Protestantism, femininity, masculinity, domesticity, and literature became sentimentalized.[5] From boyhood through adulthood, Roe Cloud observed how the middle and upper classes crafted forms not just of spirituality but of sentimentality to sanctify their motives and their social power.

It is a matter of historical importance that while Roe Cloud was being socialized as an ambitious leader at Yale, he also was taking an advanced course in the emotional interdependencies and sentimental expectations gestated by the early twentieth-century white upper-middle-class family. This chapter, like those that precede and follow it, is about a form of *education*. Sometimes one learns lessons from one's education that were not included in or even contradict the lesson plan. Roe Cloud's sentimental schooling with the Roes, especially Mary Roe, as pictured partially in their archived letters, constituted an integral dimension of an education that, one way or another, complexly reaffirmed his enduring allegiances to and alliances with Indians.

Class, racial, and gender ideologies often circulate through even the most private relationships and shape self-conceptions in ways that Americans too often are brought up to misunderstand, or mystify, only as personal or individual. The intimate yet thoroughly social experiences I consider here were not only part of Roe Cloud's history with the Roes, in a more encompassing way they were an episode in the cross-cultural and cross-racial history of the sentimental family. I move toward clarifying Roe Cloud's bicultural position as an Indian who negotiated, and learned from, the ways in which an upper-middle-class machinery of sentimental domesticity affected his sense of self, structure of emotional investments, framework of needs, and scope of aspirations.[6]

The notion that the family constitutes a socializing machinery—that inculcates values, manners, emotional styles, self-regimentation, guilt, and shame—was stated openly in the "outing program" that Pratt originated at Carlisle. For all of Pratt's fulminations against race and racism, he was inspired by the idea of slaves living with, laboring for, occasionally learning from, and sometimes forming affective attachments to, their owners. Federal Indian boarding schools across the country developed outing programs influenced by Carlisle's. Pratt encouraged his students to leave Carlisle for months, in some cases years, to live with and labor for local families. He knew that such private units would be able to "immerse" students in regimes of everyday life more comprehensively and less mechanically than officially institutionalized school culture. Pratt grasped domesticity as a selfhood-making, citizen-making, and worker-making factory: "We make our greatest mistake in feeding our civilization to the Indians instead of feeding the Indians to our civilization." Outing programs not only farmed Indians out as cheap laborers, they "fed" them to the digestive system of domesticity and sentiment. Many students refused to be digested and opted out of outing programs. Some feigned being digested as they learned how to move tactically within and around white domesticities.[7]

Roe Cloud entered a sentimental and psychological upper-middle-class domestic machinery whose product was a cultural model of selfhood often termed "individuality." While the Roes were not exactly Roe Cloud's upper-middle-class outing family from Yale, they certainly fueled and benefited from his youthful commitment to labor as a missionary. Eventually he moved beyond these bonds and this vocation to take up another calling. In my view Roe Cloud, brimming with intellectual and cultural curiosity, digested more than he was digested, though the two formative processes were related.

I will explore two intersecting questions. How might the histories of family life, intimacy, and emotional life illuminate one's reading of Roe Cloud's informal adoption by the Roes? And how might the study of Roe Cloud's experience advance these histories? Historian John Demos, in asking why psychoanalysis was embraced with such enthusiasm by some Americans in the first decades of the twentieth century, has studied how the nineteenth-century cult of domesticity could establish close, psychologically intensified bonds between mother and son, and how the cult of success could place father and son in an unstated, even unconscious, competition with one another. These emotional investments and tensions produced what Demos calls a middle-class "hothouse family" replete with multilayered psychological selves. When emotional products of these middle-class families read Sigmund Freud's theory of the Oedipus complex, Demos posits, they would have recognized this triangulated set of attachments as corresponding to their own hothouse experience and therefore as a profound "psychological" account, not of historically produced social relationships, which they were, but of what seemed like universal "human nature" simply expressing itself in the family.[8]

Below, my emphasis on this history of family dynamics offers the antithesis of a psychoanalytic, psychobiographical, or psychohistorical reading of the tie between Henry Roe Cloud and Mary Roe. My approach is historical and focuses on the social making of selves who, in the twentieth century, were increasingly taught to label, read, and experience themselves as intrinsically "psychological." In class terms, the Roe Cloud–Roe letters contribute important cross-cultural perspectives on the history of the socialization of the modern bourgeois psychological self in America. Drawing on the work of Demos and other historians, I analyze the formative power of a historically specific sentimental family structure that produces, through a social setting, emotional dynamics resembling what Freud misconceived as timelessly and universally human. Historical conditions, not transcultural human nature, squeezed the American middle-class "Oedipal" family into being. Roe Cloud left one cultural system of emotion formation and self-understanding—the Winnebago tribe—and eventually entered another cultural system of emotion formation and self-understanding—upper-middle-class sentimental domesticity. The drama, sometimes melodrama, that ensued is based on the interaction, sometimes collision, of two cultural systems.[9] "Dearest Heart," Zitkala-Ša wrote

Carlos Montezuma, her beloved, in 1901, "It is as you say; the greater part of civilization is the complication of desires!"[10]

If, as Demos suggests, a full-fledged nineteenth-century "Oedipal" configuration of emotional investment entails a conscious or unconscious competition between father and son, the Roe Cloud–Roe letters do not fit this pattern. Up to a point, Roe Cloud appeared to identify with Walter Roe. Mary Roe is a more complex figure whose letters exhibit some aspects of this pattern. One fact that makes her deviate from this pattern is that Mary and Henry were not mother and son. They were dear friends who chose to use familial language—and Winnebago endearments—to relate to one another.[11] In pondering this, it is important to appreciate the fact that some sentimental advice-writers venerated deep mother-son emotional bonds as an *achievement*. In *Bits of Talk about Home Matters* (1873), Helen Hunt Jackson lavishes praise on the sentimental mother who can say of her offspring, "He is lover and friend and son, all in one." For Jackson there is nothing untoward about imagining a son as friend and lover. Instead, she characterizes such a mother as "the wisest, sweetest, most triumphant mother."[12]

Sometimes intense familial sentiment can generate what Herman Melville termed "ambiguities." Demos profiles the American middle-class Victorian mother as "sentimentalized, not erotized," but adds: "perhaps in the world of unconscious process the distance from sentiment to Eros was not so great after all." He reads this ambiguous passion not as emotionally aberrant or morally suspect but as culturally predictable. "Is it too much to suppose that many nineteenth-century women—faced with overbearing cultural constraints on their sexuality in relation to their sweethearts and husbands—proved to be rather 'seductive' in their maternal function?" For Demos this is a human potential crystallized by historical pressures on family life.[13] Some of Henry's and Mary's affectionate letters, though they only played at being son and mother, display a marked sentimental-romantic intensity. In recognizing this I refer only to the use of language and tone and hazard no guesses about actions not described in the letters. It is fair to say that the depth of feeling, attestations of interdependence, and confidential expressions manifest in some letters are what modern readers might expect to see in romantic exchanges. Nonetheless, I will offer several reasons why I think it would be mistaken

—unhistorical—to take these epistolary testaments of affection at face value. To do so would be to ignore the nexus of taboos extant in Winnebago culture (of which Henry and likely Mary were aware), their sentimental and melodramatic conventionality (mother-son letters could be intense in their emotional outpourings), and the piety of the correspondents (their bond with God as well as with one another was always their vital concern, and they practiced Christian self-scrutiny).

Why is it theoretically and historically important to focus attention on this affectionate expression? As one scholar of Indians has generalized: "North American Indians reveal no strong cases of the Oedipus complex anywhere."[14] Winnebago child rearing, like that in many other Indian tribes and cultures, was distributed among numerous members of the clan, not wholly centered on parents. Therefore, as Roe Cloud relates in "From Wigwam to Pulpit," much of his upbringing was supervised by his uncles and grandmother and was probably contributed to by members of the Bear clan, a more communal network of adult authority and emotional bonding that would be far less likely to nurture anything like a white middle-class family "Oedipal complex." If Freud, therefore, was wrong about the universality of the Oedipus complex, and Oedipal feelings do tend to be culturally specific symptoms of the middle- and upper-class family structure of emotional interdependencies, then it means that a study of the process that Roe Cloud underwent is a historical case study of his transit through a domestic machinery for the making of social selves.[15] The Roe Cloud–Roe exchanges, it will be clear, make more visible the multidimensional ways in which sentimental emotion making and emotion using reproduced class identities, class incentives, and class allegiances.

When ruminating on the intensity of feeling exhibited in passages of some letters, it is crucial to bear in mind that what Radin terms the Winnebago "formal system of instruction"—"precepts on . . . behavior to one's parents, and relatives, and how to treat one's wife and women in general, how to bring up children"—would have complicated Roe Cloud's response to structures of emotional attachment that Demos calls "Oedipal."[16] On the reservation Roe Cloud would have been taught an array of Winnebago taboos and restrictions that pertained to sexual propriety, familial obligations, and bounded behavior.[17] The Roe Cloud–Roe letters, whose frame of reference is mostly Christian, sentimental, and domestic, do not focus on Winnebago taboos and proprieties. Yet, if Roe Cloud's childhood training in kinship customs continued to influence the structuring of his emotional investments, it would have pulled him back from the middle-class "Oedipal" ties that Demos describes. Having worked with Henry among the Winnebago it is probable that Mary was aware of some tribal customs and prohibitions.

Roe Cloud viewed adoption at least in part through a Winnebago lens. When a Winnebago child died, the child's parents sometimes adopted a child of the same age who would retain membership in his or her own biological family. Winnebago adoption brought with it kinship obligations and taboos.[18] For their part, the Roes—whose son, if he had lived, would have been a few years younger than Henry—were likely familiar with missionary patterns of adoption. Jane Hunter, in her history of late-nineteenth- and early-twentieth-century female missionaries in China, goes so far as to characterize missionary work as a generalized form of sentimental mothering. Many Chinese missionaries adopted boys and girls in need, so much so that "many boards . . . ruled against official adoptions" because they compromised "the disinterested benevolence the church aimed to offer." Most adoptions were informal rather than official and permitted a "great variety in the degree and permanence of financial support." Sometimes the adoption gave both the missionaries and the adopted child a higher status in the community. And sometimes the adoption served the mission movement's public relations.[19]

Another custom to consider is that in traditional tribal cultures Indians often honored others to whom they were not biologically related with familial names (father, mother, grandfather, grandmother, son, daughter, and so on). One did not have to "adopt" a youth to be regarded as a mother or father. Sue McBeth, an unmarried Presbyterian missionary, served the Nez Perce from 1873 till her death in 1893. The Nez Perce named her "Pika" (mother). " 'Pika,' " she wrote, "has had very much comfort from her children, and has had very much care too, in the year past." McBeth called the Nez Perce males her "boys" and "sons." Alas, as one historian notes, in some cases missionaries who used this familial language could be paternalistic toward their "children."[20]

As Jason M. Tetzloff's 1996 dissertation on Roe Cloud points out, most of the correspondence in the Roe family papers—thousands of pages of letters and related material, which make up the majority of Roe Cloud's publicly available writings—documents the bond between Roe Cloud and the missionary couple, especially Mary Roe. Readers of this archive cannot avoid thinking at length about their tie. As I noted in the preface, Tetzloff's dissertation biography limits discussion of their affective bond to one paragraph that notes its centrality in Roe Cloud's life at that phase and observes the difficulty of interpreting their emotionally intimate relationship.[21]

My own reading is at once historical and literary in its sensitivity to the cultural forms, genres, and conventions that imprint feeling, motive, self-conception, and expectation.[22] Literary critics would recognize many of the Roe Cloud–Roe exchanges as distinctly melodramatic.[23] By melodrama, I am somewhat less concerned with exaggerated expressions of emotions and more interested in how social pressures induce one to identify with and enact a role in a narrative that seems to make sense of the world and its contradictions. For example, Stephen Crane's *Maggie: A Girl of the Streets* (1893) depicts melodrama as a victory-of-the-victims fantasy: "Maggie always departed with raised spirits from the showing places of the melodrama. She rejoiced at the way in which the poor and virtuous eventually surmounted the wealthy and wicked."[24] In Henry James's *The Turn of the Screw* (1897), the Governess, entranced with and exalted by romantic novelistic melodramas, finds "a joy in the extraordinary flight of heroism the occasion demanded" and casts herself as the savior of her wards.[25] Melodramatic themes include crisis, endangerment, yearning, sympathy, endurance, protection, and rescue, topoi that resonate with late-nineteenth- and early-twentieth-century Indian struggles.

Walter and Mary Roe, a white couple who played the role of parents, and Henry, an Indian who performed the part of son, enacted their own form of bourgeois domestic melodrama, race melodrama, and uplift melodrama. What some critics call bourgeois domestic melodrama often dramatizes losses, conflicts, ambivalence, and reunification in the family and in romance, though it sometimes represents the pressures of personal life under capitalism, particularly female self-sacrifice, in heightened emotional terms that divert analysis from the transformable social conditions that produce such pressures. And what Susan Gillman terms race melodrama "points to the irreducible historical identity of race itself as melodrama in the United States." Philip J. Deloria's study of Indian-white melodramatic formulas in early-twentieth-century popular culture involves the analysis of discourses of call-of-the-wild primitivism, noble savage conventions, vanishing Indian stereotypes, narratives of doomed interracial romances, and representations of assimilation ambivalence.[26] As upper-middle-class guardians, the Roes sponsored a kind of uplift melodrama in which they directed Henry how to direct himself. They made the shaping of Henry's career their "career," and this entailed issuing advice and exhortations concerning the struggle for self-management and success. The injunction to rescue oneself from oneself had melodramatic tensions (the ongoing assimilation melodrama within).[27] Of course, the Roes' Christian conversion mission—not just class conversion mission — was imbued with melodrama. Missionaries instilled melodramatic images of the interior contest between good versus evil and virtue versus temptation in Indians to redeem them. If conversion is melodramatic, the crusades of missionary-parents to uplift Indian-wards were especially so.

The late-century Protestant Indian reform movement took melodramatic as well as political inspiration from the mid-century abolition movement. Melodramatic representations of sufferers garnered support for both movements. Frederick Douglass, Harriet Jacobs, and Harriet Beecher Stowe all employed melodrama emotionally as well as intellectually to generate sympathy for the antislavery cause. When the abolitionist Lydia Maria Child censured military campaigns against Indians in 1868, she used melodramatic parental language to argue not just for peace but for assimilation: "[Indians are] younger members of the same great human family, who need to be protected, instructed, and encouraged, till they are capable of appreciating and sharing all our advantages."[28] Melodrama can mobilize actions as well as organize feelings. In 1881 Helen Hunt Jackson's A Century of Dishonor roused middle- and upper-class Protestants to "save" Indians. Jackson's critique included a legalistic brief against federal abuse of Indians and "robbery" of their land, the claim that this oppression violated international law, and an analysis of how the category of "the nation" had been wielded to obfuscate systemic injustice. She also inserted strategically melodramatic "appeal[s] to the heart and the conscience of the American people." Century of Dishonor attempted not just to activate readers critically but to cast readers melodramatically as redeemers of injured Indians: "What the people demand, Congress will do. It has been—to our shame be it spoken—at the demand of part of the people that all these wrongs have been committed, these treaties broken, these robberies done, by the Government."[29] Melodrama can imbue effort with elevated purpose, moral urgency, and spiritual value.

The windows that the Roe Cloud–Roe letters constitute, if read historically, are not transparent; rather they are made of stained glass, tinted with sentimental conventions and latticed with melodramatic form. Usually the Roes played the dominant role of Henry's spiritual rescuers and class-identity advisors, though when Walter neared death and then died, Mary recast Henry as her emotional rescuer. Roe Cloud, partly through these exchanges, acquired strategic knowledge of—and practiced—sentimental conventions and melodramatic forms. He was charismatic and effective as a bridge figure among elite whites in part because he knew that they perceived him as a melodramatic figure (from wigwam to Yale).

Much that Mary Roe wrote reads like a cultural blueprint of sentimentalized emotion. In this sentimental system, terrific emotional expectations and pressures were heaped on the family to provide a psychological and spiritual refuge from a marketplace world that was supposedly outside it.[30] In 1911 Mary sketched the family and home as safe havens, as zones of certainty, devised to protect one from external threats and violence. Mary wrote effusively of the home with melodramatic language and affect that countless middle-class mothers would have recognized and affirmed as beyond question. Legions of nineteenth-century advice-book authors sold female and male readers on the idea that the emotional warmth of the home, personified by sentimental femininity and motherhood, could heal the lacerations that the sharp edges of competition inflicted.[31] Mary must have been gratified when Henry confirmed her ability to help assuage his historical wounds as an Indian. Addressing her as a mother in February 1909, the junior valued his domestic tie with the Roes as particularly vital because he was the sole Indian at Yale and could not be among his people.[32] Henry's declaration of reliance was on sentimental cue.[33] His need confirmed Mary's therapeutic potency and mission as a protective mother. Sentimental middle-class culture stimulated and ratified such effusions of emotion, and scripted their form. Henry had enrolled in a sentimental school set up to produce and regulate class caring, class interdependencies, class insecurities, class self-images, class aspirations, class boundaries, and, it will be clear, class marriages.

ANALYZING IMPERIAL SENTIMENT

The encompassing cultural and historical question is not just what shaped Roe Cloud, but what shaped the Roes to try to shape Roe Cloud in certain ways? Laura Wexler, Amy Kaplan, Jane Hunter, Ann Stoler, and Catherine Hall have enlarged the scope of histories of domesticity to include not only matters of gender and class, but race and imperialism. Wexler holds that nineteenth-century sentimentalism—transmitted through religion, novels, poetry, conduct manuals, ladies magazines, architectural designs, furniture, songs, art, photography, and clothing styles—must be read relationally "as a tool for the control of others, not merely as an aid in the conquest of the self." The antebellum cult of domesticity that established the ideological foundation for Mary Roe's turn-of-the-century concepts of mother, home, and interdependency tried to make middle-class private life seem civilized, cozy, and innocent, while American Manifest Destiny went on a rampage banishing Indians on the Trail of Tears in the 1830s and instigating the Indian Wars. Sentimentality, femininity, and missionary evangelism could make imperial capitalism seem reassuringly self-righteous. White women, as mothers-at-home or missionaries-in-the-field, played a symbolic role in colonization-through-domestication campaigns.[34]

Herman Melville's first novel, *Typee: A Peep At Polynesian Life* (1846), clarifies such connections. Reflecting on the mid-century transformation of Honolulu, Melville's narrator censures merchants and missionaries— "self-exiled heralds of the Cross," "spiritual instructors"—for "civilizing" the natives into "draft horses" and "evangelizing" them into "beasts of burden." He analyzes his century's predatory capitalism as an emotional system and spiritual system as well as an economic system.[35] Melville saw missionary evangelism and missionary capitalism as in cahoots. Sentimentalism helps manufacture energies as well as alibis to take over others. Well-mannered and well-dressed colonization "originate[s] in certain tea-party excitements, under the influence of which benevolent-looking gentlemen in white cravats solicit alms, and old ladies in spectacles, and young ladies in sober russet low gowns, contribute sixpences towards the creation of a fund, the object of which is to ameliorate the spiritual condition of the Polynesians, but whose end has almost invariably been to accomplish their temporal destruction." Sentimental infrastructures take genteel forms of "neat villas, trim gardens, shaven lawns, spires, and cupolas" that displace islanders from their own land. The "Anglo-Saxon hive" that threatens Polynesians had already assaulted "Paganism" on the mainland, "extirpating" much of the "Red Race." Yet Roe Cloud, the Roes, and many others in their camp could have countered such critiques by emphasizing the material as well as spiritual good that religious and sentimentally motivated reformers, teachers, and missionaries performed. In 1915, when criticizing Albert Hensley's effective evangelizing of peyote Christianity among their fellow Winnebago, Roe Cloud insisted that the only worthwhile Carlisle students were those who had been reformed by missionaries.[36]

FORMING EMOTIONAL INVESTMENTS
AND EMOTIONAL SELF-IMAGES

The Roes welcomed the Yale student into their family circle at an important historical juncture in 1907: white middle-class sentimental families were exhibiting signs of becoming modern psychological families. Here I will touch on only a couple of characteristics of this complex mix (a combination which is still developing interestingly in this new millennium). Nineteenth-century sentimental discourse defined the family as the private space in which one's most meaningful relations, emotional commitments, and character were established. The family formed the stronghold of what historian Philippe Ariès termed the "emotional revolution"—the compensatory feelings revolution that was intertwined with the industrial revolution and its production of class identities. Nineteenth-century middle-class families responded to the anxieties of "capitalist expansions," sociologist Eli Zaretsky argues, by expanding "inner life" (certainly by intensifying class preoccupations with the idea of inner life). This sentimentalization of "inner life" focused in part on melodramatically defining sexuality as that which needed to be hidden and controlled, and in doing so made sexuality seem like an inner force that necessitated domestic monitoring and taming. In these respects the sentimental family set the stage for the psychological family in which emotional ambivalences and conflicts were taken as evidence and expressions of class belonging and subjective complexity.[37]

This history of the "emotional revolution" contextualizes aspects of the Roe Cloud–Roe relation. But, as Frederick Hoxie's study of Crow culture suggests, the history of Indian structurings of emotional investments also helps frame the significance of the Roe Cloud–Roe bond. In the nineteenth century, when the sentimental revolution inflated expectations that love was unique and the locus of meaning, "the Anglo-American idea of romantic love . . . was not the central focus of [Crow] family life." Crow culture officially encouraged female chastity but, like many other Indian cultures, it really allowed sexual experimentation fairly early in pubescent life for both boys and girls. And "marriages," Hoxie writes, "were more significant as alliances of extended families than they were as unions of individuals." Emotional allegiances were socially dispersed, sexual alliances were quite mutable, and, as noted, the young had many kinfolk who literally were called father and mother. These social relations were not conditions within which sentimental romantic love and Oedipal complexes seemed like universal facts of life.[38]

Late-nineteenth-century white Protestant Indian reformers, some of whom were interested in financial as well as emotional investments, explicitly plotted to reorganize Indian structures of romantic and family life. These reformers realized what historian Stephanie Coontz has stated succinctly: the family is "culture's way of coordinating personal reproduction with social reproduction."[39] They tried to prescribe certain kinds of masculine and feminine roles for Indian students, forms of intense romantic bonding between them, and a sentimental domesticity that would produce a nexus of emotional interdependencies. Reformers, politicians, and bureaucrats wanted a structure of male and female emotional interdependence to aid in the creation of economic dependencies and in the transformation of Indian males into compliant workers.

Hence in 1881 Carl Schurz, who had recently stepped down as Secretary of the Interior, advocated the sentimentalization of Indian male and female romantic bonds so as "to stimulate their attachment to permanent homes" and thus to better "individualize" tribally held reservation land. He recognized that the intense emotional investment in private life and the desire for private property were symbiotic. "Indians will occupy no more ground than so many white people; the large reservations will gradually be opened to general settlement and enterprise, and the Indians, with their possessions, will cease to stand in the way of the 'development of the country.'" Similarly, Merrill Gates, who had served as a president of Rutgers University and Amherst College, and as the presiding member of the Lake Mohonk conferences, exhorted his fellow reformers in 1884 to do all they could to erode Indians' fidelity to tribal cultures, and in its place foster their "consciousness of the family hearth" and "true family feeling." Sentimentalization would form law-abiding possessive "individuals" and property owners. In short, reformers hoped that the sentimental system of emotional attachments and allegiances would supplant the "tribal system."[40] The hope was that Franklinian self-reliance and sentimental family reliance would combine to replace tribal reliance.

Early-twentieth-century social and economic changes significantly affected the structuring of Indians' emotional commitments. The authors of the Meriam Report who surveyed Indian family life in the late-1920s observed, in words that may well have been co-written or approved by Roe Cloud: "The two-generation family composed only of husband, wife, and children is relatively less significant than in our social organization. The several generations mingle more intimately in the households and the camps. . . . The family has a relatively greater obligation to the larger group than among whites. Home life is not so exclusive as with us" (572). Yet they also pointed out that the individualizing of land under the allotment system, and the labor market pressures placed on Indian workers, in tandem, were beginning to structure a more economically and emotionally privatized Indian family (more like what the late-nineteenth-century white Protestant reformers had wanted). There was a consequent "weakening of clan responsibility for dependent women and children" (572) and increased strain on an ethos of giving that traditionally made a virtue of redistributing both goods and emotional care to members of the tribe. By the early twentieth century, as Crashing Thunder's autobiography suggests, the Winnebago, like other tribes, had endured considerable pressures on traditional emotional arrangements.

PRACTICING INNER LIFE

Over the past few decades anthropologists have analyzed emotions as what Michelle Rosaldo calls "social creations." Rosaldo's cross-cultural research led her to contend that emotions "are no less cultural and no more private than beliefs." Notions of the inner self, or even the idea that humans have inner selves, are not universal. The Ilongots, Rosaldo explains, "do not conceptualize an autonomous inner life in opposition to life-in-the world." Rosaldo and other anthropologists read feelings and experiences of "interiority" as culturally ordered in relation to structures of social power, contradictions, and conflicts. Some cultures control their members by positing an inner self in need of social control. Many "relatively egalitarian" cultures, Rosaldo generalizes, do not assume the "need for controls, nor do individuals experience themselves as having boundaries to protect or possessing drives and lusts that must be held in check if they are to maintain their status or engage in everyday cooperation."[41] This research challenges commonplace American premises that "individuals" naturally or psychologically have particular kinds of inherent desires and drives. Catherine Lutz notes that the Ifaluk of Micronesia do not believe that they have access to their own "insides" or the "insides" of others and consequently are not, unlike many well-trained American "individuals," culturally preoccupied with "insides." Rodney Needham concludes that "inner states" should be studied as "social facts like other facts."[42]

Such cross-cultural perspectives help one more complexly identify the ways in which imperial power often seeks not just to coerce but reinvent selfhood. "Since prayer has come into our cabins, our former customs are no longer of any service," one colonial-era Indian lamented. "Our dreams and our prophecies are no longer true,—prayer has spoiled everything for us."[43] Leslie Marmon Silko's (Laguna) *Ceremony* (1977) charges: "Christianity separated the people from themselves, [it encouraged] each person to stand alone because Jesus Christ would save only the individual soul."[44] This spiritually individualized formation of self and self-interest contrasts with what Arnold Krupat in 1992 and Jace Weaver (Cherokee) in 1997 characterized as the traditional Indian kinship imagining of self: "I-am-We."[45]

Ilongot children, Rosaldo points out, require adult monitoring and tutelage "not to save their souls, but for a much more worldly reason—to survive." The white world Roe Cloud negotiated coupled soul surveillance and social survival, yet souls were defined by a capitalist structure that had invested heavily in individualizing conceptions of selfhood and motivation in particular ways.[46] Anthropologists of different cultural selfhood systems would view the forms of "individuality," competitive drive, and soul language that Roe Cloud studied at Yale as cultural blueprints of "inner" selfhood.

Indians were caught in a crossfire of cultural assumptions about what constituted their "innerness." Although Pratt insisted that Indians had no inherent racially based incapacity and, like whites, simply had to be trained, he racialized the inherent when advising Dr. Montezuma: "Be what the Indians call you, a white man, not only white in conduct outside but white in the inside." By implication, Montezuma's "civilized" white "inside" conflicted with an "uncivilized" Indian "inside" that he had not fully expurgated. Even the Society of American Indians could indulge in associating Indians with a romantic "inner" self. This is clear in Power O'Malley's painting, The Descent of Man, which the society displayed in its headquarters. O'Malley's Descent depicted a short-haired Indian professional-in-training in a three-piece suit writing with a quill at his desk daydreaming of tribal Indians riding with quills in their headbands, perhaps on the warpath. The society's journal melodramatically commented in 1916: "There is perplexity in the Indian's face—shall he go forward to a professorship and into a profession and win a banker's daughter, or shall he fly back to the plains and become the warrior-horseman, the wise man of the tribe, the free wanderer of wide stretching prairies."[47] Presumably, in some cases the "banker's daughter" would be white. A precipitous Indian "descent" could undermine efforts to woo a "banker's daughter." Yet the very wish to woo the "banker's daughter" could trigger white suspicions that the Indian professional-in-training might surreptitiously plunge into a "descent."

Perhaps the anachronistic "warrior-horseman" image could spur college-class Indians to fight on new kinds of battlefields. But they also knew that this Wild West image could disqualify them as harboring a call-of-the wild within and that white worries about this could thwart rather than advance their endeavors. African Americans also negotiated a primitive within racial stereotype. In 1929, George Schuyler, an African American intellectual, mocked the white fear that the black professional secretly yearns to "strip off his Hart Schaffner & Marx suit, grab a spear and ride off wild-eyed on the back of a crocodile."[48] Roe Cloud knew that with most whites he was always on exhibit and led a symbolic life. White power brokers could wonder: was he really the Yale Indian, or would an atavistic Indian inherent self surface and pose a threat? Would the Indian within be too dangerous, too instinctual, too sexual, too resentful? Roe Cloud had to preempt any white anxieties such as these from forming and thereby impeding his missionary and fundraising efforts. Mary also, playing the role of mother-protector, sedulously monitored Henry to stop this from occurring.[49]

Historians and anthropologists of cultural structurings of emotions, placed in conversation with one another, challenge one to read Roe Cloud's "private" and "intimate" experiences with the Roes as a complex historically situated cross-cultural encounter. To some extent the Roes tried to shape Roe Cloud's imagining of himself as having "individuality" (within a certain class mold), as being "psychological" (within a nexus of sentimental expectations and interdependencies), and as having certain "inner" needs and desires that had to be managed (to achieve status within their social group). Basically, they too had been socialized this way.[50] The Roes, as members of their social group, gave Roe Cloud advanced class lessons in the sentimentalization of emotional performance. Yet he was never wholly defined or confined by this instruction, never stopped being a Winnebago, and was never away from an Indian community for long.

Key queries that arise from the analysis of Roe Cloud's social experience in this domestic machinery of emotion making—latency making— include: What did it do for him? What did he learn and unlearn from his sentimental exchanges with the Roes? How did these white upper-middle-class advanced selfhood lessons affect his dealings with members of the educated classes? Did the Roes, in ways they had and had not intended, empower Roe Cloud as a strategist on behalf of Indians?

CONVENTIONS OF SENTIMENTAL INTIMACY

Below I focus on correspondence that traces the play of conventions and the presence of history in the Roe Cloud–Roe emotional bond. It is vital to stress that hundreds of letters between Roe Cloud and the Roes convey the goodness, devotion, and piety that made their relation with one another life-enhancing, gentle, and sweet. Much that I referred to in chapter 1 illustrates this. Hamlin Garland, in his critique of missionaries, was right to single out the Roes' "kindliness." Henry's and Mary's exchanges, in particular, were at times mutually sustaining lifelines. As mentioned, Henry behaved very much like a son when he sent Walter and Mary a draft of his Ten Eyck speech and anxiously awaited their comments. And the Roes were thrilled to learn about Henry's election to the Elihu Club. Henry looked forward to Mary's attendance at his commencement. He loved and admired them not simply because of their righteousness, benevolence, and charm, but because of their sense of Indian mission. Henry's Winnebago and Christian ethos of service resonated with their Christian ethos of service. If on one level the Roes fit the sentimental model of the family that intensifies emotional bonds within the home, on another level they exemplified another strain of sentimentality: social altruism and reformism.[51] The Roes invested their intellect, emotions, spirit, and labor in those who needed help in the world. One of the poignant aspects of the letters is that even this touching love, respect, and support were not immune from the workings of class, racial, and gender ideologies.[52]

Henry and Mary worked together on the Winnebago Reservation as well as reservations in Oklahoma and elsewhere during several summers, parts of the school year, and after his Yale graduation.[53] It was not uncommon for them to be separated from one another for weeks or months, and letters articulated their adopted bond. Their correspondence clarifies, among other things, how the making of the managerial individual—eager to lead—and of the psychological individual—eager to believe in, express, and prove one's own seeming uniqueness as defined in relation to an intimate other—could work in concert.

Following the typical maternal-sentimental pattern, Mary endeavored to make Henry emotionally loyal to their bond. Part of her protective project entailed monitoring and suspending his relationships with white women. His letters do not suggest that he knew any young Indian women directly associated with his Yale circle. As Henry confided his romantic interests in young white women, Mary intervened melodramatically as his rescuer, and gradually the Winnebago reassessed his role in this redemption narrative.

What they experienced, however, was so much more than a two-way power relation. Henry and Mary responded tenderly to one another's needs. It may be that the pressures of Yale heightened the undergraduate's need for people who would play the role of parents, perhaps in such conditions, white parents. And what better justification for their calling could the Roes ask for than proselytizing beside the man they called a son, a Christian Indian, an eloquent Yale Indian?

If Mary's fervor for performing the role of Henry's beloved mother was a sentimental mothering that sometimes took on intense expressions, her yearning for affection should be comprehended compassionately in the context of a few biographical factors.[54] Mary's bond with Henry was especially strong partly because, as mentioned earlier, she had lost her only child, Albert, in infancy in 1889, a son who would have been only a few years younger than Henry had he lived.[55] Their mother-son role-playing helped give her an outlet for what she conceptualized only in biological, not social, terms as her suppressed maternal drive.[56] This senti-mentalized maternal drive was channeled into an ambition to protect and manage Henry by lavishing affection on him. In 1909 Mary wrote the undergraduate that she derived great pleasure from writing him long let-ters and signing them as his mother.[57] Sometimes she unburdened her cares in these letters, and Henry performed the role of therapeutic com-forter. For instance, in 1910 Mary confided to Henry that she had entered menopause and was distressed by the physical and psychological distur-bances it created.[58] Her nervousness about this was intensified by her husband's poor health and finally his impending death. Just before Dr. Roe succumbed to Addison's disease, she lamented to Henry that her husband's illness had left her disconsolate and feeling much older.[59] The enormous sacrifices she made in her altruistic life, on behalf of Indians and her husband, had taken their toll.

Mutual confessions and mutual monitoring evident in the Roe Cloud–Roe correspondence were typical of sentimental evangelism. "Christians would engage in mutual supervision," writes historian Catherine Hall, "the constant checking on each other by brothers and sisters in Christ."[60] Their epistolary support for one another extended a domestic project that sought to regulate intimacy and emotional commitment. Yet it also gave voice to contradictions and pressures that challenged domestic happiness.

Viewing the American capitalist family historically, Joel Kovel reads it not just as a socially compensatory "bastion of love and security," but as a social "arena of intense and insoluble struggles" in which "emotional demands forced on the nuclear family" often wind up "sacrificing" the "individuality" of "the mother."[61] In a couple of missives Mary confessed to Henry, who would periodically voice his own bachelor frustrations, that her life had spiritual and intellectual though not other conjugal gratifications. Her adoration of and loyalty to her husband exacted a longstanding suppression of physical needs.[62] Walter's health had been compromised after he contracted tuberculosis in 1889. They then moved to Texas so that Walter could convalesce and take up his ministerial duties. In writing to Henry, Mary typically referred to her husband as Father. Five months before Walter's death, she sadly hinted of the future without her mate. She wrote that if Henry were with her she would have him come close to her so that she could tell him more intimately that, apart from her husband, she loves him most and that he should not be jealous about the affective significance of others in her life.[63] Many of Henry's attentive letters must have reassured her in her role playing as a mother and as a woman, and may have done much to sustain her in her tribulations, disappointments, and sacrifices. Another aspect of their tie was that Mary gave Henry some modest loans to help him get through Yale and his seminary education: he was financially as well as emotionally in her debt.[64]

Henry gave her a Winnebago name that described her slight physical stature and her familial role in his life.[65] She also bestowed on Henry a Winnebago endearment that conveyed his abundant kindness.[66] Their letters exhibit not just gentle endearments but examples of sentimental hyperbole. Sometimes Mary expressed intense needs for Henry's attention.[67] Mary, under duress, could be candid about her own temptations and battles. Writing to the Yale senior, she confided the challenges she faced in managing her unfulfilled physical impulses.[68] Her letters announced her emotional reliance on Henry and in doing so sought to ensure his reliance on her. Mary, who performed the melodramatic role of maternal guardian and rescuer, implied that she also needed comfort and protection. In May 1915 Mary alluded to her awareness that her love for Henry sometimes exceeded her comprehension of it.[69] Even as she affirmed her abiding love for her husband, she testified to Henry's importance in her life as a son.[70] Occasionally, in efforts to contextualize this intensity, Mary reasserted the mother-son form of their affection.[71]

Readers of these letters are likely to ask: What does one make of such hyperbolic sentimental-romanticism? Clearly, these sentimental epistolary reciprocities helped sustain Henry and Mary. Dr. Roe seldom mentioned Henry in his diaries. The correspondence and diaries I have perused give no indication that he felt any reason to be concerned about their conventional, at times colorfully melodramatic, sentimental play.[72] A photograph in the Roe family papers shows Walter sitting and holding a book, while Mary and Henry stand behind him almost protectively. The mood seems peaceful.

CREATING LATENCY, CONTROL, AND INCENTIVE

Walter and Mary subscribed to the standard Christian-sentimental belief that humans are highly susceptible to temptation and thus in need of severe, vigilant regulation.[73] Mary warned Henry against succumbing to instinctual urges and represented the effort as a spiritual, moral, and intellectual struggle.[74] Such statements endeavored to socialize the Winnebago into believing that he had a particular kind of instinct-filled inner self, a latency in need of policing. Demos notes that it was conventional for sentimentalized parents to cultivate the child's "capacity to experience inner guilt" as a mechanism of character formation.[75] This concept of selfhood fits the model of controls that Rosaldo sees as the product mainly of inegalitarian cultures: controls are deemed requisite because the culture defines interiority as harboring "drives and lusts" that jeopardize "status" and "everyday cooperation." The Roes, Rosaldo would be quick to point out, did not simply control Henry's desires, they encoded or classified his desires as being in need of control.

This was their protective mission as upper-middle-class parents. In their minds, Henry's future, his success, was at stake. The Yale Indian was in his mid-twenties and expressed interests in courting young women. A Yalie capable of diligently surveying and controlling his desires could better manage other men and succeed. So Mary assured him that if he wed too soon it might compromise his intellectual and career development. It was her feminine and maternal responsibility to serve God, she believed, and to come between Henry and romantic possibilities she considered unpropitious.[76] Her sentimental and Christ-ordained goal was to help manage Henry's self-management.[77] This too fits the conventional sentimental

incentive-building script. These controls (and notions of instinctual latency), Demos writes, gave purpose to Civil War soldiers: "Mother for
whose sake the war must be won, Mother whose influence keeps her son
from yielding to various forms of battlefield temptation, Mother whose
past self sacrifices justify the supreme sacrifice of life itself, and so forth."[78]

Helen Hunt Jackson's characterization of Señora Moreno's sway over
Felipe, her son, in *Ramona: A Story* (1884), foregrounds sentimentality as a
form of management practice in a world that deprived too many women of
power and control. Moreno, the Spanish Californian matriarch, adminis-
ters her sentimental control over her son "without [his] ever finding it
out": "Never to appear as a factor in the situation; to be able to wield other
men, as instruments, with the same direct and implicit response to will
that one gets from a hand or a foot,—this is to triumph."[79] Mary was much
more playful and well intentioned than the manipulative Moreno. She felt
that Henry's self-management would be cultivated efficaciously if the pretend mother played the role of her pretend son's portable conscience. In
December 1909, in the same missive in which Mary tried to prepare Henry
for the interracial challenges he would take on as an Indian manager of
white men, Mary narrated her melodramatic game-like fantasy of regulat-
ing Henry to regulate himself. She imagined herself shrinking in size so
that she could take up her maternal guard in his garments and monitor
his behavior. That way he would remain cognizant of her and the self-
regimentation she hoped he would achieve at all times.[80] Such impulses
were in no way atypical of missionary monitoring. "A constant commentary on the most intimate practices of daily life was part of the evangelical
agenda," Catherine Hall relates. "Were there signs of sin—in sexual im-
morality, indulgence in drink, the wrong kinds of feelings for unsuitable
people, improper activities on the Sabbath or in the workplace?" Hall calls
this "the fantasy of the all-seeing, all-regulating, all-supervising hand and
eye."[81] And so Mary's fantasy of a miniaturized self transported her to
Henry's chest pocket, a rescue post that would allow her to ensure that he
was not staying up too late when studying.

Mary's management of Henry's self-management took on racial meaning. In her zeal to save him from what she took to be his Winnebago
instinct-filled inner self, she implanted the idea of moral declension, something she could help prevent. She tried to give him the weapon, sentimental

self-control, to combat the latent impulses that she viewed as inherent in Indians.[82] Recycling cultural stereotypes of primitiveness, she signified Indianness as instinctual temptation and, by implication, Protestant whiteness as potential salvation. Roe Cloud's class sentimentalization was simultaneously his racial sexualization. She assumed the class and racial power to either bestow on him or withdraw from him the feeling that he was an honorary Yale individual. The scenario was pure melodrama: if Henry's interests in other women were too precipitously romantic, then Mary, his guardian, could rush to his rescue and make him feel too Indian, too naively, instinctually, racially vulnerable to seduction. Henry's sentimental restraint—in effect, coating his heart with sentimental ice—became tantamount to a reaffirmation of his upper-middle-class Yale and sentimental status.[83]

Hall's study of nineteenth-century missionaries in the West Indies suggests that this attempt at racial and class management was the product of training rather than an idiosyncratic psychological tendency. Missionaries labored to "organize and legislate both their own emotional lives and those of their congregations—regularizing marriages in an attempt to stop intimacies 'out of place.' " In her work on missionaries in the East Indies, Ann Stoler argues that the intermarriage of whites and colonial subjects of color was "so heavily politicized because it was understood to destabilize both national identity and the Manichean categories of ruler and ruled." White female middle-class missionaries, as regulators of sentiment, she adds, had a particularly important stake in censoring any sexual inclinations their converts might have that would compromise "racial segregation": "In the nineteenth-century Netherlands Indies, white women could lose their legal rights to European status if they married native men, on the argument of colonial lawyers that their feelings (rather than acts) betrayed cultural dispositions that were less Dutch than Javanese." Female missionaries served as "the boundary markers of empire."[84] The effort to influence Roe Cloud's romantic investments was an enactment of a sentimental missionary role that predated Mary Roe's interventions.

Henry's college and graduate school romances pushed sentimentality's limits. When Henry expressed his affection for Ethel and her interest in him, at Oberlin, this was Mary's cue. Mary, nursing her sick husband, wrote him nervously that she wanted to hold him close and discuss the matter. What she felt it necessary to do, it seems, was protectively in-sinuate racial insecurity in his Yale-Winnebago self-image. Mary asked whether any white woman would dedicate herself to working for Indians (by implication, as she had).[85] She told Henry about a discussion she had had about Ethel with a woman whom she admitted did not impress her as having a capacious or forgiving heart. Mary's acquaintance described a conversation she supposedly had with Ethel and, on the basis of this, characterized the young woman as shallow and indefinite about her goals. Ethel, so the acquaintance claimed, sought her counsel about the pos-sibility of taking an Indian husband and intimated that the Indian would soon propose.[86] Mary's efforts to recast Henry's interracial romance as an Indian problem were enough to arouse his suspicions of Ethel's sincerity and probably also to activate what he sometimes regarded as his rather self-critical tendency to undervalue himself.[87] There are indications that Henry may have left Oberlin not just for academic reasons but to disen-tangle himself from a romantic tie.[88]

Before Mary ended the Ethel affair she had saved Henry from Jessie by reminding him that pity and love are not the same. This hit Henry hard. Henry denied that he had fallen in love, but thanked Mary for her guidance about the responsible way to interact with Jessie and other young women. His self-admonition suggests that he had come to harbor concerns about whether such women were attracted to him as a man or to his exotic stature as an Indian or because they felt altruistic compassion, rather than passion, for him. If they were simply drawn to his Indianness, then he melodramatically had to shield them from being swept away by their youthful enthusiasms.[89] Margaret and several others were also disquali-fied. Henry wrote that he had called on a young woman in New Haven and thus did not send Mary his usual letter. He apologized, confessed that he had been more fascinated with the woman than he should have been, and, somewhat ambiguously, associated the whole episode with a pattern of attraction that he linked with the color red.[90]

How taboo was romance between an Indian man and a white woman in middle- and upper-middle-class Protestant reform culture? Michael Cole-man infers that "the silence of the Presbyterians on intermarriage is omi-nous." His research on nineteenth-century Presbyterian missions yielded no evidence of sexual relations between male or female missionaries and

Indians.[91] Yet Indian late-nineteenth- and early-twentieth-century reform culture was complex. "Taboos against interracial mixing certainly existed," Katherine Ellinghaus acknowledges in *Taking Assimilation to Heart* (2006), "but in the context of indigenous assimilation they could be overlooked by some in favor of an emphasis on acculturation and self-support." Some educators and missionaries interpreted middle-class Indian-white marriage as a socially symbolic union offering dramatic proof that Indians could be civilized, Americanized, and individualized as workers, competitors, and family-centered men and women.

In 1886 Alice Robertson, a missionary whose sister and aunt had wed Indians, wrote that such unions demonstrate "that there is nothing inferior in the Indian." Elaine Goodale Eastman began her career as a teacher of Indians at Hampton Institute. In 1889, a year prior to meeting Dr. Charles Eastman, whom she would marry in 1891, she published a story in which a white physician encourages an Indian man: "I don't know why a white girl shouldn't marry an Indian if he was a good fellow." And Pratt, who held that Indians and whites did not have inherently different racially based capacities, asked rhetorically: "Why should not Indian men take white wives and live with the whites?" Indian-white unions were not commonplace. But some of the major boarding schools did not frown on them. Carlisle's school files yield information on twenty-seven Indian male–white female and eighteen Indian female–white male marriages, while Hampton, from 1871 to 1893, records six Indian male–white female and eight Indian female–white male nuptials. The reform ambition was to assimilate not just Indian minds and bodies, but emotions and desires. Ideally, Indian-white marriage put intimate reformism into practice. A proper marriage also could help ratify an educated Indian's class membership.[92]

Henry's contemporaries could have responded to the courtships he refers to in a variety of ways.[93] As nationally respected figures within Protestant assimilationist circles, Mary and Henry had to have known that some reformers and missionaries would read a middle-class romance between Henry and a white woman not as something illicit, but as a symbolic affirmation of Indian capabilities and the uplifting power of education. They also had to have realized that not all reform-minded benefactors and power brokers would have expressed this tolerance.

Early-twentieth-century literary and popular culture suggests that white anxieties about amorous ties between college Indians and refined white women were very much "in the air." Indeed, the white female rejection of college Indians and Indian self-disqualification were stock themes. As noted in chapter 1, Marah Ellis Ryan's *Indian Love Letters*, reviewed by the *Yale Lit.* in spring 1907, portrays a college Indian who attaches life-and-death importance to being accepted by a refined white woman. When she rejects him, he rejects himself, and, unlike Henry, loses hope and dies. Helen Hunt Jackson's *Ramona* and Zane Grey's *The Vanishing American* (1925) popularized similar melodramas of "noble savage" self-disqualification. Although Jackson's violin-playing Californian Indian eventually marries the half-Spanish and half-Indian Ramona, in defiance of her racist aristocratic aunt, he torments himself with doubts that an upper-class woman could accept him. "Could she live in a house such as he himself must live in,—live as the Temecula women lived? . . . He must leave his people, must go to some town, must do—he knew not what—something to earn more money." He asks: "Would not you rather be dead, Señorita, than be as I am to-day? . . . I know it would kill you, Señorita." Zane Grey's college Indian, an All-American baseball star, wins the heart of a white woman. But this automatically plunges him into a "brooding subjectiveness of mind." In romance, can Indians really be All American? "The noble proof of his love for Marian was not in surrender to it. He would not drag her down to his level."[94] He must protect her by disqualifying himself and rejecting her. The noble Indian elicits "sympathy," film historian Gregory Jay writes about the stereotype, without demanding "equality." Grey's college Indian, like Ryan's, "doomed" by noble primitivism, melodramatically expires.[95]

John Joseph Mathews's *Sundown*, published in 1934, revisited the college Indian rejection and self-disqualification melodrama. The Osage novelist suggests that early-twentieth-century Indian-white romantic relations at college could be ideologically charged, even without letters like Mary's to amplify anxieties. At the University of Oklahoma, the Osage undergraduate, Chal, develops a crush on the white beauty Blo, who enjoys keeping Chal yearning for romance, though unfulfilled. His quiescence and diffidence during their dates are partly the result of white students' attitudes toward Indians. After one date with Blo he damns "himself with the accusation that he would never be as other people were and that he would never really be civilized." Yet acceptance by a white woman is symbolically potent because it can confer the sense of belonging that Chal craves. "All the time he was attempting to be like the others, and he was unhappy when he felt that he was not like them." Over time, however, Chal tires of this mimicry.[96]

In life beyond literature white women sometimes invited and then rebuffed Indian mimicry. "The very fact that you are of another race is a barrier between you and any white woman your equal," one white woman admonished Dr. Carlos Montezuma. "You *must* look for a cultured and beautiful Indian." Montezuma seems to have internalized this racial disqualification when he wrote the father of Lillian Underwood, a white woman, requesting his daughter's hand in marriage. The marriage prospect must strike him, Montezuma confessed to Lillian's father in his letter, as "an outrageous idea." And when Jason Betzinez (Apache), a former Carlisle student, wooed Anna Heersma, a white Dutch missionary whom he eventually married, he flagellated himself: "no house, nothing to offer a wife."[97]

Variations of these plots and anxieties proliferated on the silver screen. Philip J. Deloria has analyzed the plots of numerous college Indian and Carlisle Indian romantic-rejection movies produced while Henry was consulting Mary about his romances. D. W. Griffith's *Call of the Wild: The Sad Plight of the Civilized Redman* (1908) features a "football hero from Carlisle Indian College" who unlearns much from a white woman: " 'Good enough as a hero, but not as a husband.' " Still primitive inside, he hears the "call of the wild" and returns to his tribe to wreak revenge (yet spares her life when he captures her). In *Strongheart* (1914), the Columbia University Indian, a football star, woos a white woman until the call of the plot banishes him to the reservation to tend his dying father. *The Great Alone* (1922) is about a Stanford Indian, also a gridiron star, who, when rejected by the white woman, takes up with a mixed-blood. In *Blazing Arrows* (1922) another Columbia Indian triumphs in cross-race romance (after some failures) only to discover that, appropriately, he is white. Closer to Henry's own storyline are films made by James Young Deer (Winnebago) and his wife Lillian St. Cyr (Winnebago), known as Red Wing. *Young Deer Returns* (1910) rejects the stereotypical rejection and self-rejection plot. The Carlisle baseball star rejects his white paramour after her father, whose life he had once saved, initially dismisses the athlete's marriage request. He goes home, weds an Indian, and lives happily ever after. In Young Deer's *Red Eagle, the Lawyer* (1912), the Indian professional, rescued by an Indian woman, overcomes white land-grabbers and marries his helpmate. The famous Winnebago filmmakers, Deloria argues, helped revise the "cultural expectations" of movie fans. In their cinematic America, Indian-Indian and Indian-white matches could beat the odds, equality could encompass romance, and love's redemption could defeat rejection.[98]

It should be noted that Roe Cloud's Winnebago upbringing would have schooled him in the notion that parents often arranged the marriage of their child. Moreover, clan membership regulated who could marry whom. Hence he would have been at home with the cultural idea that a young man's marriage was not strictly a matter of his own preference. But he also would have been accustomed to the qualification that if a son disagreed strongly with his parents about whom he could wed that they would accede to his wishes. In addition, he would have been aware that Winnebago males usually married once they were mature enough to do so.[99] In his late twenties, Henry may have reached a point where he stopped consulting Mary about his romantic prospects (sending her epistolary cues to protect him from women and from himself) and courted women without her knowledge. Certainly by 1914, the year he met the woman he would marry, he ceased seeking Mary's approval.

MELODRAMATIC PLAY

If Mary decreed that romantic relations with white women could not be a part of Henry's always contingent Yale and Christian individuality, her hyperbolic sentimental-romanticism offered him compensations. Mary entreated him to confess to her his needs.[100] She wrote of her deep affection for him, representing this as God-ordained maternal passion.[101] The invocation of God sanctified and clarified her own sentimental expression of love. To ensure that Henry discontinued his friendship with a discontented wife who overly appreciated his sympathies, whom Mary dubbed Delilah, Mary alluded to their own affectionate gestures. Again, when referring to their endearments she reasserted their maternal meaning.[102] And again, she formulated the problem as the Winnebago's inner nature.

All this left Henry in an emotional quandary. Fundamentally, Mary had turned his interest in refined white women into a test of his sentimental evolution. His chastity became the condition of his class and racial belonging. He had to prove that piety, morality, and sentiment, not sexuality, motivated him. Yet Mary's emotional grip on Henry provided him, at least for a time, with a sense of security. Henry admitted that she could overwhelm him with her sentimental power.[103] He wrote that he knew she would never rebuff him, perhaps as some young women had in Yale circles.[104] Henry playfully asked if he could escort her to the junior prom.[105] The woman he called mother—not Mary—was about 46 when Henry wondered about whom he might take to the prom. However, his performance of this restraint became exasperating. As early as 1911, Henry, while studying in the seminary, notified Mary that his willingness to defer romantic involvements was wearing thin.[106]

Henry exercised considerable emotional agency in this melodramatic play. Sometimes he sought to gain psychological sway over Mary. Someday, Henry noted in 1912, he might take a wife or enter an occupation different from what Mary had in mind for him.[107] Two months before the ailing Walter died in 1913, Henry wrote her again in this vein. He observed that his tie to her was not romantic and that she, in truth, was not his biological mother. Thus she need not hold back her fondness for others.[108] But the illness and death of her husband fueled Mary's need for a son who would carry on her husband's mission.

Henry's most histrionic and curiously self-parodic critique of the performance dimension of their relationship took the form of a titled dialogue between what seem to be two lovers that he sent Mary, composed five months before Dr. Roe's demise. The occasional gestures toward mock-Shakespearean language suggest perhaps that on some level he saw the male as a kind of Hamlet figure and the female as Gertrude. His unnamed male character proclaims his love. The unnamed female character tells him to be quiet and not request that she spurn others. Then the male refers to the emotionally tumultuous nature of their sometimes covert, sometimes overt, yet dizzyingly ambiguous relationship. In his own voice Henry asks that Mary give him up as her pretend son if it means ignoring others or if it means obscuring their pretend mother-son bond as she seeks out others.[109] His stagy hyper-melodramatic enactment of *Sturm und Drang* reads like a twentieth-century parody of the romantic "Byron-ism" or "Wertherism" that Henry's early selfhood-guide Samuel Smiles believed was anathema to the maintenance of pragmatic individuality and character.[110]

PSYCHOLOGICAL INDIVIDUALISM VS. INDIAN SELFHOOD

At moments the Winnebago saw that he was being partly transformed, by Yale and by Mary, into an upper-middle-class psychological individual, and began to reconsider this process critically and cross-culturally. Worn out by prolonged debates at Yale about Elihu Club prospects, Henry specified the neurasthenic nature of his emotional exhaustion.[111] Henry's characteriza-tion of himself in this way in 1910 is historically significant, because, as Tom Lutz observes, the early-twentieth-century medical discourse of neu-rasthenia was not just a cultural encoding of mental and emotional suffer-ing, it was a "marker of status and social acceptability." Harvard's Henry Adams and William James, for example, both endured "neurasthenia." According to this cultural discourse, immigrants, Catholics, Jews, and members of the working class lacked the subjective complexity, and fragil-ity, to be affected by neurasthenia. And only the " 'advanced' races" pos-sessed the subjective capital to join the neurasthenic club—no African Americans or Indians allowed. For Henry to represent himself in neuras-thenic language meant something then that it no longer means today. It signals his own tendency to read himself, or at least describe himself, through a cultural lens that Mary, who also portrayed herself as nervous, and probably some of his classmates, had adopted. Sensitive Anglo-Saxon "brain-workers, but no other kind of laborer," Lutz observes, got to be "nervous." Yet Lutz also notes that in the early 1900s neurasthenia "had spread through the international bourgeoisie as far as Kyoto, Calcutta, and St. Petersberg."[112]

This does not mean that Henry surrendered his Winnebago kinship understanding of himself, only that he felt and thought about the pull of new ways of imagining, classifying, and experiencing emotional life. In another instance Henry apologized to Mary for writing a letter he decided not to send and associated his composition of it with hysteria. Mary had upset him because she indicated that she might not attend his Yale commencement. Henry suggested that Indians do not respond to stress or disappointment in this affectively extreme fashion. Here he implies that Indians have what we might now term different cultural structures of emotions and that his structure had only partly changed at Yale and with the Roes.[113]

As I have noted, early-twentieth-century class identity formation, gender construction, racial division, and imperial discourse are bound up complexly not only with the ongoing development of sentimentalism, but with modern representations of the middle-class family and individuality as "psychological." When Henry and Mary were exchanging letters, Taos and Santa Fe were becoming artist colonies for bohemians who sought cultural contact with Indians as a treatment for what they took to be their overcivilized suppression of instincts and creativity. Increasingly, many members of the middle and upper classes would translate their social dilemmas and preoccupations into "psychological" terms. Whites now needed Indians as human touchstones to "discover" their repressed or latent individuality. This therapeutic use of Indians supercharged the Southwestern tourist industry. Yet these white pilgrims—as much as they felt instinctually indebted to the Indians they danced with, painted, wrote about, and profited from—mostly distinguished themselves from these tribal "exotics." Modern white neurotic complexity sometimes took the place of sentimental moral superiority in the social hierarchy of selfhood that continued to elevate whites over Indians. If Indians offered whites a primitive enrichment of psychological complexity, whites still judged Indians as too primitive—too tribal, too collective, too unevolved—to embody white "psychological" depth.[114]

How much Roe Cloud became attuned to this "psychological" turn in the white encoding of Indians—much of his missionary work was in the Southwest—is unclear. But Henry invoked race again to Mary in 1912 when he contended that races categorized as civilized and races classified as uncivilized love differently and that his affection was influenced decisively by his membership in the latter category. He averred gently that the privatization of emotional investments that structured the affective relations of white individuals and families did not fulfill a scope of love that he needed. That scope was a greater, more communal attachment and commitment to others, not a love expressed mostly through charged familial bonds. He believed that God created humans who appreciate a range of characteristics found in a range of humans. Concentrated love, he ventured, can obfuscate this more expansive need for affection. Here the Winnebago who was educated in kinship values that emphasized interconnectedness recoiled from the constraint of the middle-class family circle. And here the Winnebago Yalie who could entertain varying beliefs and self-conceptions withdraws from the dominant model of emotional investment linked with the middle and upper classes. Yet it is the Christian as well as the Winnebago Indian who asserts himself—though it may be that the Winnebago framed his comments in Christian, rather than Winnebago, terms that Mary would fully understand, respect, and heed. That said, later in his letter he added, with a melodramatic flourish, that he was still drawn to their intimacy.[115]

Fanon was familiar with the sort of socially conditioned emotional bind that characterizes aspects of Henry's complicated intercultural relationship with Mary. Reflecting on colonial structures of racialized self-deprecation, he writes that the Antillean "feels (collective unconscious) that one is a Negro to the degree to which one is wicked, sloppy, malicious, instinctual. Everything that is the opposite of these Negro modes of behavior is white." Tragically, this can lead not only to self-hatred but hatred of one's race. Consequently, one ignores race (the Carlisle focus was on embracing Americanness, conventional gender roles, one's capacity as a worker, and so on) or embraces race (the catalyst for the race pride that helped engender pluralism and later multiculturalism). "Either I ask others to pay no attention to my skin, or else I want them to be aware of it. I then try to find value for what is bad." Fanon proposes what Henry may have aspired to achieve: "to rise above this absurd drama that others have staged round me, to reject the two terms that are equally unacceptable, and through one human being, to reach out for the universal."[116] The human who made the lasting difference for him was Elizabeth Bender.

ELIZABETH BENDER

That Henry, always shaped by his Winnebago upbringing, had also become partly reliant emotionally on Mary's sentimental intensity seems clear in some of the letters he continued to write her after he met Elizabeth

Georgian Bender (1889–1965), his future wife, in the autumn of 1914, and even after Elizabeth announced to Mary in July 1915 their engagement. All this changed. One of Mary's diary entries in 1917, a year after Henry married Elizabeth, records that Henry asked Mary to let him go his own way.[117]

Bender, a Bad River Band Chippewa, had studied at Hampton, then taught children from the Blackfeet tribe, and after that began to teach domestic science at a Carlisle that had been rocked by notoriety and scandals in 1914. Carlisle made international headlines when Jim Thorpe (Sac and Fox, Potawatomi), the former Carlisle athletic star, was forced to return the Olympic medals he won in 1912 because he had played some summer baseball for a pittance of a salary and was thus classified as professional. And then in 1913 some Carlisle students and graduates signed petitions that the superintendent, Moses Friedman, had mistreated students, some of whom he called "savages."[118]

In the aftermath of this turmoil, Bender published an essay in Carlisle's *Red Man*, "Training Indian Girls for Efficient Home Makers" (1916), that envisioned home as a leadership-instruction enterprise organized to sustain the nation. Some of her domestic premises are in sync with the sentimental conventions that structured Mary Roe's views. Carlisle girls practiced in a "model home cottage" under Bender's supervision to make sure they played their role well.[119] Bender believed that a fundamental goal of education was the building of character and that religious training was essential for this, and for those reasons she, like Roe Cloud and Mary Roe, was quite critical of Carlisle.

In November 1915 Elizabeth sent a sagacious and sympathetic letter to Mary because Mary had not written very much in response to their letters. Elizabeth presented herself as Mary's daughter and wanted Mary to love her the way she did Henry. Her generous letter also demonstrated her ability as a homemaker, a savvy builder of her conjugal unit. Elizabeth's plural pronouns staked out her marital turf; she was eager to share Henry, but was wary of Mary's protective possessiveness. She reaffirmed Henry's love for Mary while acknowledging compassionately that Mary had reacted badly to the prospect of their marriage. Elizabeth's conciliatory reassertion of Mary's maternal bond with Henry was also her gentle means of signaling to Mary that Henry had entered into a different primary relationship, as Elizabeth's beloved and future husband. In one passage Elizabeth presented herself as having a key influence on Henry's emotions, or at least on Henry's emotional response to Mary. Elizabeth pledged to make sure that Henry would always remember Mary.[120]

How Mary viewed Henry's alliance with an Indian woman—rather than with a white woman, like those Mary had fended off to rescue Henry from unpropitious alliances—is not certain. But Henry's own complex attitude toward this may suggest something about Mary's take on the union. Although Henry succeeded in courting and proposing to Elizabeth without consulting Mary, he also wrote several letters to Mary that show his emotional unrest during this transitional phase. In one letter Henry wrote that though Elizabeth is of Indian ancestry, she was raised similarly to a white girl, does not speak Chippewa, and is unfamiliar with Indian forms of domestic life.[121] He did not go on to mention in this missive that Elizabeth was half white—her father was a German homesteader who had settled in Minnesota.[122]

A few months before his engagement to Elizabeth, Henry sent Mary a stirring testimony of his affection for Mary. It mixes familial language, sacred references, melodramatic fervor, and some sentimental-romantic imagery.[123] Henry wrote his most conflicted letter to Mary during his honeymoon with Elizabeth in June 1916. The upper-middle-class feminine distinction and style that Henry had come to value in Yale circles still appealed to him.[124] Henry's sense of his own Yale persona and class-belonging seems to have relied partly on feeling subjectively potent enough to maintain Mary's deep affection and maternal approval. The religious, sentimental, and Yale codes and conventions that Mary embodied appear to have been what structured some of Henry's emotional dependencies, which included his need to think of himself as able to wield influence among whites. More powerful, compelling, and enduring, however, was his love for Elizabeth and their membership in a racialized group that affected Henry's ability to be received in all circumstances as a Yale individual. Elizabeth was Henry's companion at the restaurant in Wisconsin where they were directed to eat in the kitchen and use a pail rather than the washroom because they were misidentified as African American. Together they reasserted their class standing and defiantly joined the Harvard Club luncheon. Their love thrived for three and a half decades.[125]

Mary's diaries clarify that Henry's and Elizabeth's conjugal passion was alive and strong. Elizabeth appears in Mary's entries during the Thanks-giving holiday in 1915. Months later Mary depicts the bride-to-be as emo-tionally on edge a couple of days before her nuptials. On their wedding day, June 12, 1916, Mary seems reconciled and gives them her benedic-tion. She wanted Henry to be happy. But her uneasy bond with them continued.[126]

Encounters described in the diaries bring to mind popular stereotypes of competitive relations between mother-in-law and daughter-in-law. In November 1916 Mary reports that she and Elizabeth experienced some friction with one another. A week later Mary opines that Elizabeth is difficult to satisfy. And a few days after that something Elizabeth said or did made Mary weep. By Thanksgiving Mary charges Carlisle's teacher of domestic science, perhaps only in her diary, with getting up late and falter-ing as a housekeeper. This domestic scrutiny, as Catherine Hall notes, was common among missionaries. "Did women clean their homes well? Were children sleeping separately from their parents? What states of feeling were being lived in these homes?"[127] However, Mary's criticisms have an edge. Although she depicts Elizabeth as impolite, Mary sketches herself as self-effacingly determined to befriend her in support of Henry. The next day Mary's resolve is shaken. Mary complains to Elizabeth and categorizes what she reads as Elizabeth's offensive emotional posture as an Indian behavioral trait. In early December Mary concludes that Elizabeth is not yet capable of contenting herself or making anyone else content. Near the New Year, as Henry and Elizabeth pack, Mary prays that God will enable her to endure tolerantly under this stress. Yet the tension gets to her on New Year's Eve day when at church Elizabeth elects not to take the sacra-ment of communion.

Mary's memoranda for the year yield clues to an underlying source of her problem: raw, intense, heart-ripping loneliness. On New Year's Eve night the newlyweds adjourned to their room leaving her. Mary repaired to her own room, walked the floor, and prayed. Yet their laughter and joy, audible through the wall, interrupted her supplications.[128] Mary self-defensively classified their demonstrative pleasure as Indian childishness. The Indian couple was unambiguously blissful. Mary's onrushing loneli-ness, even when it takes the form of peevishness, is poignant in its sad-ness.[129] Some of her letters and diary entries in the years leading up to this entry in 1916 contribute to a still-unwritten American history of loneliness. Mary also is a moving figure in the still-unwritten American history of middle-aged widows.

The years proved over and over that Henry and Elizabeth had reason only to be proud of each other, their love, and their four accomplished daughters. They became intellectual partners in the Indian cause. Elizabeth as well as Henry was honored with a biographical page in *Indians of Today* (1936), published by the Indian Council Fire to feature "outstanding individuals" who have exemplified "the progress of the American Indian race." The editor notes that Elizabeth had studied for two years at Wichita University and the University of Kansas and that she is, as was Mary Roe, "outstanding as a lecturer in the interests of Indian people, and is in great demand as a speaker before prominent women's and missionary organizations." Elizabeth, like her husband, devoted herself unselfishly to the struggle to open higher education to Indians. In 1931 she observed that although Indians, more than any other group, had been forced to negotiate unceasing waves of transformation over the last hundred years, increasing numbers of Indian youth, remarkably, are making their way to the American Indian Institute's high school in their early teens. Hazel Hertzberg writes glowingly that Elizabeth, who "came from a prominent Chippewa family," was "one of the few persons active both in the Society [of American Indians] and in this century's second major reform Pan-Indian organization, the National Congress of American Indians, founded in 1945. For several years she directed the NCAI's American Indian Development self-help program."[130] Elizabeth, like Henry, concentrated constructively on what could be done for Indians.

Her mettle in dealing with private and public problems was perhaps a family characteristic. Also written up on his own page in *Indians of Today* is Elizabeth's brother, Charles Albert Bender, known as Chief Bender, a former Carlisle student who became one of the greatest American League pitchers of the early twentieth century (Philadelphia Athletics, inducted into the Baseball Hall of Fame). "When hostile fans would whoop derisively in imitation of Indians, 'Chief' Bender delighted in walking close to the stands, on his way from the field to the bench, proclaiming scornfully —'Foreigners!' "[131]

Elizabeth received national attention. In 1940 she served as a delegate to

the White House Conference for Youth and Children. She established a
national Indian women's club. Shortly after Henry's death in 1950, Elizabeth earned the distinction of being named Oregon Mother of the Year and
then proceeded to win American Mother of the Year.[132] In a wise piece she
wrote for the press in May 1950, her modesty and dedication to her children shines forth. For Elizabeth mothering meant not in any way sub-
merging her Indian identity.[133] Henry and Elizabeth put the Indian way
first even as they helped develop the meanings and possibilities of being
Indian in new conditions.

READING HISTORICALLY SYMBOLIC
ROLES AND RELATIONSHIPS

Perhaps some scholars would read Mary Roe as representing a charismatic
and seemingly sacred Great White Colonial Mother who promises to nurture her colonized "children" in return for their loyalty, assimilation, and
adoration.[134] Sentimental culture's imperial and class investment in white
femininity set Mary up to play this powerful melodramatic role.[135] In Mathews's *Sundown*, the young Osage protagonist entertains the sentimental
fantasy that civilization—which, he was told, was coming to the reservation—is a "woman with her laces, fluttering handkerchiefs, and sicken-
ing perfumery. . . . He used to visualize this lady drooping in the intense heat of the Agency." Overwhelmed, "Civilization, pale and beautiful,
[would be] lying on her bed and people standing around her. Curiously, he
didn't see the fullbloods standing around the bed of the lady, but sad-
faced mixedbloods" (66). Charles Eastman also may have experienced
some of the sentimental pressures that Henry felt in his bond with Mary.
He and his white assimilationist wife, Elaine, seem to have separated from
one another in 1921 partly, if his biographer's inference is right, because
he finally felt too uncomfortable with her expectation that he serve as "a
living vindication of the reformer's dream."[136] A white woman reformer,
Elaine Goodale Eastman believed, could inspire Indians "with admiration
and almost awe, and . . . persuade them to study and to think and to give
up some of their old bad habits when an equally good *man* would not
influence them at all."[137] Conscious of the socially symbolic dimensions of
some colonial "psychological" relationships, Memmi asserts: "the whole

world is within the couple."[138] It is understandable that in this historical moment some Indians could have viewed attempted assimilation as
being like both an abortive romance—seemingly promised but not quite
consummated—and a pretend foster adoption—never really legalized.

And yet, such an abstract, schematic, allegorical account of Mary Roe's
role and potency would be neither sufficiently sympathetic nor historically
complex enough in its inattentiveness to her own struggles as a woman, a
middle-aged woman and by 1913 a widow, within a social structure that
offered women too few opportunities.[139] Long before she met Henry, she
developed her extraordinary talent to rouse others with her oratory, ideas,
presence, and piety, and enjoyed great celebrity on the missionary social
circuit (which traversed Vassar, Yale, wealthy homes, and Christian associations).[140] She and other remarkable Protestant women in her era ener-
getically took up what Patricia Hill calls a "romance of missions" that
permitted them to travel and have adventures. This "romance" allowed
them, as missionaries or evangelical administrators, to move beyond the
narrow patriarchal restrictions of middle-class femininity and acquire executive skills in "public speaking, fund-raising, and organization management."[141] Mary, as an enterprising builder and manager of the spirit in the
Progressive Era, was culturally equipped to attempt to influence what and
who Henry identified with, and to try to make the Roes' mission his—for
a time.

As I suggested above, if one central question is, what did white middle-
class culture do to Henry Roe Cloud, another is, what did white middle-
class culture do to Mary Roe? She too was caught in the vortex of history
and ideology. The sentimental influence that this caring and ambitious
woman sought to establish over Henry—overseeing his attempted romances with white women, teaching him to imagine himself as having
a particular mold of inner self susceptible to temptations—was part of
middle-class identity training. Her well-intended directorial impulses fit
what Carroll Smith-Rosenberg terms the "emotional logic," if not "cognitive logic," of a cultural pattern.

Several historians—Smith-Rosenberg, Stephen Nissenbaum, John Kasson—have analyzed the nineteenth-century middle-class tendency to fret
over and control the body, sexuality, and the emotions (fears surrounded
masturbation, menstruation, alcoholism, meat eating) as a displaced ef-

fort to control an American world experienced as whirling out of control. As I said earlier, for Mary, and for millions of sentimental middle-class mothers, the family had to seem like a precinct of order, a protection from America's dangers and instabilities. True to standard Protestant and sentimental form, Mary worried about managing her own corporeal impulses as well as Henry's. In her performances as a woman and a sometimes melodramatic mother-protector, Mary had to serve as what Smith-Rosenberg calls the "savior of home and society" and a "symbol of order." The maintenance of order could require the sexual policing and emotional regulation of one's intimates. What Smith-Rosenberg sees in this zeal to establish order is a socially symbolic system understood and felt by people within this system only in a personal, unhistorical, "sentimental" or "psychological" way. "Change and chaos assumed a sexual form," Smith-Rosenberg concludes, hence the "physical body" stood in place of the "social body" as the locus of control. How did this compensatory and displaced yearning for order—emotional order, sexual order—relate to Henry? For one thing, he was a male playing the role of son. Many of the nineteenth-century discourses Smith-Rosenberg has analyzed are preoccupied in particular with controlling the young male's sexuality as a potentially socially disruptive force. Competition demanded that the young man's energies be harnessed and channeled into hard work, success, and family support.[142] Mary, however, wanted to manage the self-management of an Indian male. Her rhetoric of God-ordained self-regulation did not simply seek to control an inner self that existed, a self already fully formed by white culture. Rather, her admonitions and prescriptions helped culturally manufacture that self, call that self into being, as a product of sentimental regulation.[143]

Henry's self, his Winnebago kinship self, "I-am-We," negotiated new models of self-conception at Yale, with the Roes, on the missionary circuits, and elsewhere. Recall his two comments about Indian dancing discussed in chapter 1. In his 1911 letter to the Roes, Henry reads Indians performing the Buffalo Dance in psychological and literary terms as dancers unleashing their drives. And his 1909 *Yale Courant* article categorizes the performance of other Indian dancers as being on a "barbaric march." Could it be that Henry, as an Indian, came to symbolize not only the tribal, barbaric, instincts that Mary thought she had to control in herself, but those that dominant white culture believed it had to manage and channel to sustain itself? Connecting domesticity, imperialism, and the ideology of self-government, Amy Kaplan writes: "The narrative of female self-discipline that is so central to the domestic novel might be viewed as a kind of civilizing process in which the woman plays the role of both civilizer and savage." One female teacher in the Carlisle-like Indian boarding school depicted in Frances Sparhawk's novel *Chronicle of Conquest* (1890) outlines the white challenge: "We Anglo-Saxons have been a thousand years getting the savage out of us, and there are occasions when it doesn't seem as if we succeeded well." For many assimilation-era reformers, the campaign to get the Indian out of Indians and the project to get the Indian out of whites were indeed linked.[144]

Henry's stated preference for uncivilized love of the many over civilized privatized love of the few suggests that at times he grew impatient with being rendered a symbol of that which must be controlled. However much Henry was re-acculturated to fear lapsing into tribal, barbaric, call-of-the-wild instincts, he eventually rebelled against insulating his heart and postponing romance. For all the love and respect he bore the Roes, his "I-am-We" self-definition and mission ultimately prevailed. What Henry moved beyond, understood historically, was not just a person—a friend he loved and admired—but a sentimentalized carrier of patterns and displacements of which she herself could not have been fully aware. Two different "emotional logics" from two different cultures encountered one another—producing much affection, sometimes clashing—in a moving and illuminating cross-cultural drama.

Some prominent Indians—Ely Parker (Seneca), Eastman, Sherman Coolidge (first president of the Society of American Indians), Montezuma, Thomas Sloan, and Chauncey Yellow Robe (Lakota Sioux)—had married white women. William Jones, educated at Harvard and Columbia, was engaged to the white Caroline Andrus, who taught at Hampton Institute. He died in the Philippines before they could be married.[145] Despite the fact that these were middle- or upper-middle-class alliances sanctified and applauded by some white Protestant reformers, the dominant culture still placed them under symbolic pressure. Philip J. Deloria's analyses of early films helps clarify what the Indian man–white woman union could destabilize: "If race and gender made one another authoritative, with the 'natural' dominance of men dovetailing and exchanging meanings with the 'natural' dominance of white people over Indians, then inverting either race or gender upset the entire economy of meaning. How, within an audience's expectations, could the formula '(Indian) man controls (white) woman' make any sense? Men might control women, but Indians should not control whites."[146] Henry's romances risked transgressing a symbolic dominance within which Mary, as a woman, also played a subordinate role.

Some of Henry's experiences with Mary during and after Yale may have made him recollect a tale his grandmother once told him, a version of a story about the dilemma of a "praying Indian" (that may first have been circulated by Ottawas and Ojibwas in the 1830s).[147] Upon dying, her cautionary tale went, a Christianized Crow takes the fork in the road that leads to the Christian heaven and is told: " 'You have mistaken your road. Go back and take the other road.' He was a white man in dress, but his Indian features betrayed him." When he follows the other road to the Crow heaven, he finds that in his Americanized form he is rejected there also. " 'Now,' said my grandmother, 'I do not command you to stop being a "preaching listener," but if you want to be forever a wanderer in the other world, you can continue in the road you have taken.' "[148] If Henry "dressed" white, "his Indian features" announced rather than "betrayed" his mission. He remained a "preaching listener," although characteristically he expanded what he listened to and learned from. And if at times Henry explored the white road, it was in the service of opening new Indian roads.

Some of Fanon's thoughts on colonial reorganization in the Antilles of the black professional- and managerial-class male's desire and self-image may help elaborate the significance of this tale. Fanon suggests that the male Antillean's anima "is almost always a white woman," while his animus is "always a white man." Having internalized whiteness as the greatest social, professional, and subjective value, the only "solution for the miserable Negro" is to "furnish proofs of his whiteness to others and above all to himself." Even his dreams are invaded with colonial representations of race and racial value: "It is in fact customary in Martinique to dream of a form of salvation that consists of magically turning white." The Antillean's colonized interiority habitually "requires a white approval." Fanon's provocative solution to this social and psychological trap is radi-

cal and exceedingly difficult, perhaps impossible to achieve or even imagine: "I propose nothing short of the liberation of the man of color from
himself."[149]

As Roe Cloud's own talented family grew and flourished, he did not
exactly follow the Roes' early plans for him and become their version of a
leader, competing with Eastman for fame, and elected not to consecrate
himself mainly to preaching the gospels of Christ and the gospel of assimilation. It is not clear how often Mary and Henry wrote one another in the
1920s and 1930s. The Roe family archive contains few Roe Cloud–Roe
letters from this period. But Henry wrote her on Mother's Day in 1939—a
devoutly humble, yet somewhat plaintive, expression of gratitude. As Mary
had, when comparing him to Eastman and Montezuma, he used the metaphor of the torch. He thanked Mary for her spiritual stability and for
exhorting him to exert self-control to better serve Indians. He promised to
hold the torch she had given him and pledged to call on God's might,
rather than his own, which he distrusted in and of itself.[150] His anxiety
about avoiding the pitfalls of temptation is evidence of the Christian,
sentimental, and psychological interiority that the Roes helped bring into
being, a cultural and class experience of selfhood which, mixing with
Henry's "I-am-We" Indian identity, still made itself felt. Mary continued
her missionary work in Colony, Oklahoma, until 1924 and lived there until
1932, when the Reformed Church terminated the mission. In 1941 she
perished in a car crash. When Henry died in 1950, after giving his life to
the Indian cause, he and Elizabeth had ten grandchildren.[151]

THE ROES AND ROE CLOUD'S INDIAN MISSION

In concluding, I wish to develop a point made in the introduction: Henry
and Elizabeth retained the middle name *Roe* Cloud. The non-hyphenated
Roe Cloud publicly drew attention to and venerated the association. Their
name preserved Henry's legacy as the Roe Cloud legacy. The Roes, Roe
Cloud knew, were a factor, by no means the sole factor, in the Roe Cloud
success story.

It is telling that Elizabeth and Henry reacted to Mary's enactments of
the clinging mother-in-law stereotype not with rejection, but with sus-
tained compassion and kindness. Perhaps this partly expressed the heal-

ing spirit that the Roes had stood for and preached. As noted, Elizabeth, with the mother-son model in mind, tried initially to cast herself not as Mary's victorious competitor for Henry's emotional attention, but as Mary's daughter. Both Henry and Elizabeth felt a sense of Indian obligation for the woman whom Henry addressed persistently as a mother. They never lost contact with Mary, who was an active supporter of the Roe Indian Institute and later, with its name change (which she backed), the American Indian Institute. All three served on The Mohonk Lodge's Board of Directors in the 1930s. Elizabeth, like Henry, no doubt had considerable insight into the multidimensionality of Henry's bond with the Roes.

To appreciate this, it is worth revisiting Henry's 1939 Mother's Day epistle to Mary. Notwithstanding her previous efforts to influence his romantic life, Henry's missive clearly assigns Mary the role of she who guarded him from stumbling, despairing, and yielding to his impulses. Henry also is specific about what Mary had helped facilitate: his tireless devotion to Indians. The Roes assisted in making this a sacred mission.

Henry's Mother's Day letter was infused not just with familial sentiment—and perhaps an unstated forgiveness for Mary's melodramatic insecurities and efforts to shape his imagining of himself and what he needed to control in himself—but with unambivalent thankfulness. What was he so appreciative of, even in 1939, and what was its larger significance, perhaps its strategic significance? I suspect that what drew Henry to the Roes in the first place was the spiritual illumination he acknowledges in the letter, the holy illumination that would support him in his campaigns to guide others. Roe Cloud envisioned Indian education not only as intellectual development and as preparation for work, but as spiritual healing. The Indian education he wanted to provide for Indian students was suffused with evangelical passion. His chosen name, Roe Cloud, was one signifier of his Indian Mission. Although this mission may have been one that Roe Cloud, with his Winnebago upbringing, conceptualized somewhat differently from the Roes, despite their use of the same religious language and framework.[152]

If Roe Cloud's connection with the Roes spurred his motive, his incentive to educate Indians, it also enriched, as did Yale, his comprehension of the classes whose aid he had to enlist. For Roe Cloud saw the importance of winning the hearts and minds not only of Indians but of white people whose social power could be channeled into the support of Indians. What he learned from the sentimental and melodramatic intensity of his encounters with the Roes, in part, was how the American reproduction and enactment of middle- and upper-middle-class identity takes particular emotional forms. The class system of emotional investments, interdependencies, incentives, and aspirations in which he found himself enmeshed, at Yale and with the Roes, opened insights into what made the educated classes tick. Roe Cloud was more successful at fundraising than any Indian of his era. He tried to direct members of these powerful classes to his Indian mission and build their incentive to be just.

Intriguingly, what Roe Cloud may have learned from the Roes was how to be a more persuasive Indian missionary not just to Indians but to white people who ruled.[153] Roe Cloud's project as a bridge figure relates to what Arthur Parker once termed "Indianizing the white man"—in the white man's and woman's own sentimental, religious, reform, and class languages.[154] Perhaps Roe Cloud's emotional and sentimental, not just intellectual, education taught him that whites too needed to be healed, as well as taught, to set America aright.

❦ three ❧

CULTURAL
INCENTIVE-AND-ACTIVISM
EDUCATION

ROE CLOUD'S EDUCATION as an educator was by no means static. The sum of what he learned in his youth led him to try to help Indian students develop "Christian motive" and character, a work ethos, and an individualistic self-reliance so that Indians could more effectively serve Indians and improve America in the bargain. This was Roe Cloud's Indian revision of the incentive-building machinery blueprinted in so many mid- and late-nineteenth-century advice books. Roe Cloud, like countless missionaries, saw his Indian students as Indian workers. He also envisioned them as thinkers. Thus he sought to infuse students with the ambition to explore sectors of the intellectual universe introduced to him at Mount Hermon, Yale, Oberlin, and Auburn. What grew more prominent was his dedication to teaching Indian students about a field not investigated in the schools he attended—Indian cultures. Eventually the Indian education he had in mind pointed in the direction not only of cultural knowledge and celebration but cultural activism. The study of Indians in the early twentieth century is an important part of the American history of activism and organizing strategies. Roe Cloud's development as a modern Indian activist, institution builder, public figure, and bureaucrat casts light on ideological shifts in this Indian-white history.

ONWARD CHRISTIAN WORKERS:
THE AMERICAN INDIAN INSTITUTE

Financial need forced Roe Cloud to spend one of his five years at Mount
Hermon working on a farm. Notwithstanding Samuel Smiles's tendency
to misrepresent drudgery as work, in "From Wigwam to Pulpit" Roe
Cloud seems to have realized quite well which category better described
his agronomic efforts: "As I followed a mule team all day long on the New
Jersey farm I used to tack on the hump of the plow before me card after
card on which I had written the Greek conjugations. In this way I mastered my Greek grammar and made good headway on Xenophon's 'Ana-
basis.' . . . The farmer said I was not plowing as large a section as I might,
and knocked the cards from the plow" (13). During his college years he
held a variety of jobs, including selling books door-to-door in Connecticut. The residents were not as anti-intellectual as the farmer. But they were
much more keen to discuss Indian arrowheads they had found than buy
books. In so doing, they displayed stereotypical fascinations with seemingly vanishing Indians (14).

Neither job was as bad as what he had endured as a young boy. In an
address to the 1914 gathering of the middle- and upper-class Friends of the
Indian at Lake Mohonk, he testified how much he reviled his two-year job
of "turning a washing machine in a Government school." That kind of
routine toil "is not educative," he affirmed. "It begets a hatred for work,
especially when there is no pay for such labor. The Indian will work
under such conditions because he is under authority, but the moment he
becomes free he is going to get as far as he can from it."[1] Roe Cloud
got as far as he could from it, but never forgot it. Such experiences in-
duced him, at Mount Hermon and Yale, to obtain an education that a
minority of not just government-run but private schools wanted Indians to
have: intellectual, cultural, and social mobility training in Latin, Greek,
and English.[2]

For the young Winnebago, however, it was his education in Christianity, even more than his myriad experiences at work or his studies
of Greek, that inspired him to be productive, ambitious, and hopeful.
Though Roe Cloud framed Christianity as indispensable to Indians partly
because it offered them spiritual priorities within a civilization that failed

to measure up to its treaties, promises, and religion, he also tactically represented Christianity as immensely valuable to employers and to an emerging Indian professional and managerial class interested in resignifying Indianness.[3] In a speech to the Society of American Indians on "Some Social and Economic Aspects of the Reservation" (1912), he rather pragmatically defined industriousness as the character habit that would best save Indians, and Christianity as the most effective builder of incentive and self-reliance.[4] Roe Cloud's Christ was capable of making the ideology of self-help spiritually significant and attractive to Indians who might otherwise discount it as another manifestation of white American cupidity and stupidity. He embraced Christ—good shepherd not just of people, but of what would come to be called personnel—as the greatest creator of economic motive.[5] His Christ, businessmen learned, could best facilitate the move from wigwam to workplace.

Of course, Carlisle had long claimed to be an efficient builder of Indian incentive and Indian workers. Both Pratt and Roe Cloud aimed to use education to uplift, individualize, and motivate Indians and to integrate them more productively with whites. Even at Yale, Roe Cloud believed that he could outdo Carlisle in this mission. In 1910 he predicted that his trip to lecture at Carlisle would be explosive. He looked forward to criticizing Carlisle's educational premises and practices.[6] But after his visit he seemed appeased and satisfied with several talks he gave there.[7] Roe Cloud felt not only that Carlisle put too little stress on religious training, but that this omission lowered the quality of its students. In 1914 and 1915 tensions erupted between Roe Cloud and Pratt when the latter's congressional machinations had succeeded in preventing the Presbyterian church from getting $10,000 from the sale of land in Oklahoma Indian territory. Roe Cloud depicted Pratt as obsessed by his vision of Carlisle and gloated that he had been terminated as superintendent.[8] Carlisle and schools like it, he argued, were unable to tap into the social and pedagogical power so evident in evangelical gatherings, in which Indians experienced an emotional and spiritual pressure to acknowledge their sins and convert. He recognized the importance of cultivating an emotional commitment, a spiritual resolve, to labor. And he saw the development of work habits and the knowledge of skilled labor not just as useful and economically pragmatic pursuits, but as conducive to good character formation and moral growth. He therefore tried to institutionalize an evangelism of work that respected Indian identity, even as Indians manifested this identity in a range of new forms.[9]

On the one hand, it was incumbent on Roe Cloud to view such evangelical campaigns as deployments of God's supreme power and as manifestations of the humility of Christian soldiers in the presence of His power. Writing to Henry in 1909, Mary de-individualized human success and achievement. Her understanding was in sync with many traditional Indian concepts of spiritual power. She counseled humbling oneself before the power of God and defined this spirit as true accomplishment.[10] On the other hand, self-conscious altruism and service increased the Christian soldier's spiritual and subjective capital: the more one sacrifices, the more one accrues spirituality and with it the potential to produce incentive, industriousness, and the will to endure.

Roe Cloud and Dr. Roe had this spiritualization of incentive in mind when they proposed that Yale found a college preparatory program in which Indians could enroll. The successful Yale-in-China high school program offered an example of what could be done. In 1906, the year Roe Cloud matriculated at Yale, the Yale mission established the Yali Daxuetang or Yali Academy.[11] Several of Roe Cloud's classmates were from China and returned to their homeland after graduating. Although Anson Phelps Stokes, secretary of the university, had politically progressive sympathies, he and President Hadley rejected the sophomore's proposal. Roe Cloud acknowledged Yale's conservative reputation when he rationalized the university's decision.[12] Dr. Roe, with help from Roe Cloud, continued to solicit funds for the founding of a Christian high school for Indians and collected several thousand dollars by the time of his death in 1913. This crusade stands out as even more remarkable considering that in the early 1910s only a little over 15 percent of Americans in their mid-teens enrolled in high school and that about one-third of this group received mainly vocational training.[13]

Roe Cloud persevered and succeeded in the campaign to raise money for the fledgling Roe Indian Institute. He served first as its special representative and later as president, building the institution, located in Wichita, Kansas, from 1915 to 1930. Roe Cloud's manifold criticisms of Carlisle included the charge that too few of its students ever made it to college.

The Roe Indian Institute, renamed in 1920 the American Indian Institute, aimed to rectify this. Roe Cloud's school, like the Society of American Indians, shows the influence of the Progressive Era faith in what Richard Hofstadter called the belief in "the formation of a responsible elite," reformers who would act as effective mediators between the ruling classes and the people.[14] Pratt, corresponding with Arthur Parker, predicted that the school would not succeed and that if Roe Cloud had attended his own school he too would have failed. True to form, Pratt believed that Roe Cloud's school would segregate rather than integrate Indians and whites. The prep school stressed academic study, but also included training in agriculture and the trades. Roe Cloud felt it important that each student labor for the school.[15] The school—in some respects, not unlike Carlisle—conceptualized Indian education not just as the cultivation of the intellect but as a character-building and incentive-building project. Numerous graduates of the Institute went on to study at the University of Oklahoma, Wichita State University, Fairmount College, and Friends University, but not East to Yale, Princeton, Harvard, or to the original Indian college, Dartmouth.

Roe Cloud, like the evangelist Dwight Moody, founder of Mount Hermon, was a gifted fundraiser. Thompson's 1944 newspaper profile of Roe Cloud saluted him for having raised a total of $500,000 for the American Indian Institute, "the largest amount of money ever raised by an American Indian."[16] But some of his correspondence indicates that the Institute, despite its president's efforts, had a difficult time staying afloat financially. The 1926 edition of the Yale class of 1910 volume has Roe Cloud writing with his usual upbeat style. Roe Cloud had the jaunty, ironic, self-deprecatory yet self-assured Yale tone and idiom down pat, apparent in the series of Yale class of 1910 classbooks to which he contributed (1910–35).[17] He registered optimism about the Institute, though seemingly discouraged with his students, or with what white society had done to them: "The young school now seems robust and healthy, but its forward progression is very slow. What I choose to term 'Race Inertia' cannot be overcome quickly. Right now I am heading a drive for $75,000 to feed the infant institution in the hope that it will get up and walk."[18] Years earlier he had defined race inertia not in evolutionary but in social terms: Indians' forced reliance on governmental support, he maintained, would impair their capacity to rely on themselves.[19] If any rich Yalies substantially helped the "infant institution" to "get up and walk" in the mid-1920s, I have found no evidence of this. Most of its financial support seems to have come from wealthy families in Wichita, some rich Indians, the Daughters of the American Revolution, and Protestant denominations.[20]

By the time Roe Cloud wrote his former Yale classmates about the young yet wobbly Institute, his school had accumulated assets of more than $100,000. Yet his daunting fundraising challenges persisted. In 1927 Roe Cloud and the Presbyterian Board of Home Missions worked out a plan so that the Institute's property and funds could be transferred gradually to the Presbyterians. However, the Depression complicated this Presbyterian takeover, and Roe Cloud still had to raise money to fund one-third of its operating budget in 1930. The Institute folded seven years after Roe Cloud officially resigned in 1932.[21]

Roe Cloud's alumni file contains several Institute pamphlets he sent Yale from the late 1910s to the early 1920s, all of which were composed to stimulate the interest of potential contributors. "Progress at the Roe Indian Institute" (undated, received 1918) gives a brief biographical profile of the late Dr. Roe, who is likened to Tuskegee's Booker T. Washington. It says that Roe wanted the nonsectarian institute to train Indians throughout the hemisphere in Christian leadership, character, self-reliance, and the work ethic. Dr. Roe also envisioned the Institute as a conference and research center, which it never became. Some plans for the Institute, such as these, make it sound more like the ambitious basis for an Indian university than a high school and link Roe and Roe Cloud more with Du Bois than with Washington. Perhaps Roe Cloud and Roe dreamed of using the Institute to help materialize some contemporary Indian demands for an Indian intellectual center.[22]

At the same time, several parallels between the Institute's educational philosophy and the Carlisle and Tuskegee approach are patent. All students had to do physical labor a couple of hours a day—some beyond the precincts of the school—to earn their keep, whether or not they could pay the full tuition. The school's proximity to its neighbor, Fairmount College, where Institute students used classrooms and the library, and its campus location just outside of Wichita, ensured that students would benefit from salubrious associations with whites. Perhaps thinking of his relationship with the Roes, Roe Cloud stressed that such associations could benefit Indians intellectually and spiritually. Institute students, like Carlisle's and Tuskegee's, were inculcated to encode struggle, failure, and disappointment—and, by implication, exploitation—as character-building challenges: systemic disadvantages permitted or even decreed by the government could become advantages if they toughened the will of Indians to endure and succeed.[23] However, Roe Cloud's Institute, unlike Pratt's Carlisle and Washington's Tuskegee, placed more emphasis on studying what Washington termed the "mere books" that would open the possibility of college education.[24] In its stress not only on work-study approaches and character formation but on academic preparation, Roe Cloud no doubt had the intellectually serious Mount Hermon in mind.[25] Again, this respect for intellectual achievement links him with Du Bois.

Yet, "The Strategic School for the Native American" (undated, received by Yale in 1921) was even more explicit about fashioning workers, not just enlightening students, at the newly named Institute. On the title page of the pamphlet, highlighted in a rectangular field, is an almost militaristic pitch written to excite the business class of interwar America. It spells out unambiguously the school's commitment to shaping Indian laborers and contributing to America's output. Employing a martial metaphor, it asks supporters to help arm the school for this warlike campaign. This almost seems to advocate the following, if I may revise Pratt's notorious plea, "Kill the Indian in him, and save the man": Educate and Christianize the Indian to save the worker. The American Indian Institute, the pamphlet attests, is dedicated to educating students who will then school other Indians to value and enjoy labor.[26] Here again, Roe Cloud emphasizes channeling Indian initiative back into the Indian community. "Why Should I Help the American Indian Institute?" (undated, received by Yale in 1921) announces that the school has been set up to explore how the 300,000 Indians in the United States, the 100,000 in Canada, the 30,000 in Alaska, and the 20,000,000 or more in Mexico, Central, and South America might become eager laborers.[27] The Institute pledged to revivify the ambition and incentive that the reservation system had smothered in Indian youth.

Needless to say, this promotional literature was designed to spark the incentive of potential contributors. It featured worker production as its paramount selling point, even more than the religious instruction (which partly served as a means to that end). The Institute's students were influenced to take religious vocations seriously, though after leaving the school they could follow with greater resolve whatever paths they selected.[28] An Indian's attempt to work was often not without its challenges, especially in the West, and so it was precisely the "Christian motive" that was underscored as giving students the spiritual strength, status, and transcendence to overcome the trials that awaited them. Spiritual education, thus, was presented as an education in establishing and maintaining a stable way of life and productive aspirations.[29] The Institute president, perhaps more than Christ, served as the most moving example of what could be achieved. Roe Cloud was cited as one who exemplified how spiritual reliance empowered self-reliance. Self-making depended on spirit making.[30]

The Institute's promotional pamphlets also resemble Washington's writings because they are nonthreatening and display no sense of entitlement or outrage. At Harvard and in his writing, Du Bois was publicly indignant about the exploitation of and discrimination against his race. Decrying the "criminal foolishness of your fathers," he predicts trouble: "If you do not lift them up, they will pull you down." His warning is an ultimatum: "You have no choice; either you must help furnish this race from within its own ranks with thoughtful men of trained leadership, or you must suffer the evil consequences of a headless misguided rabble."[31] Du Bois suggests that a "Talented Tenth" is requisite to maintain social stability. However much Roe Cloud hoped that some of the Institute's graduates would help build an Indian "Talented Tenth," the promotional materials I have seen do not foreground this. Roe Cloud was surely aware that Washington's unassuming and reassuring style contributed to his success as an outstanding fundraiser.

The pamphlets showcased Roe Cloud not only as a worker but a class networker. They presented the Institute as a worthwhile investment, focusing on its growing acreage, the value of its physical plant, its endowment, and its specific financial needs and long-range goals. The literature frequently mentioned the president of the Board of Trustees, a wealthy professor of theology at Vassar, and the Board's treasurer, president of the Hudson River Line and director of Irving National Bank, New York City.[32]

Still, Roe Cloud may have been somewhat disheartened, perhaps even overwhelmed at times, with the project. Fewer students enrolled than he had hoped. The highest number of students ever in attendance in one year was forty-six. Some students had to drop out for financial reasons. Too few of the school's graduates who did attend college had the financial means to complete their course of study.[33] In such conditions the efficacy of self-help was put under pressure just as it was on the New Jersey farm whose fields Roe Cloud plowed without the compensation of educative index cards.

The school launched its newspaper, The Indian Outlook, in 1923. Although its conventional self-help themes echoed those in some of the government's Indian school publications, its title signaled the Institute's effort to represent a distinctly Indian perspective. The image chosen for the newspaper's masthead is a drawing of a barebacked and befeathered Indian in breechcloth and moccasins who, back to the viewer, is seemingly experiencing the epiphantic moment of seeing for the first time a 1920s cityscape with skyscrapers, not mountains, and airplanes, not birds, high above him and dominating the heavens. In his right hand he is holding a bow as he would a walking stick—there are no arrows or bowstring. Standing in the foreground he is as tall as the skyscraper in the distance. Yet the tilt of his left hand suggests that he has been thrown slightly off balance by the world before him. The scene, which also shows ships in the harbor, a railroad, telephone poles, and factories and warehouses, seems to say: this is the inescapable modern reality with which Indians, who cannot afford to be anachronistic, must contend. The light showering through the clouds evokes the sublime, as do Thomas Cole's or Frederick Church's romantic paintings of mountains as witnessed by white "explorers."[34]

When Carlisle transported its students from western reservations to the Pennsylvania school, the trains often stopped at large cities like Chicago, where new towering skyscrapers sent the message that white American society was here to stay and Indians, reduced to a small minority, must resign themselves to it. The Indian Outlook's masthead image, suffused with the Indian's amazement, excised some of the fright that this urban encounter could trigger. Overall, the white metropolis, arching over the Indian explorer, appears more like a rainbow of possibility than one of forbidding structures.[35]

Roe Cloud's effusive editorials drove home the importance of the work ethic, self-sufficiency, incentive, ambition, and leadership—replete with "inspirational" Samuel Smiles' style quotations from American and European intellectual, cultural, and political figures.[36] Reviewing the hardships suffered by Indians over the last century, Roe Cloud claimed perseverance as an Indian virtue.[37] He depicted God as the greatest energizer.[38] Occasionally his service-above-self exhortations sounded like those of Yale's President Hadley. Roe Cloud's editorials elevated character building over knowledge as the most pressing goal of early Indian education, because character would enable students to thrive, not just survive, in a white world.[39]

Sometimes this character rhetoric led to what seems to be a distinctly conservative grasp of social relations, as is apparent in the second issue. Here Roe Cloud, apparently without irony, wrote that Indians should be thankful for all the economic, medical, domestic, and educational support that the government has bestowed on them. Most historians would not describe the Bureau of Indian Affairs in the 1920s as a benevolent organization deeply dedicated to Indian welfare. Given the poverty, poor health, illiteracy, and white land-grabbing rampant on government-ruled reservations, it is noteworthy that Roe Cloud describes the government's policies as just, as kind, and as proof of American democracy in action.[40] Should one take such assertions at face value? Or should one consider the context —the particular student audience to which his remarks were directed? Roe Cloud sought not just to disseminate knowledge but to cultivate spirit. He found self-pity, the tendency to fixate on one's position within systemic contradictions, self-defeating. Perhaps such statements should be read as indicative of Roe Cloud's distrust of a pedagogy that ignites resentment. He may have wanted his students to view the government and capitalism more as resources and opportunities than as insurmountable exploiters of Indians. Pratt, for all his hoopla about capitalist self-making, had no compunction about indicting the Bureau of Indian Affairs and doubtless won the respect of some students because of his truculence.[41] For Roe Cloud, however, it seems to have been spiritually as well as socially unstrategic to have students embrace the role of angry victims.

Roe Cloud's sense of what students needed in order to endure the long struggle led him to develop an American Indian Institute program that departed significantly from the older patriotic melting-pot assault on Indian cultures. The school encouraged students to learn Native arts and crafts and be proud of their racial heritage. Roe Cloud took part in annual campus pow-wows.[42] Some of his remarks in *The Indian Outlook* hold that America could learn much from Indian cultures, traditions, and values.[43] In these instances Roe Cloud's public stance began to shift from a concentration mainly on multiracial access to what dominant white culture defined as education to a protomulticultural reformulation of the sort of intellectual, critical, and cultural education that Indians require in multiracial America.

PLURALIST MANAGEMENT AND ECONOMIC MOTIVE MAKING: FROM THE MERIAM REPORT TO COLLIER

Gradually Roe Cloud moved somewhat away from his official self-help orientation and reevaluated the usefulness of government intervention, especially in the establishment of educational possibilities for Indians.[44] One of the important lessons he learned from his challenges at the American Indian Institute was extrapolated from an insight he published in 1914, directing critical attention not on Indians as a race with inherent characteristics but on the system's contradictions that afflicted Indians.[45] It was the systemic production of economic and cultural inequality—system inertia—not a superfluity of government support that shaped race inertia. Roe Cloud recognized that Indian students required more than Christian exhortations to self-help to get to and graduate from college—they needed federal support in the forms of scholarships and loans. When Roe Cloud served on the Committee of One Hundred in 1923, convened by the Secretary of the Interior, Hubert Work, to make recommendations to Congress about the "Indian Problem," he advocated the establishment of federally funded scholarships for Indians in college. Congress ignored the proposal.[46]

However, the Bureau of Indian Affairs finally responded to the higher education plea and began transforming some Indian schools into high schools in 1923. Until that year the American Indian Institute was one of only three high schools for Indians in the country. The founding of government high schools advanced the demise of the Institute. This development in federal policy as well as the Institute's ongoing funding challenges motivated Roe Cloud to leave the school to work for the Bureau as a field representative at large in 1931.[47]

If Roe Cloud's move toward government service and the advancement of beneficial federal intervention in Indian life took place when he worked on the Committee of One Hundred and fought for the passage of the Indian Citizenship Act of 1924, a far more decisive step came a few years later when he was recruited to join a new group sponsored by the Secretary of the Interior to address the crisis in Indian-government relations. Roe Cloud gained national eminence in 1928 as one of ten coauthors of the Institute for Government Research's (Brookings Institute's) influential, *The Problem of Indian Administration*. Lewis Meriam, an Institute statistician, oversaw the development of what came to be known as the Meriam Report. It was submitted to Secretary Work. This weighty tome helped propel the fundamental reorganization of Indian Affairs in the 1930s.[48] The volume, as the title announces, shifts the focus from the Indian Problem to Indian Administration as the problem. As mentioned earlier, Roe Cloud was the only Indian among the authors. Fayette McKenzie, whom Roe Cloud knew as the white initiator of the Society of American Indians, was a contributor to the study (he had left Ohio State to become president of Fisk University in 1915).[49] Their research was conducted on reservations from November 1926 to June 1927. Roe Cloud served not as an expert in one area but as a general expert in all aspects of Indian life and its relation to the government. He made many of the investigations possible by functioning as an intermediary between the "experts" and Indians across the country.[50]

It is difficult to believe that Roe Cloud did not contribute to the chapter on education, mainly written by Will Carson Ryan, a professor of education at Swarthmore College.[51] The first section title in this education chapter headlines one of the report's key criticisms of what Indian education had failed to sponsor: "Recognition of the Individual" (346). Its findings echo Gertrude Bonnin's earlier fictional indictments of the manufacturing-plant aspects of Indian boarding schools.[52] Deploying the 1920s "expert" language of psychology, emotions, personality, social work, and personnel, the report blasts the militaristic "routinization" (351) and factory-like standardization of government-school students as systematically undermining (393) the development of "initiative," "independence," and "self-reliance" (351). The authors respect the tribal diversity as well as individual diversity of Indian students, whom they represent as possessing an individuality, emotions, and personality as well as affective attachments to distinct cultural traditions and forms of family life that must no longer be "violated" (406). Rather than conceptualizing Indian youth, as Pratt did, as "raw material" that lack "character," or as child workers available for hiring out as cheap labor on the pretext of vocational training, as was the case in some Indian school "outing" programs (389), the authors recategorize them as psychological subjects with desires and preferences. As early as 1913 Roe Cloud, in an address to reformers, lamented the system's failure to instill incentive in Indians, bemoaned the absence of Indians in public office, and urged that new psychological and pedagogical developments be employed to deal with Indians.[53] The Meriam Report followed up on many of Roe Cloud's concerns.

Its authors recommended, among other things, that teachers be better educated (359–60) and paid more (347–48), that Indian students be instructed mostly at day schools and not be removed from their families to attend boarding schools (403, 412), and, with praise for Roe Cloud's American Indian Institute, that more schools offer high school–level education and prepare greater numbers of pupils for college (420). They target what Indian schools termed "citizenizing" as the major goal of education, even more than "reading, writing, and arithmetic," or learning English. But they define citizenship not as the relation of Indian students to government bureaucracy or American "civilization," but as Indians' active participation in their own community, having employment in a "socially worthwhile vocation," and enjoying a "comfortable and desirable home and family life" (373). The report also attempts to de-racialize the "Indian problem" in part by comparing the debilitating effects of white and Indian poverty (570–71). This critical emphasis resonates with Roe Cloud's social thought when it took the form of systemic critique.[54]

Notwithstanding these incisive criticisms, the report also sometimes recycled racist stereotypes about Indians' "lack of aggressive qualities," their "sensitive nature" (384), and their "personality handicaps" (390). On occasion the study seems as if it was using modern ideas about cultural pluralism, psychology, and personality—the buzz words that were supplanting Americanizing, civilizing, and individualizing—to develop a more effective and psychologically subtle socialization through education than the militarized assimilation that many government boarding schools had set out to achieve. Some of the authors, with no discernable sense of irony, argue that Indians are "human being[s] like the rest of us" and have created cultures that are "quite worthwhile for [their] own sake" (354). They engage cultural relativism to better "use what [Indians have] as a starting point for [making them into] something else" (398).

Indeed, the same affective and managerial logic that informed late-nineteenth-century assimilationist reform writings on the Indian family and gender is still present in the Meriam report, in which the production of familial economic and psychological interdependencies is grasped as crucial to fostering the "incentive to industry" (576) and the economic motive in Indian workers. Hence boarding schools, unlike day schools, are criticized for disrupting the growth of familial emotional interdependencies and allegiances that can induce Indians to participate in the labor market, even when they "are seldom trained for the more interesting occupations and . . . are impatient of routine" (571). The strategic insight is that the social cultivation of an intense, family-centered personal life is foundational to the creation of workers who will compliantly undertake alienated labor for love, an accommodation defined psychologically as adult (the older assimilationist-era word would have been civilized): "In relieving them of their children the government robs them of one of the strongest and most fundamental economic motives, thereby keeping them in the state of childhood" (576). The report registered moral indignation about the systematic social degradation and "pauperization" of Indians, and compiled pragmatic policy reforms of Indian administration. Yet at least some of its authors, most of whom were academics, still subscribed to a doctrine of progress that allowed them to believe that they were aiding "the development and advancement of a retarded race."[55]

The Meriam Report served as a bellwether that signaled an official bureaucratic policy shift from the premises of older white Protestant Indian reformers. The Carlisle newspaper often reprinted the Reverend Henry Ward Beecher's Biblical-sounding analogy about the digestive aim of Americanization: "When a lion eats an ox, the lion does not become an ox but the ox becomes a lion. So the emigrants of all races and nations become

Americans."[56] Beecher and Protestant Friends of the Indian, such as Merrill Gates, Lyman Abbott, and Charles Painter, would have been shocked by the pluralist turn evident in parts of the Meriam Report. While the Meriam Report did not abandon notions of Americanization—as cultural and economic digestion—its social science–oriented pluralism was less brazen and predatory. Although the Roes exemplified aspects of Protestant Indian reform, their support of Indian arts and crafts and their kindliness distinguished them from some of their self-righteous peers. Yet Roe Cloud moved on. His involvement in the Meriam Report marked him as a man who would help usher in a modern regime of federal Indian administration and more modern Indian reformism within this administration.

Roe Cloud's contributions to the report consolidated his links to the government. In 1929 he criticized the Bureau of Indian Affairs, arguing that it compromised the individualistic incentive of Indians, but also maintaining that the government had to take responsibility for better educating Indians, by white standards, to make them more effectively self-reliant.[57] This critique as well as his investigations for the Brookings Institute helped pave the way for his work in the Bureau of Indian Affairs. From 1931 to 1933 he was the Bureau's special field representative. John Collier became Indian Affairs Commissioner in 1933. From 1933 to 1935 Roe Cloud served as superintendent of the Haskell Institute in Lawrence, Kansas—the largest Indian high school in the country. Roe Cloud was the first full-blood Indian to get this appointment. After his tenure at Haskell the Bureau appointed him Representative-at-Large for Indian education.

Collier rose to national prominence as an advocate of Indians rights in 1922 when—with support from Tony Luhan, Mabel Dodge Luhan, and other Taos artists and intellectuals—he spearheaded the Pueblo resistance to the proposed Bursum Bill, which would have robbed much of the Pueblo Reservation of their water rights. He transformed their resistance into not just a national campaign, but a national organization that did not equate Indian reform with Indian assimilation.[58] Collier's brand of reform celebrated tribal cultures and their preservation. Roe Cloud and Collier would have encountered one another on the Committee of One Hundred in 1923, which discussed such matters as Indian education. It is understandable that Roe Cloud, having had some experience with the new style of Indian reform on that committee and in his work for the Meriam report, came to realize that he would have to engage tactically with Collier, and with those who thought as Collier did, in this shifting ideological climate. The rise of Collier also meant that education for Indians, which many older Protestant Indian reformers had viewed as a machinery of ideological assimilation, was not accorded quite the prominence it had once enjoyed as a reform priority.[59]

Roe Cloud's role as an Indian whose job came to entail legitimating Collier's pluralist management of Indians was challenging. On the one hand, he did not dress or act like the traditionalist Indians whom Collier and others romanticized as a spiritual tonic for alienated whites. On the other hand, the polished Yalie could serve as Collier's intermediary with traditionalist Indians. Roe Cloud's credentials could enhance his authority and effectiveness as Collier's representative. And yet Roe Cloud's eminence could blow the whistle on Collier's pluralist paternalism. Roe Cloud's presence complicated Collier's romantic construct of Indianness. Arthur Parker articulated what Indians like Roe Cloud would have to negotiate in this new regime: "How would the white man like it if the Indians demanded that all white men who came upon their reservations must dress in Colonial uniforms and appear like the picture of Sir Walter Raleigh or of ancient Britain? Such white men want a show, a circus, a make believe Indian, and have but faint sympathy for the up to date Indian who living like a civilized man struggles in civilization for competence."[60]

What Roe Cloud's relationship with the controversial Collier really was remains a topic for future research. Here I offer some evidence to consider on this matter. In apparent support of Collier, Roe Cloud campaigned to win Native votes for the Indian Reorganization Act in 1934—traveling to reservations all over the country—and was photographed as the first Winnebago to vote for the act.[61] Several Indian leaders, especially Christians who were aghast at Collier's termination of coerced religious instruction in government Indian schools, were critical of Roe Cloud's support of Collier. Some vowed never to back any future bid Roe Cloud might make to become the Indian Affairs Commissioner. As Philip J. Deloria notes, the Indian New Deal "drained power away from the churches and created more rigid boundaries between church and state." Roe Cloud's rejoinder to Indian criticisms was loyal: "I think that John Collier is maneuvering the Indian race and our Government in such a fashion as to bring about a situation where the deep-seated characteristics and the nobilities of the

Indian can be molded anew into a fresh vigor and life." But his public comment also registered a trace of his still vague ambivalence about Collier: "Somehow, if I cannot explain it in words or define it in specific terms, I feel that John Collier has got a real program."[62]

There is only one letter from Roe Cloud to Collier extant in the Collier papers at Yale. When Roe Cloud served as superintendent of Haskell in 1934, he wrote Collier to thank him for visiting Haskell and more especially for sending A. C. Monahan, a Bureau administrator, to Homecoming. Roe Cloud's eloquent letter is gracious in its praise of Monahan, who brought not only helpful suggestions to the school but a warm humanity and a use of the healthy aspects of cultural playfulness. Roe Cloud and Monahan joked together and demonstrated that even bureaucratic labor could be infused with a life force. This joyous spirit helped make Collier's and Monahan's visit to the school inspirational. It also energized incentive at Haskell. In effect, Roe Cloud made a case that the most efficient managerial and personnel strategies were those that made work fun. The Haskell staff and students could be enthusiastic about working with and for someone like Monahan. In this letter Roe Cloud did not represent religious spirit as that which could make Indians diligent workers—his American Indian Institute incentive-building tactic—rather he singled out humorous and life-enhancing interactions as that which could do the trick.[63]

However, in a private letter of 1945 Roe Cloud criticized his former boss in a way that suggests the complexity of his own position on Indians and assimilation. He wrote this missive just as many were wondering who would be appointed the next Commissioner of Affairs. Roe Cloud may have been contemplating his own non-candidacy. The Senate Indian Committee, he noted, was more interested in business values than in preserving Indian communal ways. In Roe Cloud's view, the committee compelled Collier to step down because his utopian romanticism had prevented Indians from fully entering the modern marketplace as producers. Collier's divorce from his wife of many years, he added, also fueled their criticism of him. Roe Cloud closed by lamenting that Indians had been and would be yet again subjected to forms of government manipulation and experimentation.[64] His letter champions neither the Senate Indian Committee nor Collier.

Could it have been Collier who restrained Roe Cloud, a nationally visible high-ranking Indian in the Bureau, from rising higher than he did? Collier's early 1930s correspondence with Lewis Meriam sheds some light on this. A couple of years before Collier became Indian Commissioner and worked with Roe Cloud, he saw the Winnebago Yale graduate as a poor candidate for a mouthpiece. In 1930 Collier nominated Gertrude Bonnin, who had published her fiction under her Sioux name, Zitkala-Ša, and Richard Bonnin (Dakota Sioux), her husband, as well as Roe Cloud to Meriam as persons who could effectively implement a Brookings study of law and order and economics among the Pueblos. Almost a year later, however, Collier registered doubts. Collier not only demeaned Roe Cloud's intelligence, he revealed the sort of psychological control he himself thought requisite to wield over Indians. He questioned Roe Cloud's intellectual ability and his capacity to establish what psychologists call an emotional transference with the Pueblos. Collier himself was not always adroit at attaining a psychological influence over Indians in his efforts to assert himself as a leader with whom they should identify. His choice of the psychoanalytic term transference, which in this usage signifies the formation of a psychological management relationship, is telling. Would Indians have been disheartened, or would some have been amused, to discover that Collier's objective was to set up an emotional transference with them? (Years before Roe Cloud had advocated employing an emotionally intense evangelism to reach Indians' hearts and as the most effective way to create Indian incentive.) Collier then oddly discounted Roe Cloud's full-blood Winnebago identity as a factor that would facilitate his dealings with Indians. Did Roe Cloud's ability—his Indianness, his Yale Indianness— make Collier defensive and complicate his preferred image of Indians?

Just three years later Collier patently relied on Roe Cloud's full-blood Indian identity as well as his intelligence to make a political difference when he deployed the Winnebago as a promoter of his New Deal legislation among diverse tribes throughout the continent. He strategically made use of Roe Cloud's intellectual, cultural, and class status. Bureau personnel often introduced him to Indian groups as a graduate of Yale. Collier knew that Roe Cloud conferred both authenticity and distinction on his Indian Reorganization Act campaign. And Roe Cloud understood Indian diversity.

Meriam, who had gotten to know Roe Cloud during the compilation of the 1928 report, disagreed briskly with Collier's condescending and unsubstantiated appraisal. He commended Roe Cloud's ability to get the Indians' perspective better than most and underlined the importance of having an Indian of his stature hold a high-level appointment in the Bureau. In general, he added, it was high time that more Indians receive appointments to elevated rather than lowly positions—in effect, working-class positions. A few months later he wrote Collier to applaud Roe Cloud's appointment as the Commissioner's personal representative and suggested that some Indian school superintendents would be more on their toes knowing that Roe Cloud could visit or investigate their institutions.[65]

Collier certainly offended some nontraditionalist Indians because of his propensity to romanticize Indians as a primeval redemption for whites, a problem that Roe Cloud alludes to in his letter of 1945.[66] It may indeed have been that Collier, who did not make helping more Indians gain access to college a prominent issue on his agenda, occasionally felt uncomfortable with some university-educated Indians, Indian warriors in suits, who did not seem like the brand of authentic Indian from whom he and other whites derived therapeutic solace.[67] The admixture of paternalism in Collier's Indian romanticism may have prevented him from apprehending just how ambitious and interested in social power, and self-determination, many traditionalist and non-traditionalist Indians were on and off the reservations. Though he may have concluded that Indian higher education, like the Court of Indian Affairs that he initially lobbied for and gave up on, was not what Vine Deloria Jr. (Dakota Sioux) and Clifford M. Lytle have termed a "saleable" product within the political climates that prevailed in the Depression-era Congress and among some members of tribes.[68]

Alas, Collier's sense of the appropriate scope of Indian education as consisting of basic literacy and vocational training seems unambiguous in "Indian Education Should Be Practical" (1934). Here Collier quotes Indian Affairs Commissioner Leupp's 1905 assertion that Indians fated to be farmers, wagon wheel menders, and so on, require just elementary schooling that teaches them minimal literacy skills. Collier, who studied at Columbia and more informally at the Collège de France, embraced Leupp's myopic educational vision for Indians and stated that, twenty-nine years later, it was in harmony with his Indian New Deal administration's educational premises.[69]

Thompson's passing claim in "From Wigwam to Mr. Bigwig" that from 1931 to 1933 Roe Cloud devised "a plan for Indian rehabilitation, a plan which under the official title of Indian Reorganization act, was passed by congress in 1934," is tantalizing. Did Roe Cloud, in his capacity as a new Indian Affairs special representative (1931–33), help conceptualize the bill? Vine Deloria and Clifford Lytle write that "the Collier bill [the original long version of the Indian Reorganization Act] had been drafted by non-Indians, with virtually no Indians participating in this initial phase."[70] But did one Winnebago contribute to an earlier formative phase and influence Collier? Some evidence of the relationship between Roe Cloud and Collier during the Haskell years and after, when the Winnebago's position in the Bureau declined, raises more intriguing concerns and questions.

PROTOMULTICULTURAL ACTIVISM AND VOCATIONALISM AT HASKELL

In 1933 the Bureau of Indian Affairs announced the closing of Haskell Institute one year shy of its fiftieth anniversary. Founded in 1884, in Lawrence, Kansas, it was one of the oldest and most renowned boarding schools. It boasted not only a high school, till 1923 the only federal Indian high school, but some post–high school programs. Haskell was notable for its victorious football teams, its Indian-funded 10,500-seat football stadium, its strong emphasis on vocational training (with particularly good instruction in agricultural and printing skills), and the wide representation of tribes in its student body. Since Carlisle's closure in 1918, it became the most famous Indian school and competed with many college sports teams. Even in the mid-1930s, however, it was still beset by typical boarding school problems such as contagious diseases, especially trachoma and tuberculosis, and the exploitation of students who labored for Kansas families in the "outing" program. In 1919, during a lecture in the auditorium, students contrived to plunge the school into a blackout and mount a rebellion in which they threatened to "string up" the superintendent. Student agitation helped sway the Bureau to establish a junior college program in 1928, but the conservative Bureau administration eliminated it in 1932. The 1928 Meriam Report's catalogue of myriad boarding school abuses and shortcomings prompted Congress to consider terminating institutions like Haskell and reallocating funds to reservation day schools.[71]

Yet the Bureau reversed its decision to shut down Haskell and appointed Roe Cloud superintendent, beginning in August 1933. Roe Cloud had been recruited to join the Bureau a couple of years earlier when, under reform pressure, it began to place some Indians in positions of responsibility and visibility. The Commissioner of Indian Affairs originally wanted the nationally eminent Winnebago to serve as his assistant for human relations. Could it be that Roe Cloud failed the civil service test for this post because, intellectually, he was far beyond such bureaucratic exams? The Bureau got around this by appointing him field representative at large, a loosely defined new position that required no bureaucratic quiz. It then made Roe Cloud's visibility even more visible to affirm publicly that the Bureau was making an effort to better obtain Indian perspectives in its rule. One of Roe Cloud's assignments was to investigate Haskell in late 1932 and early 1933. He exposed the Athletic Association's illegal procurement of contributions from oil-rich Indians, often young ones manipulated by corrupt white guardians. Much of this money could not be accounted for in the records. Some of it financed part of the construction of Haskell's heavily mortgaged stadium. During almost two years at the helm, Roe Cloud fired a football coach (twenty-six staff members did not return in fall 1933), severed the school's link with the National Guard, and endeavored to hire more Indians.

Curiously, Roe Cloud's investigation also recommended that Haskell devote itself not to a college preparatory program but to improved vocational training. When Roe Cloud took control of the school, however, his pedagogical contribution may have been more multidimensional. Numerous articles in the school newspaper suggest that Roe Cloud was interested in beginning to transform a vocational school invested in athletics and military instruction into a vocational school that doubled as a leadership and cultural activism training center.

Roe Cloud's proposal about better vocational training may have helped him get his administrative foot in Haskell's door. In 1935 the Bureau's Education Director, Will Carson Ryan, with whom Roe Cloud collaborated on the Meriam Report, convened a committee to reassess educational policy. It determined that Haskell and other schools should focus on vocational instruction. This sort of education, they believed, would abet the economic development of reservations. No doubt this concern became more urgent because of the Depression. On the one hand, administrators believed that vocationalism would address what Indian students really needed to know to "modernize" reservations; on the other, it could serve to reinforce Indian participation in a beleaguered economic system that had not been advantageous for the vast majority of Indians.[72]

But if Roe Cloud had aspirations for his students that exceeded the Bureau's plans, he had little time to turn them into an institutional initiative. In May of 1935 Commissioner Collier announced rather vaguely that Roe Cloud would take a leave as superintendent for quite awhile in order to expand his administrative responsibilities and facilitate the implementation of the New Deal Indian Reorganization Act of 1934 (the leave turned out to be forever).[73] Collier benefited a great deal from Roe Cloud's smart and strenuous efforts to persuade Indians across the country to vote for this legislation. In fact, the first phase of this road campaign took Roe Cloud away from Haskell during much of his tenure as superintendent. When Roe Cloud stepped down, Collier praised him publicly as the nation's top Indian leader. Yet, could Collier have reassigned Roe Cloud partly because he wanted to dim the spotlight on him?[74]

Characteristically, Roe Cloud assumed the editorship of the school newspaper, *The Indian Leader*, something the previous superintendent had not done, and took its title seriously. Roe Cloud set the tone by publishing an anonymous article about himself that stressed the importance of leadership and of what is now called affirmative action in the Bureau, especially appointments of well-known Indians to high-level posts. The article quoted parts of his opening address to the students. In this address Roe Cloud acknowledged that he and other Indian staff were under scrutiny and that his appointment was the Bureau's test to determine whether Indians would give their allegiance to an Indian superintendent.[75]

Roe Cloud not only drew attention to his culturally symbolic importance as the exceptional Yale Indian, he published a series of over a dozen how-to articles by Annette M. Lingelbach, an essayist and poet from Iowa, on leadership studies, cultural activism, and, in effect, on how his students could become their own versions of Henry Roe Cloud. This series replaced a series that ran the previous spring on "Vocational Education."[76] Far from encouraging readers to aim for careers in plumbing, carpentry, leather-work, masonry, painting, or automotive mechanics, the Indian Leadership series outlined how young Indians could use culture strategically to foster social change. Indian students could learn traditional Indian dancing and legends, compose music, recover the history of and write their own Indian poetry and fiction, study biographies and autobiographies of Indians, practice oratory, submit book reviews, and establish contact with politicians in order to cultivate and disseminate a historically informed and socially critical race pride and Indian cultural prestige that would help alter the attitudes and prejudices of both Indians and non-Indians. The Indian leader's historical sense would shape his or her incentive to be a modern social agent and win Indian and white support. This series advised students to read Indian history, examine Indian customs and communal practices, and determine the influences that Indians as groups and individuals have had and might have on American culture.[77] The project of cultural vocationalism was intended not just to preserve Indian cultures but to edit them for modern achievement. It urged students to frame not only the problems Indians face but the solutions that Indians can try to bring about in Depression-era America.[78]

In these articles students encountered numerous discussions of what we might now term multicultural public relations tactics that rely on Indian performances of Indianness for whites, tactics not unlike those Roe Cloud must have learned at Yale and afterward as a fundraiser and administrator. Students were encouraged to read books about Indian lore and compose lectures, talks, or presentations that could be given in schools, clubs, churches, and other cultural organizations.[79] The series held that learning about culture, specifically Indian culture, could be enticingly instrumental. Students in training to be Indian leaders could gain experience by writing poetry and then reading it in public. Culture—the creation of beauty—was viewed as a route to achieving social and political influence among non-Indians. Such performances also would enhance Indians' respect for, love of, and loyalty to Indians.[80]

The series conceptually divides the world into races—not nationalities, classes, genders, regions, personality types. In the modern bureaucratic world, the diverse tribes and bands categorized as Indians were also expected to classify and reimagine themselves as a race. Leadership students are counseled to strive for not only individual distinction or tribal distinction but racial distinction.[81] By studying the lives of Indian leaders, as one would study lives chronicled by Plutarch, students could find examples that illuminate how to choose and fashion a socially responsible Indian individualism. The overriding message is that an Indian education in the strategic uses of Indian culture and the formation of race identity can help one transform not simply the social status, cultural image, and self-image of Indians, but more comprehensively American modernity. Through the example of Sitting Bull, for instance, students are taught the power, necessity, and responsibility of Indian social critique. In response to a request to comment on what struck him most about modern civilization, the great Sioux chief related what Lewis Hine had photographed so disturbingly in factories and sweatshops: young girls and boys laboring for a living.[82]

In Roe Cloud's version of *The Indian Leader* the focus on racial difference or racial singularity is often represented as the means of strategic integration into rather than segregation from America. The plan goes as follows: once Indians accept the category of race foisted on them, they will be able to redefine it so as to celebrate their racial distinction. This distinction potentially strengthens their position as they take up the challenges of the larger culture. Thus the Choctaw educator, administrator, and statesman Gabe E. Parker, in his speech at Haskell, deployed ideas of racial essence, character, instinct, and habit to contest the stereotype of the naturally indolent male Indian. He used modern psychological discourse to endow Indians with industrious instincts. But he also pointed to the age-old necessity of hunting and conditions of warfare as social factors in the cultural development of an Indian work ethos. He sought to reclassify Indians as owners of weapons who traditionally had respect for property. Hence Indians, rather than being primitive communists out of step with modern capitalist America, were instinctually and culturally well equipped to be productive contributors to modernity.[83]

A piece by Oscar H. Lipps, the penultimate superintendent of Carlisle, exhibits both the newer 1930s pluralist turn and older constructions of race, assimilation, and the modern. Indian schools, he argued, should promote programs that respect cultural diversity. He urged that the best of Indian arts and customs be appreciated and taught. Yet he advocated assimilation, rather than amalgamation, and insisted that Indians must merge with the larger American population. The principal problem for Indians, he maintained, is what he considers their racial sloth. Therefore Indians should be trained to value work over recreations such as hunting and fishing.[84] Lipps, like Pratt, tried to stimulate Indians' incentive to labor within dominant American versions of modernity. Gabe Parker had the same aim, but sought to achieve it by encouraging race-conscious pride, not shame.

An adulatory anonymous piece on Marie Martinez, the celebrated San Ildefonso Pueblo potter, attributes significance not only to her talent and to her recovery and development of traditional Indian designs, but to her contribution to regional pottery production, and thus to the great economic growth of San Ildefonso and the other pueblos. Nonetheless, the article stresses, her fame has not compromised her Indian values and bribed her into viewing herself as an individualistic artistic genius. She has declined prizes for her creations, insisting that other potters also do excellent work.[85] Martinez was not just selective about the ways in which she participated in the modern, she was contributing to the formulation and formation of an Indian-influenced modern.[86]

The logic of racial essence enabled members of the race whose ostensible essence was the subject of ideological contestation to introduce the idea of authenticity—here meaning that only Indians can define the nature of Indianness or claim authority to Indianize themselves, albeit in a vast and sometimes contradictory range of ways. In his 1934 commencement address, David Parsons (Choctaw) employed the notion of racial character to fuel students' ambitions to compete in higher education, the arts, and business.[87] He began by recapitulating traditional Indian critiques of a white socioeconomic system that standardizes labor (9). By contrast, he observed that the Indian students' ancestors were Homeric warriors whose ingenious military tactics have been studied and imitated by generals (10). Rather than miscasting Indians as antagonistic to the modern, Parsons focused on their salutary contributions to inventing the modern: weaving, metalworking, jewelry making, pottery, cultivating herbal medicines, and discovering quinine, digitalis, and cascara. After Rome had declined and before Charlemagne took the throne, he reminded Haskell's students, the Mayan Indians brought civilization to new heights. He called for a renaissance of Indian greatness.

Parsons, like Gabe Parker, suggests that this revival of race ambition should channel Indians into rather than away from the capitalist battle-ground. He embraced competition as a means of reconstituting Indian racial power. And Parsons, as did Lipps, cites Japan as the model of an empire that selectively fuses modernity and tradition. This racial proto-multicultural incentive building, like Pratt's individualistic incentive build-ing, banked on the premise that adaptation was inevitable: Indian strength and character must adopt and adapt modern forms of expression within the workplace and marketplace (12). Consequently, he advised, students should analyze the biographies of great men—Leonardo Da Vinci, Ben-jamin Franklin, Henry Roe Cloud, and others—in order to develop Indian forms of self-reliance (though with no great emphasis on tribal reliance). Parsons' social critique of the modern was a bicultural—or more accu-rately multicultural, given the number and heterogeneity of Indian cultures —means of inducing students to operate and succeed as agents within the modern. Like a business professor, he concluded that to be success-ful, Indians must not envy their competitors; they must study and outdo them (13).

ROE CLOUD'S COSMOPOLITANISM
AND COLLIER'S VOCATIONALISM

Roe Cloud included some of his own essays in The Indian Leader. Clearly, he was thinking through how best to rebuild Indian identity within the midst of American and Bureau of Indian Affairs dominance. Perhaps taking his cue from the Society of American Indians, Roe Cloud used the modern categories of race and race pride, not just the categories of Indian peoples and Indian nations, to articulate this reconstruction.[88] As one might ex-pect, he encouraged students to be intellectually ambitious, not only voca-tional. He asserted that Indians have given modern American culture what it lacks—a cultural antiquity that, if valued, can help modern white Amer-ica develop a culturally diverse and culturally mature personality. Indian cultures, he maintained, traditionally shape a racial character that tends to be more self-composed, self-possessed, and self-regulated than white character.[89] America needs such racial qualities to advance. He implied that the so-called New World is just as much an Old World as the Old

World, even if historians fail to or are unable or unwilling to take account of this.[90] Roe Cloud implored students not to allow the ruling race to efface the Indian past from Indian memory and the construction of Indian agency.[91] At the same time, he urged Indian students to learn not just from traditional Indian cultures or from mainstream American culture, but from cultures everywhere. His intellectual protomulticultural cosmopolitanism, which he may have honed in Yale's Cosmopolitan Club, rejected the monocultural Americanization of the older government boarding school approaches. He criticized assimilationist and ethnocentric productions of knowledge that tried to compel Indian students to betray their racial pride, values, and history. Progressive educational systems, he felt, had to learn from and teach cultural difference and cosmopolitanism.[92] American Indians had to be World Indians.[93]

Roe Cloud's protomulticultural cosmopolitanism included social critique. He saw the undervaluing of Indian cultures as part of a more encompassing structure of exploitation. One implication of his argument is that students would do well to place their understanding of the Indian predicament in the context of systemic class exploitation. In America, he acknowledged, the wealthy dominate the poor.[94] Indians must contend with federal bureaucratic management that mislabels itself democracy.[95] To counter this, Roe Cloud proposed an Indian education in what amounts to domination-and-resistance studies that would scrutinize why multitudes obeyed the wealthy few and why intellectuals for so long have been excluded from political power. He concluded that contemporary Indians should study histories and analyses not only of their own battles, but of battles for freedom and rights throughout the ages.[96]

Still, Roe Cloud proposed an Indian protomulticultural modification of the assimilationist inevitability argument. While he considered it inevitable that Indians integrate into American culture, he also thought it imperative that Indians import Indian ways of thinking, valuing, and living into the mix of the dominant culture.[97] In part his refrain was similar to that of assimilationists like Pratt: to resist American inevitability is tantamount to refusing to be developed.[98] But he added a protomulticultural twist: to retreat from this development means surrendering the opportunity to redevelop American society Indian-style through cultural and political citizenship. He envisioned an America in which racial interdependency and exchange would replace racial stratification in the power structure. By blending America's cultures, America could be a better, richer, fairer, more fascinating culture for everyone.[99] Only by creating, editing, and retaining race identity, he believed, can the requisite intercultural fusion take place. At Haskell he turned recreation halls into lodges bearing Indian names, sponsored Indian dances, authorized the teaching of Indian languages, and reprinted books of Indian legends.[100]

In many respects Roe Cloud's understanding of protomulticulturalism resembled that of Commissioner Collier. One article reprinted from the Bureau's newsletter, *Indians at Work*, announced the new commitment to design school architecture inspired by traditional Indian aesthetics.[101] Collier grasped that Indians made up a vastly diverse world and that as commissioner he would have to contrive forms of what is now called diversity management, not monocultural management.[102] Years before, Eastman recognized that, to be effective, Indian "race leadership" would have to speak to "the large number of different Indian tribes with their distinct languages, habits, and traditions, and with old tribal jealousies and antagonisms."[103] Indians, as a race, Collier wrote, in an article reprinted in *The Indian Leader*, are much more culturally diverse than what government, reform, and welfare organizations have understood. Consequently, new government programs must be both flexible and experimental.[104] In his address given at Haskell's fiftieth anniversary festivities, Collier suggested perceptively that Roe Cloud embodied this flexibility: on the one hand, he is loyal to the Indian history and tradition that manifests itself in the present; on the other, he engages what Indians need to know and do in modern conditions.

In addition, Collier, like Roe Cloud, felt that Indian cultures could and should revise what dominant American ideologies and institutions defined as modernity. He predicted that what was then termed "modern" — informed by pinched individualistic values, property interests, and marketplace competition—would not survive over the next centuries. His immediate political anxiety was that some Indians who imagined themselves narrowly as modern and individualistic would not support his tribe- and reservation-oriented Indian Reorganization Act. He was right. Collier contrasted his vision of a multicultural modernity with the contemporary social formation of the modern.[105] He praised the Irish for combating

English colonialism by both looking back in time to embrace Ireland's heritage, language, art, and values, and looking ahead to create a social and cultural renewal reliant on cooperation.[106] Collier viewed the recognition and respect for Indian singularity, and diversity within this racial singularity, as a key to changing Indian Americanization and modernization. In opposition to Carlisle-style look-out-for-number-one individualizing schemes, he advocated new group forms, racial group forms, of individuality production.[107] For Collier, pluralist modernizing was a more subtle, humane, and efficient Americanization tactic than mass-cultural homogenizing. Collier conceptualized protomulticulturalism as an enlightened management project capable of cultivating new forms of economic incentive for diverse social groups to contribute to America's modernization.

Roe Cloud, taking seriously the idea that Indians deserved a real "new deal," advanced his more protomulticultural revisionary view of what education could be. An Indian-run Indian education that taught the value of Indian self-determination would have been difficult for early-twentieth-century Indian intellectuals to put on the popular agenda.[108] They needed to get their feet in the door of white institutions and begin to create Indian institutions, like Roe Cloud's American Indian Institute. Cultural, political, and economic self-determination could be on the Indian intellectuals' agenda in the 1930s partly because the Bureau of Indian Affairs sponsored tribal structures of "self-government" that many Indians found insufficient or problematic (in effect, government-ruled Indian self-government).

Where Roe Cloud significantly differed from Collier was in his stress on higher education for Indians as a fundamental way to make this newly valued diversity diverse at all levels of society. When defending the Indian Reorganization Act at reservations around the country, Roe Cloud cited, among other things, the bill's establishment of "scholarship loans"—an oxymoron, one either has a scholarship or takes out a loan—to universities.[109] But The Indian Leader reprinted the text of the Wheeler-Howard Indian Reorganization Act, which made it plain, perhaps to Roe Cloud's suppressed dismay, that of the proposed $250,000 allocations for loans, at least $200,000 was slated to support attendance at trade schools and not more than $50,000 was to underwrite matriculation in high schools or colleges.[110] In his original version of the bill, Collier had requested only

$50,000 for education, but $15,000 of that sum would have been for outright scholarships for Indians to attend high school, college, and professional school.[111]

The Collier Bureau, perhaps partly in response to ideological pressures, like previous Bureau administrations, was committed to vocationalism, a policy that kept most Indians in what might be described broadly as the Indian working class. At times Collier declined opportunities to support Indian higher education even in modest ways. In 1935 he turned down a request by Robert Yellowtail, an early supporter of the Indian New Deal, that students from his Crow Reservation be allowed to reside at Sherman Institute (Yellowtail's alma mater) in Riverside, California, while attending universities—on university-provided financial aid and scholarships—in the area.[112]

It must be said that Collier's administrative approach, which took on urgent reservation matters like soil erosion and conservation—about 90 per cent of Indians lived in rural conditions—as well as economic and arts development, was usually much more helpfully and intelligently pragmatic than previous Indian administrations in its efforts to proletarianize Indians. Yet, as I have suggested, Collier's New Deal approach sometimes recycled features and values of the Old Deal. For instance, Roe Cloud once requested that some students who were about to transfer from Haskell to public school be given some new clothing to look appropriate. Collier advised Roe Cloud to provide new garments only in cases of obvious "actual need" and recycled the hackneyed self-help recommendation that students must learn the "principle" of working to pay for what they get.[113]

The Roe Cloud who favored multiracial educational opportunities had told Rodman Wanamaker that Christianized Indians have better incentive and make better workers, and that it would pay for him to bestow his philanthropy on the American Indian Institute.[114] By the 1930s the more conspicuously protomulticultural Roe Cloud came to believe that racial discourse, not just individuality discourse or self-help discourse or Christian discourse, produced better incentive and better workers. Nevertheless, The Indian Leader suggests that Roe Cloud wanted to shape not workers only, but leaders and cultural activists with broad-ranging, cosmopolitan, intellectual ambitions. Collier, like Roe Cloud, claimed that he wanted to educate leaders, but leaders institutionally trained as plumbers, carpenters, painters, leatherworkers, and home economists. His New Deal administration advanced from vocationalism to protomulticultural vocationalism. This amounted to a schooling that encouraged the compensatory maintenance of "race identity" as one worked, often in the same old jobs and same old social stratum.

MARY ROE, JOHN COLLIER, AND HENRY ROE CLOUD

It is hard to gauge the extent to which Roe Cloud's evolving views of Collier were influenced by Mary Roe's criticisms of the Indian New Deal. In 1935, writing to a friend who also knew Roe Cloud, Roe acknowledged that both Collier and President Franklin Delano Roosevelt introduced some benevolent social initiatives. However, she added, neither Collier nor Roosevelt fully grasped the implications of their reforms. She complained that Collier had frustrated many knowledgeable and industrious advocates of Indian advancement. Collier's idealism, she concluded, was out of touch with what could and should be done for Indians.[115]

Roe collected several critiques of Collier, published and unpublished, that lambasted him for sponsoring primitive, tribal, and communistic aspects of Indian life.[116] Collier, the critics objected, thwarted missionaries' efforts to Christianize Indians and instill in them the incentive to work.[117] In these critiques worker development is seen as being necessarily intertwined with soul development, as it was in Roe Cloud's earlier writings. One critic, G. E. E. (Elmer) Lindquist, Roe Cloud's roommate at Oberlin Seminary and colleague at the American Indian Institute, lamented that the Indians were yet again being subjected to the administrative whims of the state (recall that in his 1945 letter that criticized Collier, Roe Cloud regretted that Indians had long had to put up with changing styles of federal manipulation).[118] Roe especially appreciated an article by an attorney, Flora Warren Seymour, "Federal Favor for Fetishism" (1935), published in *The Missionary Review of the World*. Seymour contests Collier's pluralistic evaluation of that which is worth preserving in Indian cultures. She lists Indian taboos as evidence of Indian customs that should not be countenanced by government agencies. Roe inscribed her approbation of Seymour's critique of Collier on the title page.[119] In 1934 one of Roe's friends on the Winnebago Reservation, who was critical of Collier's self-government reforms, wrote her that the Winnebago value having a say in government rule beyond the tribe. William Ohlerking, another friend, noted that he encountered Roe Cloud at a Bureau-sponsored pow wow—likely a reference to one of the pow wows that Roe Cloud led to win support for the Wheeler-Howard act.[120]

Weighing the views of some of his old friends, what might Roe Cloud have been thinking about as he spoke at Indian New Deal pow wows? After all, he had turned toward social science—anthropology—after his seminary training. His American Indian Institute exhibited signs of both what it grew out of—the dominance of Protestant reform—and the future—an Indian New Deal that accorded greater respect to Indian cultures, traditions, and identities. Mary Roe's views represented not just an older way of thinking about reform, but an older approach to identity building and incentive building. And yet the New Deal was not always so liberating, for Roe Cloud and for other Indians, as it made itself out to be.

Shortly after Roe Cloud left Haskell, on permanent leave, Mary Roe wrote a friend that she was happy about Henry's departure because he had experienced some difficulty in that post. She expressed her wish that Roe Cloud would change his course and employ himself in literary or religious projects to realize his full potential as an Indian leader. Roe implied that these paths would be far greater contributions to enhancing Indian life than working for Collier's Bureau at Haskell.[121]

THE BAD DEAL

In 1936 Collier designated D'Arcy McNickle to supervise a group of five educated Bureau Indians to serve as field representatives. This unit took over Roe Cloud's job of promoting the Indian New Deal to Indians. Roe Cloud, who had been appointed supervisor of Indian Education, was much older and far more eminent than these Indian colleagues. He was assigned clerical tasks that dissatisfied and marginalized him. Then in 1939 Collier informed Roe Cloud that he had to leave his current post and offered him the superintendency of the Turtle Mountain Agency at a drop in rank and pay (just when he was paying his daughters' college tuitions). Roe Cloud was worried about his health during the Northern Plains winter months and declined. He finally accepted the superintendency of the Umatilla

Reservation in Oregon at an even lower salary. Roe Cloud argued with Collier about this shabby treatment, objecting that his boss had once benefited tremendously from his arduous efforts to stump on behalf of Indian New Deal initiatives. In one letter of protest to Collier, Roe Cloud sheds some light on Margaret Thompson's tantalizing but unsupported statement in "From Wigwam to Mr. Bigwig" that he played a foundational role in the conceptual development of the Indian New Deal. Roe Cloud cites a memo he had sent Collier that laid out the ideas on which the commissioner established his Indian reorganization reforms. He warned Collier that he had retained a copy of the memo. Collier still refused to give his underling a fair deal. If Roe Cloud had formulated the basis of the Indian New Deal, it is ironic, perhaps tragically ironic, that he campaigned so effectively in his trips to reservations across the continent for a program that he had to attribute to Collier. Again I am driven to wonder if on one level Collier viewed Roe Cloud partly as a rival.[122]

Jason M. Tetzloff has traced a pattern in Roe Cloud's administrative career that became visible in the late 1920s. Delighting in investigative analyses, eloquent speaking and storytelling, writing (many of his memos, letters, and articles are beautifully crafted), hands-on negotiations and interactions, good humor and graciousness, Roe Cloud had little intellectual patience for trivial paperwork, minor details, bureaucratic deadlines, red tape, and routine thinking. As Tetzloff contends, this may account for his transfer from Haskell and his later bureaucratic demotion. My speculation is that Roe Cloud, who was as learned as Collier, and who exemplified the realization of a certain kind of Indian white-collar class potential, would not more than could not adopt the government bureaucratization of his mind, spirit, and purpose. What some Bureau career-functionaries may have thought of a Yale Indian capable of expressing his point of view to them in Greek, Latin, German, Sioux, Winnebago, or English, is left to one's imagination.

One week before Collier arrived for Haskell's fiftieth anniversary celebration in November 1934, *The Indian Leader* began running not another leadership series but a new series similar to the one featured before Roe Cloud took over the school. This series, "Vocational News," ran until Roe Cloud exited in May 1935. The series continued the term after the Bureau borrowed Roe Cloud from the superintendent's position. It was not until the 1950s that Haskell was authorized to develop programs to train some of its students for college. During the 1960s and 1970s, it gained junior college status and altered its name to Haskell Indian Junior College. Haskell built Roe Cloud Hall—a dormitory that, seen from above, evokes the shape of a cross—in 1997. The school is now Haskell Indian Nations University.[123]

Pratt protested that Indians were "Bureauized." The erudite and elastic Henry Roe Cloud had to deal with this modern imposition of power at high administrative levels.[124] But he never ceded that power enough power to let it stop him.

◄ coda ►

THE INDIAN ETHOS OF SERVICE

THE INDIAN COUNCIL FIRE'S 1936 publication of *Indians of Today* printed brief biographies of some distinguished Indians who made it into or close to the professional and managerial class: politicians, lawyers, businesspersons, authors, scholars, artists, actors, athletic stars, theologians. Some attended college, and some went on to complete graduate work in law, medicine, or academic subjects. The institutions at which they studied include Yale (Roe Cloud), Princeton (Gansworth), Dartmouth (Eastman and others), Earlham College (Bonnin), Columbia Graduate School, University of Pennsylvania, University of Toronto, McGill University, Stanford Law School, Oberlin, Mount Holyoke, University of Oklahoma, University of Kansas, and University of Minnesota. Several belonged to the Society of University Indians of America. But many had not attended college. Some of those who did not have so-called higher education had excelled as artists, actors, performers, or leaders of their communities—such as the superb artist, Fred Kabotie (Hopi), and the world-renowned Carlisle Olympic champion, Jim Thorpe.

The group was not, or in the case of some of its members was not trying to be, orthodox as a class-in-formation. Their criteria for conferring Indian Council Fire distinction was sometimes quite standard, akin to what one might find in Roe Cloud's Yale classbooks (academic pedigree, economic success), and sometimes not. Eighty-four photographs accompany the ninety-seven biographies: fifty-two photographs show subjects in the usual American suits and dresses, thirty are in traditional Indian garb, and two wear "cowboy" hats. Those honored show great pride in their Indian ancestry: thirty-three are full-bloods. Mollie Spotted Elk (Penobscot), who attended the University of Pennsylvania and had to drop out because of financial hardship, went on to a celebrated career as a dancer and actress and "firmly believes that the only typical and original things America has to offer to the world of Art, Music, and Literature are the contributions of the Indian."[1] One Indian Council Fire administrator explained the group's "color line": "We do not admit to membership any Indian who is mixed with Negro blood. . . . The white race does not class mulattoes as whites. Why should the Indian?"[2]

It is easy to imagine Roe Cloud as being very proud of the group's achievements, yet still holding to his conviction that more of them and more Indians outside this accomplished group should have had the opportunity to study at college and then advance with greater knowledge and prestige, as defined by the dominant culture, however they chose. Even though Arthur Parker, an eminent member of the Council Fire, was a successful, self-taught ethnologist and museum director, he sometimes dissimulated about having academic credentials. Some biographical sketches, even recent ones, have him attending Harvard and the University of Rochester.[3] As mentioned in chapter 1, when the Society of American Indians was gathering momentum, Parker corresponded with Fayette McKenzie about the possibility of founding an Indian college, one that would sponsor modern Indian literature and equip Indians to be Indians in contemporary ways. Both Roe Cloud and Parker knew that academic degrees function as passports that may facilitate class mobility and access to power. Paradoxically, in modern America activists on behalf of *equality* have benefited from the acquisition of *class* identity through academic honors. All of Roe Cloud's daughters took the college route, and some went to graduate school. Elizabeth Marion and Anne Woesha were the first American Indian graduates of Wellesley and Vassar, respectively. Ramona Clark also graduated from Vassar. And Lillian Alberta attended the University of Kansas.[4]

Roe Cloud's evolving self-image reveals a good deal about the historical dimension of the slippery bridge between class status and racial status. "Class and ethnicity have always been linked in the United States," George

Lipsitz emphasizes, "each identity is experienced through the other—as well as through gender, sexuality, religion, and many other social identities."[5] As I have suggested, Carlisle and government schools like it were established not simply to manufacture "individuals," but "individuals" who would be funneled into a genteel, well-mannered, easily supervised skilled and semiskilled working class. It should come as no surprise that in the last few years of its existence Carlisle sent students to work on Ford assembly lines.[6] From early childhood, Roe Cloud, whose Winnebago reservation was under siege in various ways, resisted being channeled into polite Indian worker–individuality. He absorbed the Bible and self-help books and soon moved on to Greek. From Yale, his missionary work with the Roes, and some of his experiences in later life, especially with the Society of American Indians and with fundraising, Roe Cloud learned that with the acquisition of higher education and class he had more power to signify and contextualize Indianness as socially distinctive. Probably for many reasons, what he labored strategically to achieve during his career, at least in part, was not the performative, ill-fitting, critically aware off-whiteness of Luther Standing Bear, but an impeccably groomed and outfitted class act.

One Roe family archive photograph of Roe Cloud taken in 1940 shows him on horseback, not like a cowboy or a traditionally dressed Indian, but like a man of means who owns a horse and sports a tasteful leisure-cowboy style riding habit. The photograph's anonymous inscription conveys this staging of distinction, profiling Roe Cloud as a judge attending the Pendleton Roundup. Not far from the Umatilla Reservation, where he was superintendent, he appears in saddle with unfocused tipis in the distance. Elizabeth, as a member of the Oregon Trail Women's Club, would have been near the tipis, "providing 'living' exhibitions of Indian women tanning hides, preparing roots, and doing many other tasks that have been part of Indian life for generations."[7] Professional achievement, recognition, and self-presentation enabled Roe Cloud as best he could to extend the meanings of Indianness. Wigwams are in the picture, as they were in Roe Cloud's Winnebago childhood, but now they are rendered scenic by the camera, soft-focused and in the background. Roe Cloud is not overtly a war chief—the translation of his Winnebago name—on a horse, in a headdress, armed with weapons. Rather he is well-suited with class armor, itself a defensive and offensive weapon.[8] Perhaps Roe Cloud served as judge of Pendleton's Indian dancing contest.[9] More generally, the photograph is a visual statement of Roe Cloud's dignity, in good measure his *Indian* class dignity and authority.

Despite the passage of twenty-six years, Roe Cloud's photograph in *History of the Class of 1910* (figure 6) bears an underlying resemblance to his photograph in *Indians of Today*. Clearly, the style of the white collar has changed. In the fashion of the day, Roe Cloud's 1910 version is rounded, like the bases of two wings almost joining and nearly covering the tie in between. By contrast, the 1930s starched collar has sharp angles forming a pointed arch over the tie. And his dark 1910 suit jacket, vest, and tie have been replaced with a light-colored 1930s suit jacket, vest, and tie that complement his graying hair, combed exactly as it was in college. In the later photograph he wears unframed glasses. Read historically, both portraits convey Indian class identity. In the early twentieth century there are many examples of white people who played "Indian" in one way or another. At Yale and in the intervening years one of Roe Cloud's challenges was to help expand cultural and political concepts of Indians, class identity, and leadership so that when he was seen as white collared he would not be misperceived as playing white man. This was crucial to his efforts to craft and perform his role as a leader not just of Indians but of white Americans who affected Indians.

Memmi suggests what Standing Bear, happily flaunting his "screechy" boots, oversized suits, and ties without collars, knew decades before: the colonized, typed as off-white at best, thus generically ill-fitted, "can never succeed in becoming identified with the colonizer, nor even in copying his role correctly."[10] But Roe Cloud was involved in a resignifying process too complex to be oversimplified as copying. As Homi Bhabha stresses, the colonized or postcolonized "mimic," well aware, sometimes painfully aware, at times proudly aware, that he or she may be "almost the same but not [quite] white," can use mimicry as a form of "camouflage," and can deploy it to "rearticulate" and "disrupt" colonial or postcolonial authority. And Paul Gilroy, addressing the complexity of being socially positioned, particularly racially positioned, in multiple, oftentimes contradictory ways, reminds us that we have "always incomplete identities in an unstable field."[11]

Even so, Roe Cloud negotiated this instability with his elastic sense of humor and play, not just with the formality evident in the photographs of 1910 and 1936 I have compared. This good-natured, often self-ironic characteristic was why Thompson could playfully nominate him Mr. Bigwig in her 1944 *Sunday Oregonian* profile. The cultural wisdom that informed this stance is manifest in Roe Cloud's letter to Collier about Monahan's trip to Haskell, in which he praised the latter for appreciating that life must be enjoyed and animated with humor. These words of praise speak volumes about the emotional and spiritual resilience that helped Roe Cloud do all he did. Roe Cloud always invested in more than class.

Indianness and class are also exhibited in a Roe family archive photograph of Elizabeth and two of her very young daughters. Her girls are wrapped in a blanket, and Elizabeth is draped in a patterned blanket. They appear to be sitting on the floor of a well-appointed, middle-class living room, perhaps a photographer's studio, with a carpet beneath the Indian blanket. The wall furnishings are made of carved wood, and the forest in the background is either a mural or decorative wallpaper print. In this protective class interior, Indianness is emotionally warm, familial, tasteful, and well-bred.

Roe Cloud's correspondence and career pattern suggest that he knew that the control made possible in some circles by an Indian's class and educational position and self-image was provisional. On the predicament of the Antilleans who had been admitted provisionally into the colonial professional and managerial class, Fanon observed: "Something out of the ordinary still clung to such cases. . . . It was always the Negro teacher, the Negro doctor. . . . I knew, for instance, that if the physician made a mistake it would be the end of him and all those who came after him. . . . No exception was made for my refined manners, or my knowledge of literature, or my understanding of the quantum theory."[12] The best Roe Cloud and Fanon and Memmi and others like them could be, in Memmi's words, were "the most favored colonized . . . certain rights will forever be refused them . . . certain advantages are reserved strictly for [them]."[13]

The limited and provisional redefinitional power of this class alchemy relied on the maintenance of certain economic and cultural class differences. Professional and managerial class individuality and subjective potency, in Roe Cloud's era, as in our own, was in ways direct and indirect purchased at the expense of working-class labor. As Roe Cloud well knew from much of his own "educational" experience performing manual labor in school, some of the workers who laid the socioeconomic foundation for his elaboration of selfhood were Indians molded as self-help "individuals" in institutions like Carlisle, Hampton, and Haskell.

On one level, Roe Cloud's tireless advocacy of Indian higher education was certainly on behalf of his race; on another level, especially early in his career, before Haskell, it may have been, if Montezuma was right, also in support of his fledgling social group. His original project was no small one: building a university-trained Indian professional and managerial class that would serve Indians, but which, in some respects, also would probably help perpetuate the class structure, and thus its own "individual" distinctiveness, through its cultural and institutional allegiances (despite the fact that Indian membership in this class was by no means wholly embraced by the dominant white membership). By assisting college-potential Indians to become more strategically status conscious than Carlisle-level skilled and semiskilled workers, Roe Cloud labored to bring about not so much an enhanced intellectual and critical mobility for the race in general —an impossibly tall order, now taken up partly by a network of tribal colleges—but an educational and class mobility for some Indians—also a tall order.

Roe Cloud attempted this prodigious feat decades before affirmative action laws took effect and before "race"—re-utilized by corporate multiculturalism's "diversity management" practices in late-twentieth-century America—would be resignified to function as a "constituent element of class relations." Yet the year Roe Cloud died, C. L. R. James, the great Jamaican social theorist, reflected on early signs of this diversity-management reworking of race in government and private industry. James wrote in 1950, in remarks that bring aspects of the Indian New Deal to mind, that government bureaucracies hire a "liberal sprinkling of Negroes" to reproduce more tactically the "economic and social foundations of the country": "The inevitable result of [seemingly progressive] legislation being handed over to the administration will be that those in charge of it, Negroes or not, with their first loyalty to the administration and its primary tasks, will become adjusters, manipulators, fixers, propagandists, educators, but the safest and most dependable preservers and protectors of the essentials of the system." Industries and government were grooming the "Negro intelligentsia" to be visible signs of a progress that it was their job to limit.[14] The enlistment of allegiance and agency that worried James was a pattern, pressure, and reward system, but it was not always a done deal with guaranteed results. White-collar Indians who attained some class mobility would risk being entangled in a nexus of material, bureaucratic, stylistic, familial, romantic, and psychological interdependencies that the professional and managerial class preferred to advertise, perhaps mis-advertise, as enviable "individual" independence. Yet this mobility also gave the "most favored colonized" access to social power as bridge figures and cultural brokers between races and a shot at using this limited power in a range of ways, including expanding their class.[15]

Roe Cloud reworked class with an Indian difference—with a concept of responsibility that extended far beyond the middle-class privatization of emotional investments in the family and the individualizing of ambition. He did not involve himself in significant professional- and managerial-class activities and practices simply for himself. If he became a professional and a manager of sorts, it was to serve Indians as founder of a private Indian school, head of a government Indian school, advocate for the reform of Indian policy, Bureau of Indian Affairs administrator, and superintendent of the Umatilla Reservation. His Winnebago sense of kinship merged with his Christian sense of service to ensure this. One reason he loved the Roes was their Christian dedication to Indians. At Yale, Roe Cloud acted on President Hadley's invocations of service more seriously than many of his classmates. He was not stunted spiritually by capitalist possessive individuality. Roe Cloud's Indian ethos of service was one reason why he was good at bringing the best out of philanthropists.[16] He realized that the so-called Indian problem was in fact (what Arthur Parker once called) the "white problem," and he sought to educate and spiritually elevate white-collar whites as well as Indians.[17]

Roe Cloud stood front and center in the vanguard of early-twentieth-century Indians who used class capital and knowledge to reinvest in Indians. The Crow leader Robert Yellowtail was another staunch advocate of Indian higher education. He placed more emphasis than Roe Cloud on professional training in law and business.[18] Yellowtail simultaneously owned a large thriving ranch and channeled his energy into the superintendency of the Crow reservation. His *Indians of Today* profile charts the circuit of his commitments: "All but six years of his life have been spent upon the reservation. . . . His great ambition is for the Crow youth to gain an education commensurate with their needs in the best colleges of the country, and to return to their homes as native leaders and instructors."[19]

During his two decades in the Bureau of Indian Affairs, much of Roe Cloud's work was with thinking men and women on reservations, not at the University Club. From his years at Yale to the end of his life, Roe Cloud practiced his form of what Jace Weaver terms Indian "communitism," the fusion of commitment to community and activism. Notwithstanding his Yale praise of individualism, collegiate opposition to socialism, and youthful skepticism about government support for Indians, his life exemplifies what Krupat and Weaver consider traditional Indian self-definition: "I-am-We."[20]

It was at Haskell that Roe Cloud's educational-and-class-prestige tactic seems to have taken a protomulticulturally and politically strategic turn. There, the Roe Cloud whose early mission, influenced by the Roes, was saving souls, seems to have moved even closer toward Du Bois's understanding of his life as "part of a Problem," as embodying the "central problem of the greatest of the world's democracies and so the Problem of the future world."[21] Roe Cloud encouraged intellectual ambition and showered his charges with literary and high-cultural allusions. He integrated his stress on race pride and the study of Indian cultures and history with a vigorous, somewhat Du Boisian emphasis on producing race leaders and cultural activists.[22] At Haskell his public critique of Indians' positioning in America at large and within the Bureau of Indian Affairs in particular, even the New Deal Bureau that had appointed him superintendent, grew bolder. Doubtless, his students learned from his pronouncements and had greater incentive to think more about gaining the modern skills requisite to try to transform, not simply adapt to or absorb elements of, dominant American society. Roe Cloud, like Collier, believed in gaining social access for Indians. But for Roe Cloud that access had to be to all class and social power levels of modern America. Against heavy odds, he did what he could to make Haskell—a federal boarding school, or worker production school, much different from the college he had struggled to attend—provide access that would contribute not simply to multicultural assimilation but to contemporary Indian self-determination. This was not an approach to education and academic culture that his professors taught him at Yale.

It is fascinating to ponder how many of the needs, concerns, and strategies that Roe Cloud articulated so movingly and unflaggingly in the first half of the twentieth century resonate with those of Indian contributors to the *Tribal College Journal of American Indian Higher Education*, founded in 1989. Many scholars and activists, in considering the possibilities, practices, and goals of Indian higher education, have identified the importance of addressing and synthesizing concerns such as intellectual, cultural, economic, and political leadership training, community building, multidimensional student support, the construction of good educational facilities, the promotion of educational philanthropy, the recovery, preservation, elaboration of, and assignment of status to Indian knowledge, histories, and traditions, and teaching non-Indian America some of what Indians know it needs to know, for the sake of the world. Part of Roe Cloud's immense challenge was to use and move beyond Yale's elite production of knowledge to change institutional, bureaucratic, and cultural conditions so that something like the collective intellectual efforts, critiques, and planning recorded in *Tribal College Journal* would be imaginable and discussible someday. Roe Cloud was a groundbreaker in the effort to achieve what has only begun to be possible on a wide scale in recent times, what Margaret Connell Szasz describes concisely as "Native control over [Native] schooling."[23]

Leonard Peltier, a political prisoner for over a quarter of a century, has lamented: "Prison's the only university, the only finishing school many young Indian brothers ever see."[24] Sometimes the imprisonment to which Indians have been sentenced has been more subtle, but no less real, no less institutional. Leslie Marmon Silko recalls that when her grandfather attended Sherman Institute he had become intrigued "with engineering and design and wanted to become an automobile designer." Sherman offered him no opportunity to pursue such interests. The vocational role Sherman assigned him was that of store clerk. Storekeeping failed to fire his imagination. So he always "subscribed to *Motor Trend* and *Popular Mechanics* and followed the new car designs and the results of road tests each year."[25] The historian K. Tsianina Lomawaima's father attended Chilocco Indian school in Oklahoma in the late 1920s and early 1930s. After Chilocco he worked odd jobs to support himself while he attended high school. He graduated in 1939 with an Honor Society scholarship and was accepted at "a small midwestern college." But on campus a dean told him that the college "had no place for Indians" and drove him away.[26]

The academic dreams and hopes that Roe Cloud articulated and fought for still have a long way to be realized, despite increased educational access made available to Indians especially in the 1960s and 1970s.[27] Early 1990s statistics indicate that approximately 60 percent of Indian high school students graduate and approximately 3 percent of the original group go on to graduate from four-year colleges.[28] For many Indians, the route to college, the experience of college, and life after college are full of sky-high hurdles. "I was special, a former college student, a smart kid," one of Sherman Alexie's (Spokane and Coeur d'Alene) Indian narrators ruminates, still jarred by the pressures for which college provided no clear solution. "I was one of those Indians who was supposed to make it, to rise above the rest of the reservation, like a fucking eagle or something. I was the new kind of warrior."[29] Decades earlier, as many Indians had begun to realize that they were embroiled in a new kind of struggle on new sorts of battlefields in marketplaces, courts, legislatures, schools, universities, the media, churches, and homes, Roe Cloud had to learn how to be that "new kind of warrior." Mindful of the still-pressing need for such warriors, Peltier's Charitable Foundation has funded a scholarship for Indian law students at New York University.[30]

The sort of crossover learning and unlearning that Roe Cloud accomplished was multidimensional, complicated, fraught with contradictions though not without opportunities then and now. Philip J. Deloria captures some of this complexity in his perceptive profile of his grandfather, Vine Deloria Sr., whose ministerial efforts exemplified not an ethos of assimilation but an ethos of service. "Deloria's own life—which could easily serve as a case study in assimilation, if one chose to view it that way—suggested a more complicated scenario, one that emphasized continuing service to Indian people rather than the rapid and wholesale abdication of Indianness proposed by the government."[31] Recently an illuminating collection of thirteen autobiographical essays by Indian Dartmouth graduates— 1970s to 1990s—was published that features a foreword by Louise Erdrich

(Chippewa), herself a Dartmouth alumna. Erdrich notes that all of the volume's contributors "have returned to work in their communities." She finds this "remarkable in a capitalist society, and yet not amazing given the sources." None of the essays "is about the wish to attain status, the ambition to make large amounts of money, or the desire to become famous."[32] Their intellectual, social, and career aims, like Roe Cloud's, cannot be summed up adequately as class and economic mobility. The autobiographers do not cite Roe Cloud and his efforts to establish this Indian pattern of reinvestment.

One Dartmouth autobiographer, Lori Arviso Alvord (Navajo), also a graduate of Stanford Medical School, is a surgeon who practices near the Navajo Reservation in New Mexico. She wrote of her experiences in the operating room with Indian nurses and colleagues, in words that would have made Roe Cloud smile. "I see a varied example of a primary goal of our people: that of creating our own professionals, who will lead our communities, in order to control our own destiny as a people." Alvord, like Roe Cloud, values a kind of success that links Indian individuals to their communities, connecting Indian past with a future, and Indian accomplishment to politics—a success on behalf of collective yet heterogeneous modes of self-determination. And she, like Roe Cloud, and indeed like so many Indian students, returned, as she put it, "full circle" to help and be a part of her people. Sam Deloria (Standing Rock Sioux), the first Indian recipient of the Henry Roe Cloud Alumni Award in November 2005, graduated from Yale College in 1964, before attending Yale Law School. As director of the American Indian Law Center, he exemplifies the Indian ethos of service that the Roe Clouds championed. Henry Roe and Elizabeth Bender Roe Cloud's dreams of empowerment live on in other committed Indians, most of whom have been unaware of their life, struggles, achievements, and higher educations in several spheres.[33]

Since 2005 Roe Cloud's descendants, working in concert with Yale archivists, administrators, faculty, and, especially, the university's American Indian students and alumni, have achieved much in their efforts to heighten awareness of Roe Cloud's life and accomplishments at Yale and beyond. The second Henry Roe Cloud conference was held at Yale in 2008, at which R. David Edmunds, the eminent Eastern Cherokee historian, who has advanced the study of Indian leaders, gave the opening address. From

2006 to 2008 articles about American Indians at Yale and the legacy of Henry Roe Cloud appeared in the *New York Times*, the *Yale Alumni Magazine*, the *Yale Daily News*, and the *Yale Herald*. Despite the fact that, as a Lakota Sioux Yale student generalized, referencing the social conditions that so many Indians must negotiate, "College is just not a focus for Indians," by 2007 1 percent of Yale's student population identified as American Indian. That year Yale appointed an assistant dean of Native American students. While one Indian student regretted that "Yale stereotyping is still a reality," another praised the "support system" (that Roe Cloud never knew). Yale, following Cornell and Dartmouth, has the third greatest number of American Indians in the Ivy League (about 80). More Yalies than ever look to Roe Cloud's example. The *Yale Herald* hailed him as a "public intellectual." Ashley Hemmers '07 (Fort Mohave), who served as the president of the Association of Native Americans at Yale (founded in 1991), is resolved to return "to teach my tribe how to maneuver in different situations—how to voice its opinion, be non-confrontational, function in everyday society." She will apply to law school. Her Yale plan, like her long-range purpose, resembles Roe Cloud's. "I'm going to school with the future leaders of the country. We'll leave here knowing how to work together" (see Appendix).[34]

A pragmatic, perhaps strategic, note on which to close: Roe Cloud was judicious about what he made significant. He had a sense of what was culturally healthy. It was Roe Cloud's spirituality, humor, playfulness, charm, dignity, capacity for appreciation, and cosmopolitan disposition that enabled him to deprive oppressive social power of some of its oppressiveness so that it could not tyrannize his thoughts, feelings, identity formation, and efforts to change the world. For Roe Cloud, higher education, and the provisional class membership it sometimes sponsored, provided more room to move in relation, and relative nonrelation, to larger systemic contradictions that enveloped Indians. The spirituality he nurtured in himself and others helped him see that social power was not as all-encompassing as it made itself out to be and that, in a spiritual scale of value, that power was more failure than success, more pathetic than imposing, more weak than strong.[35] Much can be learned from Roe Cloud's grace.

To be sure, Roe Cloud knew the score first hand, the racisms and exploitations Indians were up against. Yet his history is more than a history of strained negotiations. Roe Cloud realized that a ceaseless absorption with oppositional criticism in conditions of oppression sometimes risks being taken over—consumed, defined, contained—by that which it criticizes. He understood that to imagine oneself only as *the oppressed* was on one level to internalize and surrender to, rather than effectively disempower, that oppression. Roe Cloud wanted to build status for himself and other Indians by exercising power, not by asserting victimhood. Patricia Penn Hilden (Nez Perce) observes that many Indians, *never* unaware of prevailing power relations, "tend to" repudiate "aggressive" "guilt-eliciting accusations about the past" as culturally, emotionally, and politically counterproductive." "If you can . . . draw out the pain from an individual," Paul Radin wrote, conveying Winnebago wisdom, "you will indeed be a help to your people."[37] Roe Cloud, as a teacher, intellectual, leader, activist, and healer, exemplified a cultural wisdom that nourishes love, aspiration, appreciation, and resilience rather than resentment, rage, condemnation, and self-pity. I suspect that this wisdom took form long before he arrived at Yale or met the Roes in his twenties. Much must have happened to the Winnebago that made him angry. Nevertheless, his anger seldom surfaced in the many writings I have perused. Roe Cloud wanted Indians and Indian preoccupations to be greater than the sum of their struggles. His life-affirming focus on how to *be* and *act* in the world, not only his efforts to build institutions and shape government policy, represents the foundational legacy of his higher educations.

Sometimes History Needs Reminding

The main, almost cave-like low-ceilinged entrance to Yale University's Sterling Memorial Library ushers one into the nave of a soaring gothic cathedral–like interior. The nave leads to the transept, and at the crossing, in place of an altar, stands a circulation desk ornamented with carved wood. Only one of the walls that form the crossing—supporting the gothic arch, opposite the circulation desk—is adorned with a portrait. If one stops in the crossing to admire the circulation desk, where scholars borrow books rather than take sacraments, and then turns all the way to the right, the portrait is visible. It is striking. The painting is of Edward Alexander Bouchet (1852–1918). Bouchet's gaze is angled toward the nave in the direction of the empty wall on the other base of the gothic arch. A small sign notes that Bouchet was a physicist and educator. It also explains that he was the "first African American graduate of Yale College" (B.A., 1874) and the "first African American awarded a Ph.D. in the US" (Yale Ph.D., 1876). The portrait was completed in 1983. Bouchet's portrait is directly opposite the much larger portrait of one of Yale's greatest benefactors (whose gifts include the gothic Sterling Memorial Library), John William Sterling (B.A., 1864; M.A., 1874; LL.D. 1893).

This is not the place to relate the challenges that Bouchet faced, a brilliant scholar who deserved more opportunities than were made available to him. Suffice to say here that the empty wall space on the other side of the arch could be graced beautifully and meaningfully with a portrait of Henry Roe Cloud, the university's first full-blood American Indian graduate, celebrated as one of the greatest Indian leaders of his times. This Roe

Cloud memorial would be exactly opposite the large portrait of James
Gamble Rogers (B.A., 1889), architect of Sterling Memorial Library and
many other Yale buildings erected in the 1930s. Sometimes history needs
reminding.[1]

NOTES

ABBREVIATIONS

I cite articles, reviews, letters, and notes with the abbreviations below in the end-notes. Sometimes reference data about material included in archives is not complete (for instance, publication data or date of composition is missing). I present the reference data that is indicated in addition to relevant information about the material's location in the archives.

Archives of Individuals

JC   John Collier Papers, Manuscripts and Archives, Yale University Library

RFP   Roe Family Papers, Henry Roe Cloud Papers, Manuscripts and Archives, Yale University Library

RFPD   Roe Family Papers, Diaries, Manuscripts and Archives, Yale University Library

RHPP   Richard Henry Pratt Papers, Yale Collection of Western Americana, Beinecke Rare Book and Manuscript Library

Publications

IL   The Indian Leader, Sterling Memorial Library, Yale University

IO   The Indian Outlook, Yale Collection of Western Americana, Beinecke Rare Book and Manuscript Library

IW   Indians at Work, Yale Collection of Western Americana, Beinecke Rare Book and Manuscript Library

YDN   The Yale Daily News, Manuscripts and Archives, Yale University Library

The source of the volume's epigraph is Jimmie Durham (Cherokee), "Tarascan Guitars," in his *Columbus Day: Poems, Drawings and Stories about American Indian Life and Death in the Nineteen Seventies* (Minneapolis: West End Press, 1983), 48.

PREFACE

1 Joel Pfister, *Individuality Incorporated: Indians and the Multicultural Modern* (Durham: Duke University Press, 2004), especially see 57, 120–32. Also see Alice Littlefield, "Learning to Labor: Native American Education in the United States, 1880–1930," in *The Political Economy of North American Indians*, ed. John H. Moore (Norman: University of Oklahoma Press, 1993), 43–59.

2 Pfister, *The Production of Personal Life: Class, Gender, and the Psychological in Hawthorne's Fiction* (Stanford: Stanford University Press, 1991); Pfister, *Staging Depth: Eugene O'Neill and the Politics of Psychological Discourse* (Chapel Hill: University of North Carolina Press, 1995); Pfister, "On Conceptualizing a Cultural History of Emotional and Psychological Life in America," and "Glamorizing the Psychological" both in *Inventing the Psychological: Toward a Cultural History of Emotional Life in America*, ed. Joel Pfister and Nancy Schnog (New Haven: Yale University Press, 1997), 17–59, 167–213.

3 The Roe family papers in Manuscripts and Archives, Yale University's Sterling Memorial Library, are Manuscript Group Number 774 (http://mssa.library .yale.edu/findaides/stream.php?xmlfile=mssa.ms.0774.xml).

4 Jason M. Tetzloff, "To Do Some Good among the Indians: Henry Roe Cloud and Twentieth-Century Native American Advocacy" (Ph.D. diss., Purdue University, 1996).

5 On recent efforts to advance American Indian studies and American studies, see Michael A. Elliott, "Indians, Incorporated," *American Literary History* (Winter 2006): 141–59.

INTRODUCTION   CHAPTERS IN THE EDUCATION OF HENRY ROE CLOUD

Chapter epigraphs: Leonard Peltier, *Prison Writings: My Life Is My Sun Dance*, ed. Harvey Arden (New York: St. Martin's Griffin, 2000), 19. Parker is quoted in Lucy Maddox, *Citizen Indian: Native American Intellectuals, Race, and Reform* (Ithaca: Cornell University Press, 2005), 48.

1 Paul Radin, *The Winnebago Tribe* (Lincoln: University of Nebraska Press, 1970 [1923]), 179 (first published as part of the *Thirty-Seventh Annual Report of the Bureau of American Ethnology*, Smithsonian Institution, Washington D.C., 1923); Radin, *The Trickster: A Study in American Indian Mythology*, (New York: Philosophical Library, 1956), 115, 117.

2 See R. David Edmunds, ed., *The New Warriors: Native American Leaders since 1900* (Lincoln: University of Nebraska Press, 2001). In that volume, consult Frederick E. Hoxie and Tim Bernardis, "Robert Yellowtail/Crow," 55–77. Yellowtail was just a few years younger than Roe Cloud. Hoxie and Bernardis conclude: "[Yellowtail] was the first Crow leader whose influence was not rooted in battlefield achievements but in a new type of warfare: confrontations in tribal

council halls, government courtrooms, and congressional hearings" (76).
Also see Edmunds, "Introduction: Twentieth Century Warriors" to *New War-riors*, 1–15: "In the nineteenth century many tribes had warrior societies dedicated to protecting their people and their homelands. Today such societies still function, but their warriors are armed with briefcases rather than trade muskets" (14).

3 Lewis Meriam et al., *The Problem of Indian Administration* (Baltimore: Johns Hopkins University Press, 1928). Henceforth, all quotations from this book will be followed by page numbers in parentheses in the text. Michael C. Coleman, a superb historian, writes that the Meriam Report (1928) "was produced by a team—including the Winnebago Indian Henry Roe Cloud—under the directorship of Dr. Lewis Meriam" (*American Indians, the Irish, and Government Schooling: A Comparative Study* [Lincoln: University of Nebraska Press, 2007], 53). There are two very useful exceptions to this tendency: Steven James Crum (Shoshone-Paiute), "Henry Roe Cloud, A Winnebago Indian Reformer: His Quest for American Indian Higher Education," *Kansas History* 11 (Autumn 1988): 171–84. And Tetzloff, "To Do Some Good among the Indians." Tetzloff's dissertation focuses on Roe Cloud's career as an educator, fundraiser, reform advocate, survey investigator, and Bureau of Indian Affairs employee. He notes that the Winnebago tribal rolls indicate that Roe Cloud was born in 1882, not 1884, as Roe Cloud suggested (8).

4 Joy Porter, *To Be Indian: The Life of Iroquois-Seneca Arthur Caswell Parker* (Norman: University of Oklahoma Press, 2001), 95. David Wallace Adams's profile-in-passing is: "Henry Roe Cloud, a Winnebago who eventually graduated from Yale University and Auburn Theological Seminary" (*Education for Extinction: American Indians and the Boarding School Experience, 1875–1928* [Lawrence: University Press of Kansas, 1995], 152).

5 See Catherine Clay, "Henry Roe Cloud," in *Notable Native Americans*, ed. Sharon Malinowski (New York: Gale, 1995), 80–82, 81. Also see Stuart Levine, "Henry Roe Cloud," in *Dictionary of American Biography: Supplement Four*, ed. John A. Garraty and Edward T. Jones (New York: Scribner's, 1974), 165–66.

6 Roe Cloud, "Education of the American Indian," 16, in Manuscripts and Archives, Yale University Library.

7 W. E. B. Du Bois, *Dusk of Dawn: An Essay toward an Autobiography of a Race Concept* (New York: Schocken, 1968 [1940]), 62, 15. Also see Du Bois, *The Education of Black People*, ed. Herbert Aptheker (New York: Monthly Review Press, 2001 [1973]).

8 Du Bois, "The Talented Tenth," in Booker T. Washington, W. E. Burghardt Du Bois, Paul Laurence Dunbar, Charles W. Chesnutt, Wilford H. Smith, H. T. Kealing, and T. Thomas Fortune, *The Negro Problem: A Series of Articles by Representative American Negroes of To-day* (New York: James Pott, 1903), 33–75, see 33, 46, 48, 61.

9 I am grateful to Judith Schiff at the Yale University Manuscripts and Archives

library for sharing this article, which was sent to her years before; the citation is incomplete: Margaret Thompson, "From Wigwam to Mr. Bigwig," *The Sunday Oregonian* (Aug. 20, 1944): n.p. Also see Clay, "Henry Roe Cloud," in *Notable Native Americans*, ed. Malinowski, 81. Some whites also viewed Eastman as recognizably professional. One flier advertising his lecture reads: "If it were not for his bronzed features, one would take Dr. Eastman for the typical, hospitable New Englander" (quoted in Maddox, *Citizen Indian*, 33).

10   See Philip J. Deloria, "Vine V. Deloria Sr./Dakota," in *New Warriors*, ed. Edmunds, 79–95. Deloria writes that his grandfather had many "success stories," but "also had regrets. Federal Indian policy, his church's social outreach programs, Indian Christianity in general—it wasn't that all these important things had gone so terribly wrong; it was that they hadn't gone quite right. And there was the fact that, despite his best efforts, he had been helpless on so many critical occasions" (79). Success does not always mean achieving what one sets out to accomplish against the odds. It can mean standing up and being counted, or trying to stand up and get counted, in the face of bad odds.

11   For historical perspectives on the rise of this class in America, see Barbara Ehrenreich and John Ehrenreich, "The Professional-Managerial Class," 5–45, and "Rejoinder," 313–34, both in *Between Labor and Capital*, ed. Pat Walker (Boston: South End Press, 1979), Richard Ohmann, *Selling Culture: Magazines, Markets, and Class at the Turn of the Century* (New York: Verso, 1996), and Burton J. Bledstein, *The Culture of Professionalism: The Middle Class and the Development of Higher Education in America* (New York: Norton, 1976).

12   For three fine examples of what can be done in this field, see Hazel W. Hertzberg's groundbreaking study, *Search for an American Indian Identity: Modern Pan-Indian Movements* (Syracuse: Syracuse University Press, 1971); Devon Mihesuah's, *Cultivating the Rosebuds: The Education of Women at the Cherokee Female Seminary, 1851–1909* (Urbana: University of Illinois Press, 1993); and K. Tsianina Lomawaima's *They Called It Prairie Light: The Story of Chilocco School* (Lincoln: University of Nebraska Press, 1994). And for some lucid theoretical and methodological comments on the significance of assessing class boundaries in research on Indian schools, see Genevieve Bell's brilliant study "Telling Stories out of School: Remembering the Carlisle Indian Industrial School, 1870–1918" (Ph.D. diss., Stanford University, 1998), 116–17. On reconceptualizing class, see Genovese, *In Red and Black: Marxian Explorations in Southern and Afro-American History* (New York: Pantheon, 1971), 356. Roe Cloud's Society of American Indians presentation is quoted in Hertzberg, *Search for an American Indian Identity*, 67–68. For reflections on the differences and affinities between American Indian social critique and Marxist critique, see Ward Churchill (Creek, enrolled Keetowah Band Cherokee), "False Promises: An Indigenist Perspective on Marxist Theory and Practice," in his *From a Native Son: Selected Essays on Indigenism, 1985–1995* (Boston: South End, 1996), 461–82, and "Marxism and the Native American," in *Marxism and Native Americans*, ed.

Ward Churchill (Boston: South End Press, 1983), 183–203; and Pfister, *Individuality Incorporated*, 254–56, 319–20. Also consult the wide-ranging and provocative collection of essays in the "Forum: Native Feminisms without Apology," *American Quarterly* 60 June (2008): 241–315, especially the superb introduction by Andrea Smith (Cherokee) and J. Kehaulani Kauanui (Kanaka Maoli), "Native Feminisms Engage American Studies," 241–49; and Renya K. Ramirez (Winnebago), "Learning across Differences: Native and Ethnic Studies Feminisms," 303–7. Ramirez writes that her studies of scholarship produced by "U.S. women of color" and "Third World women" have underscored the importance of emphasizing the intersectional relationship between race, ethnicity, gender, sexuality, class, and nation" (305).

13 Edmunds, "Introduction" to *New Warriors*, ed. Edmunds, 1–15.

14 Richard Slotkin, *Gunfighter Nation: The Myth of the Frontier in Twentieth-Century America* (New York: Atheneum, 1992), 13 (also see 19–21, 29–32); and Slotkin, *The Fatal Environment: The Myth of the Frontier in the Age of Industrialization, 1800–1890* (Middletown, Conn.: Wesleyan University Press, 1986 [1985]), especially 466–69 and 352–55.

15 Porter, *To Be Indian*, 111, 117, 115, 116, 119.

16 Comparing the U.S. government's Indian boarding school students to Irish students in Ireland's British government–sponsored assimilationist day schools in the late-nineteenth-century and early twentieth, Michael Coleman writes: "Indians were so culturally different that they existed quite outside of conventional class ideas. Yet like their Irish counterparts, most white American educators also saw the mass of Indians as entering civilization near the bottom: 'proletarianized' as farmers, laborers, wives, and domestics, and perhaps teachers, with a few fortunate and gifted individuals rising into more elevated social levels" (*American Indians, the Irish, and Government Schooling*, 268). Coleman represents Indians both as a group perceived by dominant whites as "culturally different" and as a group that the government itself sought to "proletarianize." Did some Indians in boarding schools recognize full well, like Coleman and a few other historians, that they were being funneled into what amounted to a (mostly rural) Indian working class ("proletarianized")? And did some of these Indians, as "culturally different" as they may have appeared to some, strive consciously and ardently to move into the professional and managerial class and the halls of power to work on behalf of Indians? My research for *Individuality Incorporated* and *The Yale Indian* suggests that this was the case and that *class identity and mobility were an Indian concern and a tactic* that should also be a concern of historians who wish to comprehend and value what many white-collar Indians tried to achieve and actually achieved.

17 Maddox, *Citizen Indian*, 4, 7; also see 17–53 for a discussion of "show Indians" and how performance suffused Indian lives and survival strategies. In addition, consult Pfister, *Individuality Incorporated*, 97–132.

18 Philip J. Deloria, "Vine V. Deloria Sr./Dakota," in *New Warriors*, ed. Edmunds, 79, 85. The psychologist James Averill analyzes cultural "rules of emotion" in "The Acquisition of Emotions during Adulthood," in *The Social Construction of Emotion*, ed. Rom Harré (Oxford: Basil Blackwell, 1986), 113.

19 Maddox writes: "The enthusiasm with which the Native intellectuals prepared to enter the public debates was tempered in time by their experience of the entrenched paternalism of white elites, who refused to acknowledge the legitimacy of intellectual traditions other than their own, even when they were represented by individuals who could speak the same progressive, developmental language of reform as did the whites." And she quotes Parker: " 'The Indian, no, does not need to be white washed or whitemanized. He needs an opportunity to develop along his own lines of individuality so far as these are consistent with modern environment. And remember we are not the bleached out devitalized enervated de-Indianized Indian or the new Indian but the same old Indian adjusted to modern environment.' " Maddox notes another performance: "Indian intellectuals had to demonstrate that they could *act* in ways that white America would approve and find unremarkable—in effect, to perform a new civic identity" (*Citizen Indian*, 15, 32, 62).

20 See Michael C. Coleman, *American Indian Children at School, 1850–1930* (Jackson: University Press of Mississippi, 1993), and *American Indians, the Irish, and Government Schooling*; Adams, *Education for Extinction*; Robert A. Trennert Jr., *The Phoenix Indian School: Forced Assimilation in Arizona: 1891–1935* (Norman: University of Oklahoma Press, 1988); Lomawaima, *They Called It Prairie Light*; Delores J. Huff, *To Live Heroically: Institutional Racism and American Indian Education* (Albany: State University Press of New York, 1997); Bell, "Telling Stories out of School"; Clyde Ellis, *To Change Them Forever: Indian Education at the Rainy Mountain Boarding School, 1893–1920* (Norman: University of Oklahoma Press, 1996).

21 Consult Pfister, *Individuality Incorporated*, 31–95.

22 Excerpted in Karl Marx and Frederick Engels, *On Literature and Art* (Moscow: Progress Publishers, 1976), 140. Weber, *The Protestant Ethic and the Spirit of Capitalism* (New York: Scribner's, 1958 [1905]).

23 See Maddox, *Citizen Indian*, 65–77. Maddox observes: "It may well have been because of this desire not to be classed with African Americans as part of the country's race problem that the Indian intellectuals and reformers did not address themselves in any significant way to the theories of race that were emerging in the early part of the century" (77).

24 Porter, *To Be Indian*, 92, 127–28.

25 Henry Louis Gates Jr. notes some of the complexities of Fanon's career that highlight the specificity of his anticolonialist efforts: "We know from his biographers that Fanon, whose mother was of Alsatian descent, grew up in Martinique thinking of himself as white and French: and that his painful reconstitution as a black West Indian occurred only when he arrived at the

French capital." Fanon, upset, never returned to Martinique. Interestingly, "most Algerian revolutionaries scant his role [in the Algerian struggle against the French] and remain irritated by the attention paid to him in the West as a figure in Algerian decolonization: to them—and how ironic this is to his Western admirers—he remained a European interloper. Though he worked as a psychiatrist in Algeria and Tunisia, in neither country did he even understand the language: his psychiatric consultations were conducted through an interpreter" ("Critical Fanonism," *Critical Inquiry* 17 [Spring 1991], 457–70, see 468).

26 See Pfister, *Individuality Incorporated*, 25–26, 141–42, for comments on the use of the word protomulticulturalism, and 136–251 on the Indian New Deal as a modern protomulticultural development. On what I term "diversity capitalism" and "diversity Americanization," consult Joel Pfister, "Transnational American Studies for What?," *Comparative American Studies* 6 (2008): 13–36, see 27–30.

27 See Pfister, *Individuality Incorporated*, 230–33; 25–27, 141–42, 225–27; 189–245; 203.

28 Porter, *To Be Indian*, 113.

29 On their first meeting, see Mary Roe's diary, Nov. 11, 1906, RFPD.

30 Hertzberg is quoted in Katherine Ellinghaus, *Taking Assimilation to Heart: Marriages of White Women to Indian Men in the United States and Australia, 1887–1937* (Lincoln: University of Nebraska Press, 2006), 46; see Hertzberg, *Search for an American Indian Identity*, 58, for elaboration.

31 Terry Eagleton makes two generalizations that resonate with my point. "Works of art which seem most innocent of power, in their sedulous attention to motions of the heart, may serve power for precisely that reason." Culture, he contends, is "a process lived in the pulses rather than in the mind" (*The Idea of Culture* [Malden, Mass.: Blackwell, 2000], 50, 113). Ellinghaus has argued that, while "histories of assimilation in the United States" have studied "government legislation and social policy," the history "of how people negotiated their lives within that framework is often neglected" (*Taking Assimilation to Heart*, 220).

32 Ellinghaus, *Taking Assimilation to Heart*, xiii.

33 For the story of a contemporary Winnebago activist and Christian spiritual leader, see Reuben Snake as told to Jay C. Fikes, *Reuben Snake Your Humble Serpent: Indian Visionary and Activist* (Santa Fe, N. Mex.: Clear Light, 1996).

34 Philip Deloria, "Thinking About Self in a Family Way," *Journal of American History* 89 (June 2002): 25–29, see 27–28.

35 See C. Wright Mills on elite networks and networking of the wealthy and powerful in *The Power Elite* (New York: Oxford University Press, 2000 [1956]).

36 Eastman, *Indian Heroes and Great Chieftains* (Mineola, N.Y.: Dover, 1997 [1918]), 80, 12, 2, 74, 52, 41, 67, 19, 77.

37 Radin, *The Trickster*, 114. H. David Brumble III reprints and comments on

Hensley's two brief autobiographical statements in his chapter "Albert Hensley: Alternate Versions of the Self" in his *American Indian Autobiography* (Berkeley: University of California Press, 1988), 130–46. Brumble emphasizes that Hensley's "autobiographies" were shaped by Winnebago oral traditions, that they differ from one another in important ways, "each tailored for a particular audience and occasion," and that they demonstrate "how early in their acculturation Indians could make use of autobiographical forms for their own purposes" (145).

38   Radin, *Winnebago Tribe*, 347–50, 372–74. Hazel Hertzberg writes that many Winnebago peyotists had some schooling: "By 1911, the number of peyotists in the Winnebago tribe had increased until it matched the conservatives, with Christians in a minority. The peyotists were 'the most prosperous members of the tribe' and the best businessmen." Roe Cloud, whom Hertzberg quotes, recognized that the peyote religion appealed to " 'the younger men of the tribe because it offered more leadership to them, whereas the conservative Medicine Lodge is composed largely of the old men of the tribe and does not offer much opportunity to the younger men' " (*Search for an American Indian Identity*, 249). She also observes that the Winnebago peyote religion "had a good deal in common with Protestantism, especially Protestant fundamentalism, and was considered by its members to be a Christian faith" (248).

39   Consult Brumble's chapter on Crashing Thunder, "Sam Blowsnake: Adapting Oral Forms to Written Autobiography," in his *American Indian Autobiography*, 118–29, and see Lamere's comment about Hensley and Rave, quoted on 125. On Crashing Thunder/Sam Carley/Sam Blowsnake, Lamere, and the Winnebago syllabic alphabet ("borrowed" from the Sauk and Fox), see Christer Lindberg, "Paul Radin: The Anthropologist Trickster," *European Review of Native American Studies* 14 (2000), n.p.

40   Quoted in Ellinghaus, *Taking Assimilation to Heart*, 63.

41   On the traditional Indian ethos of giving and redistribution, see Pfister, *Individuality Incorporated*, 104–7.

42   Geertz is quoted in Jace Weaver, *That the People Might Live: Native American Literatures and Native American Community* (New York: Oxford University Press, 1997), 39. For a more extensive discussion of kinship epistemologies, values, and forms of subjectivity, see Calvin Luther Martin, ed., *The American Indian and the Problem of History* (New York: Oxford University Press, 1987); and Martin, *In the Spirit of the Earth: Rethinking History and Time* (Baltimore: Johns Hopkins University Press, 1992), and *The Way of the Human Being* (New Haven: Yale University Press, 1999). Also see Pfister, *Individuality Incorporated*, 248–51, 105–13, and more generally the chapter, "The School of Savagery: 'Indian' Formations of Subjectivity and Carlisle," 97–132.

43   No Yale personnel have been able to locate Roe Cloud's master's thesis.

44   Here I am indebted to the work of Clyde Holler on Black Elk (Sioux), *Black Elk's*

Religion: The Sun Dance and Lakota Catholicism (Syracuse: Syracuse University Press, 1995), 213, 211. For further thoughts on this see Pfister, *Individuality Incorporated*, 127, 124. On Robert Yellowtail's religious simultaneity of beliefs —his ties to Catholicism, Protestant denominations, Crow religious societies, traditional Crow healers—see Hoxie and Bernardis, "Robert Yellowtail/ Crow," 55–77, especially 58 in *New Warriors*, ed. Edmunds. See Philip J. Deloria, "Vine V. Deloria Sr./Dakota," in *New Warriors*, ed. Edmunds, 79, 82. He writes that his grandfather's "Dakota parishioners . . . tended to reject the rigid Christian/pagan boundaries laid down by conventional missionaries, letting Christian and traditional beliefs and practices overlap and come together to create something new" (82).

45 Michael Denning's observation about E. P. Thompson's classic, *The Making of the English Working Class* (1963), addresses this challenge. "The sources are clouded, Thompson reminds us, because working people meant them to be clouded." Consequently, Thompson holds that readers must " 'read, not only between the lines of the letters sent in, but also the letters which were never sent' " (Thompson quoted in *Culture in the Age of Three Worlds* [New York: Verso, 2004], 40). This is an important interpretive goal, though it remains a speculation.

46 On the politics of representing Indians in history writing see Steven Crum, "Making Indians Disappear: A Native American Historian's Views Regarding the Treatment of Indians in American History," *Tribal College: A Journal of American Indian Higher Education* 4 (Winter 1992–93): 28–31.

47 Philip J. Deloria, "Thinking about Self in a Family Way," 27–28.

ONE YALE EDUCATION

1 In "To Do Some Good among the Indians," Jason M. Tetzloff discusses Roe Cloud's experience at Yale (21–27), mentions Roe Cloud's visits to Princeton and Wesleyan (20), and observes that Roe Cloud and others often noted his affiliation with Yale (26).

2 Quoted in Michael Coleman, *American Indians, the Irish, and Government Schooling*, 153.

3 Thomas Jefferson Morgan, *Indian Education* (Washington D.C.: Government Printing Office, 1890), 12–13. Morgan graduated from Franklin College and Rochester Theological Seminary, and later joined the faculty at Baptist Union Theological Seminary. On the backgrounds of commissioners Morgan, Jones, and Leupp, see Francis Paul Prucha, "Thomas Jefferson Morgan 1889–93" (193–203), W. David Baird, "William A. Jones, 1897–1904" (211–20), and Donald L. Parman, "Francis Ellington Leupp 1905–1909" (221–32) in *The Commissioners of Indian Affairs, 1824–1977*, ed. Robert M. Kvasnicka and Herman J. Viola (Lincoln: University of Nebraska Press, 1979). Jones was a

Welsh immigrant who, after graduating from normal school, entered the
school system as a teacher, and later became a county superintendent. He
moved on to banking and purchased the largest zinc oxide works in the
country with his two brothers, both of whom were Princeton graduates and
prosperous lawyers in Illinois (211). On education in handy tinkering, see
Leupp, "Outline of an Indian Policy," *The Arrow* 1 (April 20, 1905): n.p. Leupp's
undated comments about "ancestry and environment" and Jones's position
are quoted in Bell, "Telling Stories out of School," 83.

4 See Yellowtail, "The Indian and His Problem," *Red Man* 5 (May 1913): 412–16.
Thomas Sloan, "The Indian's Protection and His Place as an American," *Red
Man* 4 (May 1912): 398–403, see 399. Also see Steven James Crum, "Crow
Warrior: Robert Yellowtail Was a Life-Long Advocate of Native Higher Educa-
tion," *Tribal College: Journal of American Indian Higher Education* 1 (Spring 1990):
19–23. On Sloan and Yale Law School, see Ellinghaus, *Taking Assimilation to
Heart*, 3.

5 The *Quarterly Journal of the Society of American Indians* is quoted in Ellinghaus,
Taking Assimilation to Heart, 45. Writing about the 1890s and very early 1900s,
Ellinghaus argues that "a number of factors combined to make this period a
brief moment in which it was not impossible for a Native American man to
attend college, enter a profession, and marry a white woman," partly because
of "the philosophies of mainstream education that had come to fruition
during this period" (17). Perhaps the best that can be said is that institutions
like Hampton Institute and Carlisle contributed to a federal "policy that gave
some Native American men the opportunity to reach high levels of education"
(22). Still, many Indians found unacceptable those conditions under which it
was "not impossible" for "some Native American men" to matriculate in
high school and for very few Indians to make it to and through college. By
the mid-1890s, Ellinghaus notes, a few boarding schools such as Carlisle,
Haskell, and Santa Fe "offered courses of study beyond the basic eight-year
program" (20).

6 Standing Bear, *Land of the Spotted Eagle* (Boston: Houghton Mifflin, 1933),
240, and "The Tragedy of the Sioux," *The American Mercury* (November 1931):
273–78.

7 Ellinghaus, *Taking Assimilation to Heart*, 42.

8 Du Bois, *The Souls of Black Folk* (New York: New American Library, 1982
[1903]), 51.

9 In the 1650s the English "Society for the Promoting and Propagating of the
Gospel in New England" donated funds to Harvard College so that it could
educate Indians. Harvard built a two-story brick "Indian College" in the
mid-1650s. The college admitted Caleb Cheeshahteaumuck (Wampanoag),
age 15, and Joel Iacoomes (Wampanoag), age 16, who were born on the island
of Noe'pe' (Martha's Vineyard) and schooled in Cambridge, in 1661. Both

excelled in their program and studied Latin, Greek, and Hebrew. In 1665, Cheeshahteaumuck became the first Indian to graduate from Harvard, but died from tuberculosis just one year later. Iacoomes perished in a shipwreck before he graduated. Notwithstanding this beginning, Harvard took in few Indian students after these two and demolished the Indian College in 1698 (although it had to promise the Society for the Propagating of the Gospel that henceforth it would allow Indian students to study at Harvard "rent free"). Harvard did not develop a strong reputation for educating Indians. I thank Ande Diaz for sending me the article by Lorie M. Graham, "The Indian College: First Native Americans at Harvard," *Harvard College News* 9 (Spring 1997): 16–17. Dartmouth College, chartered in 1769 and opened in 1770, was established by Eleazar Wheelock, a graduate of Yale and a Congregational minister who was dedicated to giving Indians an education—at a certain level. Andrew Garrod and Colleen Larimore write: "As well as founding Dartmouth College, [Eleazar Wheelock] relocated Moor's Charity School from Lebanon, Connecticut, to the Dartmouth campus. Segregated and unequal, the former Moor's school was for the Indians; otherwise, Dartmouth was reserved for the sons of Englishmen. . . . Wheelock's first Indian student, Samuel Occum, campaigned throughout Europe to raise the £12,000 with which Wheelock launched his academic endeavor. To Occum's dismay, and without the knowledge of the college's benefactors abroad, Wheelock placed growing emphasis on the education of white students. . . . By 1969 Dartmouth had graduated just nineteen Native Americans" ("Introduction," *First Person, First Peoples: Native American College Graduates Tell Their Life Stories*, ed. Andrew Garrod and Colleen Larimore [Ithaca: Cornell University Press, 1997], 1–19, see 7–8). Momaday is quoted in Patricia Penn Hilden, *When Nickels Were Indians: An Urban, Mixed-Blood Story* (Washington D.C.: Smithsonian Institution Press, 1995), 126–27. On the links between British imperialism in India and the founding of Yale College, see Hiram Bingham, *Elihu Yale: The American Nabob of Queen Square* (New York: Dodd, Mead, 1939), and Gauri Viswanathan, "The Naming of Yale College: British Imperialism and American Higher Education," in *Cultures of United States Imperialism*, ed. Amy Kaplan and Donald E. Pease (Durham: Duke University Press, 1993), 85–108.

10 See Henry Milner Rideout, *William Jones: Indian, Cowboy, American Scholar, and Antrhopologist in the Field* (New York: Frederick A. Stokes, 1912), and Daniel F. Littlefield Jr. and James W. Parins, *A Biobibliography of Native American Writers 1772–1924: A Supplement* (Metuchen, N.J.: Scarecrow Press, 1985), 217, 235.

11 See Raymond Wilson, *Ohiyesa: Charles Eastman, Santee Sioux* (Urbana: University of Illinois Press, 1983), 32.

12 Eastman, *The Indian To-day: The Past and Future of the First American* (Garden City, N.Y.: Doubleday, Page, 1915), 66, 115, 116, 119, 125; he profiles or lists eminent Indians, 121–30.

13 On schools and the unequal distribution of cultural capital, see John Guillory, *Cultural Capital: The Problem of Literary Canon Formation* (Chicago: University of Chicago Press, 1993), 61, 77.

14 John Joseph Mathews, *Sundown* (Norman: University of Oklahoma Press, 1988), 281.

15 See Clay, "Henry Roe Cloud," in *Notable Native Americans*, ed. Malinowski, 80. Also see J. Frederick Dockstader, *Great North American Indians* (New York: Van Nostrand Reinhold, 1977), 51–52.

16 See Roe Cloud's pamphlet, "From Wigwam to Pulpit: A Red Man's Story of His Progress from Darkness to Light" (n.p: Woman's Board of Home Missions of the Presbyterian Church in the U.S.A., 1916), 7: henceforth all quotations from this pamphlet will be followed by page numbers in parenthesis in the text, unless noted otherwise. The piece was originally published in Hampton Institute's *Southern Workman* (July 1916): 400–406. A superintendent of Roe Cloud's reservation named him Clarence Cloud (Tetzloff, "To Do Some Good among the Indians," 8). He also observes that Roe Cloud spent his first years with his mother Hard-To-See, grandmother Good Feather Woman, step-father Yellow Cloud, brother (or brother-in-law?) Anson, and half-sister Susan (9). The reservation superintendent appointed "Honest" John Nunn as Roe Cloud's guardian (14). I thank Colin Hampson for his research in the Roe Cloud family records, which brought to light the ambiguity about Anson's relationship to Roe Cloud. Littlefield and Parins, in their biographical note about Roe Cloud, only mention his father in passing (*Biobibliography of Native American Writers*, 191).

17 Radin, *Trickster*, 1, 5, and *Winnebago Tribe*, 112–13.

18 Nancy Oestreich Lurie discusses the colonial fate of French envoys and the tribe in "Winnebago," in *Handbook of North American Indians*, vol. 15 Northeast, ed. Bruce C. Trigger (Washington, D.C.: Smithsonian, 1978), 690–91. Also see Radin, *Winnebago Tribe*, 6.

19 Helen Hunt Jackson, *A Century of Dishonor: A Sketch of the United States Government's Dealings with Some of the Indian Tribes* (Williamstown, Mass.: Corner House Publishers, 1973 [1880]), 256; see also 218–56, especially 222–25, 230–31, 243–44.

20 Frederick E. Hoxie, *A Final Promise: The Campaign to Assimilate the Indians, 1880–1920* (Lincoln: University of Nebraska Press, 1984), 43.

21 Lurie, "Winnebago," in *Handbook*, ed. Trigger, 700, 701. For background on Winnebago history, treaties, land claims, and ethnographic work, see two book-length post–Second World War reports by J. A. Jones, "An Anthropological Report on the Indian Occupancy of Royce Areas 149, 174, and 245" and by Alice E. Smith and Vernon Carstensen, "Report of Economic and Historical background for the Winnebago Indian Claims" (Royce Areas 149, 174, 243) reprinted in J. A. Jones, Alice E. Smith, and Vernon Carstensen, *Winnebago Indians* (New York: Garland, 1974).

22 Hoxie, *Final Promise*, 43.

23 Ibid., 80. For insight into the stakes and strategies of the U.S. assimilation project earlier in the nineteenth century, see Priscilla Wald, "Terms of Assimilation: Legislating Subjectivity in the Emerging Nation," in *American Indian Persistence and Resurgence*, ed. Karl Kroeber (Durham: Duke University Press, 1994), 78–105.

24 Lindberg, "Paul Radin," n.p. If Roe Cloud had met Radin among the Winnebago, could such a meeting have contributed to his interest in anthropology?

25 Radin, *The Culture of the Winnebago: As Described by Themselves* (Baltimore: Bollingen Foundation, Indiana University Publications, 1949), 1, 2. Also see David Lee Smith, *Folklore of the Winnebago Tribe* (Norman: University of Oklahoma Press, 1997).

26 Radin, *The Social Organization of the Winnebago Indians, An Interpretation* (Ottawa: Government Printing Bureau, 1915), 38.

27 See [Sam Blowsnake], *Crashing Thunder: The Autobiography of an American Indian*, ed. Paul Radin (New York: D. Appleton, 1920), 59, 68, 103.

28 Radin writes: "[Religion] is not a phenomenon distinct from mundane life, but one of the most important means of maintaining social ideals" (*Winnebago Tribe*, 230).

29 Consult Radin's "Preface" (vii–xi) and "Introduction" (xv–xxv) to *Crashing Thunder*, ed. Radin. See ix on missionaries.

30 It is likely that Radin and Roe Cloud were on the reservation at the same time, for Roe Cloud spent much time on the reservation during his Yale years, especially during the summers. Roe Cloud, "The Winnebago Situation," *Word Carrier of Santee Normal Training School* 38 (July–August 1909): 13.

31 *Crashing Thunder*, ed. Radin, 5, 13, 60, 65. On his performances, see 29, 11, 126. Even the Winnebago in one family—Crashing Thunder and his younger sister, Mountain Wolf Woman—were not always uniform. On Crashing Thunder's relationship to Mountain Wolf Woman, see Nancy Oestreich Lurie, "Afterword B," in Mountain Wolf Woman, *Mountain Wolf Woman: Sister of Crashing Thunder: The Autobiography of a Winnebago Indian*, ed. Nancy Oestreich Lurie (Ann Arbor: University of Michigan Press, 1961), 92–108. Lurie writes: "Crashing Thunder's need for personal recognition and ego gratification stands in sharp contrast to Mountain Wolf Woman's security in this regard" (99).

32 See Brumble, *American Indian Autobiography*, 118–29, especially 121.

33 On Genoa, see Tetzloff, "To Do Some Good among Indians," 10–12. After two years at Genoa, Roe Cloud attended the Winnebago Industrial School located in Macy, Nebraska.

34 On Roe Cloud's parents, consult Sheridan Fahnestock and Thomas Charles Sorci, "Henry Roe Cloud," in *American National Biography*, vol. 5 (New York: Oxford University Press, 1999), 85–87. Radin, *Winnebago Tribe*, 230. Radin also notes that there are parallels between the Christian idea of the one true

God and the Winnebago concept of "the supreme deity, Earthmaker" (*Trick-ster*, 115).

35 Coleman, *Presbyterian Attitudes toward American Indians, 1837–1893* (Jackson: University Press of Mississippi, 1985), 82; also see 81.

36 Philip J. Deloria, "Vine V. Deloria Sr.," in *New Warriors*, ed. Edmunds, 80–82, quote is on 81. Also see Willard Hughes Rollings, "Indians and Christianity," in *A Companion to American Indian History*, ed. Philip J. Deloria and Neal Salis-bury (Malden, Mass.: Blackwell, 2002), 121–38.

37 Memmi, *The Colonizer and the Colonized*, trans. Howard Greenfeld (Boston: Beacon Press, 1991 [1957]), 99, 101.

38 Roe Cloud, "A Santee Pupil at Yale!" *Word Carrier of Santee Normal Training School* 35 (November–December 1906): 22, and "Alfred Longley Riggs," *Word Carrier of Santee Normal Training School* 45 (July–August 1916): 14. On Santee, see Elaine Goodale Eastman, *Pratt: The Red Man's Moses* (Norman: University of Oklahoma Press, 1935), 119–20. She also notes that in 1881 Dr. Stephen Riggs, Dr. Sheldon Jackson (head of Presbyterian missions in the Midwest), Pratt, and some other "reformers" collaborated in the "preparation of a memorial on Indian rights" that they presented to the President of the United States. It supported the education of all Indian children in government schools "on the ground that 'our government cannot afford to raise anymore Indians'" (121). With Santee in mind, Eastman concluded: "In all these [mis-sion] schools, even those where the material equipment is insufficient, there is more emphasis upon character-building, more of permanence and in gen-eral higher qualifications in the teaching force than under government" (*In-dian To-day*, 75). Tetzloff notes that Roe Cloud was one of eight Winnebago boys to attend Santee and the only one who remained after a couple of weeks. Santee offered students some high school level courses ("To Do Some Good among the Indians," 14–16).

39 Consult James F. Findlay Jr., *Dwight L. Moody: American Evangelist 1837–1899* (Chicago: University of Chicago Press, 1969). Tetzloff observes that Roe Cloud studied Latin, German, and Greek at Mount Hermon, a course of study that most Indian schools not only omitted but considered unuseful for pro-spective farmers and skilled and semi-skilled workers ("To Do Some Good among the Indians," 18–21).

40 See Asa Briggs, "Self-Help: A Centenary Introduction" in Samuel Smiles, *Self-Help with Illustrations of Conduct and Perseverance* (London: John Murray, 1958), 7.

41 Smiles, *Self-Help*, 37, 35, 51. On the ideology of self-help see Judy Hilkey, *Character as Capital: Success Manuals and Manhood in Gilded Age America* (Chapel Hill: University of North Carolina Press, 1997); John G. Cawelti, *Apostles of the Self-Made Man* (Chicago: University of Chicago Press, 1968); David Brion Davis, "Stress-Seeking and the Self-Made Man in American Literature, 1894–1914," in David Brion Davis, *From Homicide to Slavery: Studies in American Culture*

(New York: Oxford University Press, 1986), 52–72; Irvin G. Wylie, *The Self-Made Man in America: The Myth of Rags to Riches* (New York: Free Press, 1954); Richard Weiss, *The American Myth of Success: From Horatio Alger to Norman Vincent Peale* (New York: Basic, 1969); Rex Burns, *Success in America: The Yeoman Dream and the Industrial Revolution* (Amherst: University of Massachusetts Press, 1976).

42 Briggs, "Self Help," in Smiles, *Self-Help*, 28. Also on Smiles, see Hilkey, *Character Is Capital*, 91, 97, 124, 138–41.

43 Smiles is quoted in Hilkey, *Character is Capital*, 108.

44 Pierson, *Yale College: An Educational History 1871–1921* (New Haven: Yale University Press, 1952), 269.

45 Ibid., 117–20.

46 Radin, *Winnebago Tribe*, 118.

47 Pierson, *Yale College*, 271–74. Pierson notes that around 1909, "individuals were beginning to suggest that the all-round Yale man should be a good student as well as a social success" (348). Also see Brooks Mather Kelley, *Yale: A History* (New Haven: Yale University Press, 1974), 315–47.

48 In the words of Pierson: "Yale's future captains of industry and finance found the informal, romantic, competitive college life incomparably exciting and important—the perfect training ground for success in our confident acquisitive society" (*Yale College*, 269).

49 For instance, consult "The University's Finances," *YDN* (September 27, 1906): 4; "Development of the College," *YDN* (September 29, 1909): 1, 2, 7; "Devotion to Ideals," *YDN* (October 4, 1909): 1, 3, 5.

50 See, for example, "The Immigrant," *YDN* (February 16, 1907): 1; "Child Labor Problem," *YDN* (March 20, 1907): 1, 3; "Socialism: Dr. Lyman Abbott's Address Last Evening," *YDN* (November 29, 1909): 1–4. Booker T. Washington, a friend of Abbott, noted in 1901 that he had served as "the pastor of Plymouth Church, and also editor of the *Outlook* (then the *Christian Union*)" (*Up From Slavery* [New York: Lancer, 1968 (1901)], 229).

51 Mary Roe diary, June 22, 1910, RFPD.

52 Hadley is quoted at length in "Devotion to Ideals," *YDN* (October 4, 1909): 1, 3, 5, see 5.

53 "Summa Cum Laude," *YDN* (March 17, 1910): 1.

54 Stanhope Bayne-Jones, "Sophomore Year," in *History of the Class of 1910, Yale College*, vol. 1, ed. Robert Dudley French (New Haven: Yale University, 1910), 19–24, see 24.

55 "Defense of Wall Street: Henry Clews Speaks before Social Conditions Class," *YDN* (March 8, 1910): 1.

56 "The Industrial Movement," *YDN* (April 11, 1910): 1.

57 See Sydney E. Ahlstrom, *A Religious History of the American People* (New Haven: Yale University Press, 1972), 295–96, and Kelley, *Yale*, 3–4.

58 Auchincloss, "Yale and the Individual," *The Yale Literary Magazine* 72 (May 1907): 317–19, see 317.

59 Auchincloss, "Yale and the Individual," 318. On the rise of American therapeutic individualism, see T. J. Jackson Lears, "From Salvation to Self-Realization: Advertising and the Therapeutic Roots of Consumer Culture, 1880–1930," in *The Culture of Consumption: Critical Essays in American History, 1880–1930*, ed. Richard Fox and T. J. Jackson Lears (New York: Pantheon, 1983), 1–38, see 34; Christopher Lasch, *The Culture of Narcissism: American Life in an Age of Diminishing Expectations* (New York: Warner, 1979); Philip Rieff, *The Triumph of the Therapeutic: Uses of Faith after Freud* (New York: Harper & Row, 1966) and "Reflections on Psychological Man in America," in Rieff, *The Feeling Intellect: Selected Writings*, ed. Jonathan B. Imber (Chicago: University of Chicago Press, 1990), 3–10; Richard Sennett, *The Fall of Public Man: On the Social Psychology of Capitalism* (New York: Vintage, 1978); Jackson Lears, *Fables of Abundance: A Cultural History of Advertising in America* (New York: Basic, 1994); Pfister, "Glamorizing the Psychological," in *Inventing the Psychological*, ed. Pfister and Schnog, 167–213; Pfister, *Staging Depth*.

60 Auchincloss, "Yale and the Individual," 319.

61 On hero worshipping see James, "The Importance of Individuals," in his *The Will to Believe and Other Essays in Popular Philosophy* (London: Longmans, Green, 1911), 255–61, see 257, James, "The Social Value of the College-Bred" (given as an address in 1907, published 1908), 309–25, and "The Ph.D. Octopus" (1903), 329–47. On geniuses and universities, see James, "Stanford's Ideal Destiny" (1906), 356–67, see especially 362–63 in his *Memories and Sketches* (London: Longmans, Green, 1912) and also James, *As William James Said: Extracts from the Published Writings of William James*, ed. Elizabeth Perkins Aldrich (New York: Vanguard, 1942), 27, 29, 42–43, 155, 164, 169.

62 James, "The True Harvard" (1903), in *Memories and Sketches*, 348–55, see 354–55.

63 C. B. T., "Yale Individuality: Prevailing Topic in Current Number of the Lit.," *YDN* (May 20, 1907): 1, 4, see 1.

64 On republican civic individualism and liberal individualism, consult Robert Bellah, Richard Madsen, William M. Sullivan, Ann Swidler, and Steven M. Tipton, *Habits of the Heart: Individualism and Commitment in American Life* (New York: Harper & Row, 1985). Johnson, *Stover at Yale* (New York: Collier, 1968). Henceforth, quotations from this novel will be followed by page numbers in parenthesis in the text.

65 As George Wilson Pierson observes, there was in fact anxiety at Yale about its institutional failure to nurture great writers. Yale's golden age of Jonathan Edwards and the Connecticut Wits (and somewhat later James Fenimore Cooper, expelled in 1806) had long passed. A significant if not spectacular Yale literary renaissance commenced just at the point Roe Cloud left Yale in

1910 (Sinclair Lewis '07, Waldo Frank '11, Archibald MacLeish '15, Philip Barry '16, Thornton Wilder '20, and others) (Yale College, 358–66, 299).

66 Ibid., 365, 366. In his chapter on Benjamin Franklin in Studies in Classic American Literature (1923), D. H. Lawrence, when evoking the transgressive exploration of one's "many selves," asked skeptically, sardonically, and, he thought, ever so radically: "Is Yale College going to educate the self that is in the dark of you, or Harvard College?" On balance, the modern answer was yes (Studies in Classic American Literature [New York: Viking, 1961], 9).

67 Veblen, The Theory of the Leisure Class (New York: New American Library, 1953 [1899]).

68 See John C. Burnham, "The New Psychology," 117–27; Sanford Gifford, "The American Reception of Psychoanalysis, 1908–1922," in 1915, The Cultural Moment: The New Politics, The New Woman, The New Psychology, The New Art, and The New Theatre in America, ed. Adele Heller and Lois Rudnick (New Brunswick, N.J.: Rutgers University Press, 1991), 128–45; Nathan G. Hale Jr., Freud and the Americans: The Beginnings of Psychoanalysis in the United States, 1876–1917 (New York: Oxford University Press, 1995 [1971]), and The Rise and Crisis of Psychoanalysis in the United States: Freud and the Americans, 1917–1985 (New York: Oxford University Press, 1995); Pfister, Staging Depth, and "Glamorizing the Psychological," in Inventing the Psychological, ed. Pfister and Schnog, 167–213, especially 179–82 (on the move from "sentimental" to "psychological" self-readings).

69 Roe Cloud to Mary Roe, Oct. 19, 1909, RFP. In thinking about Roe Cloud as the only American Indian at Yale, it may be useful to bear in mind some comments made by Siobhan Wescott (Athasbascan), a Dartmouth graduate (1989), about her response to interracial challenges in college: "Most of the time, I must demystify the misconceptions that others have about Indians; I feel like a broken record in doing so. . . . At Dartmouth, I often chose to educate myself rather than others" ("Machiavelli and Me," in First Person, First People, ed. Garrod and Larrimore, 189–99, see 191).

70 Roe Cloud, "Missionary Work among the Oklahoma Indians," Word Carrier of Santee Normal Training School 36 (September–October 1907): 18. See Geronimo, Geronimo: His Own Story as Told to S. M. Barrett (New York: Meridian, 1996), originally published in 1906 as Geronimo's Story of His Life, and Angie Debo, Geronimo: The Man, His Time, His Place (Norman: University of Oklahoma Press, 1976). Also consult Bruce P. Stark and Diane Ducharme, "Roe Family Papers" (introduction to the guide to the collection), 1–87, see 3, Manuscripts and Archives, Yale University Library. On the relationship between Roe Cloud and Geronimo's band, see Tetzloff, "To Do Some Good among the Indians," 31–33.

71 As early as 1812, the Presbyterians had turned their attention to establishing missions in the expanding American empire, and this organizational com-

mitment was consolidated by the late 1830s (see Lefferts A. Loetscher, *A Brief History of the Presbyterians* [Philadelphia: Westminster Press, 1958], 74, 78). See Coleman, *Presbyterian Missionary Attitudes toward American Indians*, 27, 80, 9, 17 (on Presbyterian education for Indians, also see 147, 152, 154–55). The missionary Sue McBeth averred in 1860: "Human nature is the same everywhere" (140). And in 1882 the missionary John C. Lowrie insisted that it was "not Race, but Grace" that mattered (165). Yet the Presbyterian "missionary crusade" exhorted Indians to reject tribal values and customs and sought to replace them with the white middle-class work ethos and "property-consciousness" (22). On the Roes' Presbyterian affiliation, see Stark and Ducharme, "Roe Family Papers," 3–5.

72 See Garland "The Red Man's Present Needs," in his *Hamlin Garland's Observations on the American Indian 1895–1905*, ed. Lonnie E. Underhill and Daniel F. Littlefield Jr. (Tucson: University of Arizona Press, 1976), 174, 173. Hertzberg, *Search for an American Indian Identity*, 47.

73 Mary Roe to Roe Cloud, Dec. 16, 1909, RFP.

74 Walter Roe to Roe Cloud, April 9, 1910, RFP.

75 "Letters Paint Portrait of First Native American Student at Yale," *Yale Weekly Bulletin and Calendar* (July 31–Aug. 28, 1989): 3. Anne Woesha Cloud North writes: "It is interesting to read of the little details of his college life that I never knew about. I expect that the Roe Family Papers will tell me a lot more about him" (3). Roe Cloud's daughter herself went on to an academic career, with a B.A. and M.A. from Vassar, an M.A. from Stanford, and a Ph.D. from the University of Nebraska. She taught Native American studies for many years at Fresno Community College, from which she retired (3).

76 Yet Phelps went on to berate this "practical motive" to peruse literature as a crass "Philistine impulse." He identified the non-utilitarian, "nobler purpose" of reading literature as the understanding of "life's problems" and the project of making oneself, one's interior self, "interesting": "A man who studies literature is forever hanging pictures on the walls of his mind; life becomes to him more interesting and therefore more happy" ("Choice of English Courses," *YDN* [March 21, 1910]: 1, 3).

77 For an insightful historical analysis of Phelps's (conservative) politics, sometimes iconoclastic demeanor, and cultural significance (he became an influential popularizer of "middlebrow" literature and literary taste), see Joan Shelley Rubin, *The Making of Middlebrow Culture* (Chapel Hill: University of North Carolina Press, 1992), 281–94.

78 Roosevelt quoted in Hoxie, *Final Promise*, 106.

79 Thompson, "From Wigwam to Mr. Bigwig."

80 Quoted in Hoxie, *Final Promise*, 107, 108.

81 Roe Cloud's Yale M.A. degree required no coursework, only a thesis (see Tetzloff, "To Do Some Good among the Indians," 29).

82 Hoxie, *Final Promise*, 116–27. Maddox captures Roe Cloud's dilemma: "The difficulty of getting the American public to take seriously the very concept of Indian intellectuals is illustrated by a notice that appeared in a local newspaper at the time of the [Society of American Indians'] 1914 meeting in Madison, Wisconsin. While the delegates, many of them lawyers, ministers, or other professionals, convened to articulate their positions on various political, legal, and social issues, the newspaper reported that 'squaws and papooses in any number are here with their braves to take in the sights and learn what the white man can do for them' " (*Citizen Indian*, 63).

83 The quotation is from Garland's "Indian Education" (1903) and appears in Hoxie, *Final Promise*, 194.

84 Hoxie, *Final Promise*, 161.

85 Ibid., 133. On McKenzie and the turn toward social science in Indian reform circles—that would become far more prominent in the Indian New Deal—see Maddox, *Citizen Indian*, 116–17, 120.

86 Hoxie, *Final Promise*, 134–42. For much more historical detail on Boas, his context, and his significance, see George Stocking Jr.'s chapters "The Dark-Skinned Savage: The Image of Primitive Man in Evolutionary Anthropology" and "Franz Boas and the Culture Concept in Historical Perspective," in his *Race, Culture, and Evolution: Essays in the History of Anthropology* (New York: Free Press, 1968), 110–32, 195–233, and Arnold Krupat's "Modernism, Irony, Anthropology: The Work of Franz Boas," in his *Ethnocriticism: Ethnography, History, Literature* (Berkeley: University of California Press, 1992), 81–100. See Lindberg, "Paul Radin," on Radin's vexed relationship with Boas.

87 Mathews, *Sundown*, 100, 153, 112, 162, 143–44.

88 Charles Eastman also seems to have been accepted socially at Dartmouth. He excelled academically and in sports (football captain and track record holder for the two mile). Yet Raymond Wilson, his biographer, concludes that he was embraced as a sort of token: "He was welcomed, if only for a few seasons, into the ranks of the privileged and well born. . . . At reunions of the class of '87, Eastman frequently led the procession, attired in Indian-ceremonial dress. In later years, three beautiful portraits of him were presented to Dartmouth by his classmates" (*Ohiyesa*, 33).

89 Tetzloff, "To Do Some Good among the Indians," 23.

90 See "Yale 1910 Statistical Questions" sheet in the Roe Cloud Yale alumni file. In response to the query "In what athletics have you participated?," Roe Cloud, then a senior, wrote "Track." In response to the next question "Have you a 'Y'?" Roe Cloud left a blank. I have perused the Yale yearbook, *The Yale Banner and Potpourri*, from 1907 to 1910, and Roe Cloud is not listed on the rosters of the track team, the sailing club, the baseball team, or the debate team. Also see Roe Cloud, "From Wigwam to Pulpit," 13. For whatever reason, at Yale he did not confirm the cultural association of Indians with sports

that Carlisle and some other Indian schools were consolidating. On Indian athletes and primitivist nostalgia, see Philip J. Deloria, " 'I Am of the Body': Thoughts on My Grandfather, Culture, and Sports," *South Atlantic Quarterly* 95 (Spring 1996): 321–38, see 329.

91 Zitkala-Ša, "The School Days of an Indian Childhood" (section titled "Incurring My Mother's Displeasure"), in *American Indian Stories* (Lincoln: University of Nebraska Press, 1985 [1921]), 76–80. The *Atlantic Monthly* first published this narrative in 1900.

92 Eastman, *Indian To-day*, 119, 120.

93 On The Wigwams, 1910, and the other debate team The Wranglers, 1910, see *The Yale University Banner, Yale University,* 1907, vol. 66, ed. Richard Beaumaris Bulkeley, Malcolm Graham Doublas, and Chauncey Brewster Garver.

94 On Carlisle's national sports reputation, see John S. Steckbeck, *Fabulous Redmen: The Carlisle Indians and Their Famous Football Teams* (Harrisburg, Penn.: McFarland, 1951); Joseph B. Oxendine, *American Indian Sports Heritage* (Lincoln: University of Nebraska Press, 1988); Michael Oriard, *Reading Football: How the Popular Press Created an American Spectacle* (Chapel Hill: University of North Carolina Press, 1993), 233–47; John Bloom, *To Show What an Indian Can Do: Sport at Native American Boarding Schools* (Minneapolis: University of Minnesota Press, 2000), xi–xxi, 1–50; Pfister, *Individuality Incorporated*, 74–79; and Sally Jenkins, *The Real All Americans: The Team That Changed a Game, a People, a Nation* (New York: Doubleday, 2007).

95 Roe Cloud to Mary Roe, March 26, 1908, RFP. Standing Bear, *My People The Sioux* (Lincoln: University of Nebraska Press, 1975 [1928]), 142, 144, 191–92.

96 Roe Cloud to Mary Roe, Jan. 9, 1913, RFP.

97 When James Fenimore Cooper portrayed the somewhat titillating unconsummated attraction between Uncas, the strapping Mohican warrior, and Cora, the dark-complexioned, rich-blooded suggestively off-white maiden, in *The Last of the Mohicans* (1826), he was even then adhering to well-established narrative limits set on literary interracial romance. The tragic payoff for the mid-nineteenth-century white reader was in their dying nobly (see Robert F. Berkhofer Jr., *The White Man's Indian: Images of the American Indian from Columbus to the Present* [New York: Vintage, 1979], 88, 94, 99). These conventions were experimented with and elaborated psychologically, and to a degree challenged, in the late nineteenth century and early twentieth. For the review of Marah Ellis Ryan's novel, see *The Yale Literary Magazine* 72 (May 1907): 349. See Ryan, *Indian Love Letters* (Chicago: A. C. McClurg, 1907), 7, 81. Abbott is quoted in Ellinghaus, *Taking Assimilation to Heart*, 11.

98 Du Bois, *Dusk of Dawn*, 37, 36, 37, 35.

99 The Federal Census of 1910 records that one Indian resided in New Haven, two in Hartford, and nine in Bridgeport. Twelve Indians lived in New Haven County. These statistics are probably not wholly accurate. By this phase, many

Indians in Connecticut were part African American, and census officials may well have counted them in the latter category. Three thousand, five hundred and sixty-one "Negroes" lived in New Haven (*Thirteenth Census of the United States Taken in the Year 1910*, vol. 2 [Washington, D.C.: Government Printing Office, 1913], 256, 253, 263). Indians have long argued that the government has underestimated the size of the Indian population at different times. By underestimating the number of Indians who populated the continent in the early colonial period, before being decimated by disease and warfare, the government contributed to the ideology that Indians could never really lay legitimate claim to the vast "uninhabited" lands that awaited "civilization." And by the late nineteenth century and early twentieth, an underestimation of the Indian population fueled the ideology that Indians, like some primitive evolutionary throwback, were conveniently yet romantically "vanishing," Carlisle school newspapers often published lists of American cities each of which supposedly had a greater population than the total number of Indians in the United States. The school hoped that Indian students would thus resign themselves more readily to the seeming inevitability of American dominance (Pfister, *Individuality Incorporated*, 48). The 1910 census acknowledges (in poor English): "The census of 1860 was the first at which Indians were distinguished from other classes. Not, however, until the census of 1890 was any enumeration made of the Indians on reservations or 'living in tribal relations,' so that statistics for the group in which they are included in the table are not comparable further back then 1890." Indians were often lumped together with Chinese and Japanese Americans or in an "all other" category or in a combination of the two ("Indian, Chinese, Japanese, and all other"). The group "all other" is "frequently omitted from the tables, as it comprises several very different subclasses and yet in the aggregate is numerically unimportant in most parts of the United States" (*Thirteenth Census of the United States Taken in the Year 1910*, vol. 1 [Washington, D.C.: Government Printing Office, 1913], 127, 125). I have found no evidence that Roe Cloud knew Indians who were part African American in the New Haven area and cannot speculate on how he may have responded had he met some while at Yale.

100 See Werner Sollors, Caldwell Titcomb, and Thomas A. Underwood, eds., *Blacks at Harvard: A Documentary History of African-American Experience at Harvard and Radcliffe* (New York: New York University Press, 1993), 78, 98, 75–76 (Du Bois); 61 ("aristocrat"); 59 (Boston Latin School). Also see Manning Marable on Trotter and Du Bois, *W. E. B. Du Bois: Black Radical Democrat* (Boston: Twayne, 1986), 14.

101 *Blacks at Harvard*, eds. Sollors, Titcomb, and Underwood, 87–89.

102 Du Bois, *Dusk of Dawn*, 45, 33.

103 Philip J. Deloria, " 'I Am of the Body,' " 328. Philip J. Deloria, "Vine V. Deloria Sr./Dakota," in *New Warriors*, ed. Edmunds, 82–83.

104 "Application for a Tuition Scholarship," 1906, in Roe Cloud's Yale alumni file.

105 See in his Yale alumni file a letter to the secretary of the alumni from Miss. J. Elizabeth Bigelow, May 16, 1950. Bigelow writes that before applying to Yale, Roe Cloud had conferred with a physician who tried to persuade him that he did not require a college education to become a doctor. Apparently, the physician had taken this abbreviated route. Bigelow, a physician's daughter, claims credit for convincing Roe Cloud not to take this foolish advice. The letter does convey how set Roe Cloud was on medical training well before entering Yale. Tetzloff points out that Walter Roe encouraged Roe Cloud to obtain a master's degree from Yale to build the cultural status he could then use on behalf of Indian uplift ("To Do Some Good among the Indians," 26; also see 27).

106 On Painter and the ministerial decision to funnel Du Bois into Fisk rather than Harvard, see Marable, W. E. B. Du Bois, 7. In 1886 Painter delivered an address in which he argued that "we never intended to keep [treaties]. They were not made to be kept, but to serve a present purpose . . . to acquire a desired good with the least possible compensation, and then to be disregarded as soon as this purpose was gained and we were strong enough to enforce a new and more profitable arrangement" ("Our Indian Policy as Related to the Civilization of the Indian," reprinted in Americanizing the American Indians, ed. Prucha, 66–73; see 69). On the Hartford Theological Seminary, see David Levering Lewis, W. E. B. Du Bois: Biography of a Race 1868–1919 (New York: Henry Holt, 1993), 82.

107 See Du Bois's letter of inquiry of 1887, written while he was at Fisk, in The Correspondence of W. E. B. Du Bois, Volume 1: Selections, 1877–1934, ed. Herbert Aptheker (Amherst: University of Massachusetts Press, 1973), 6. On Oberlin's antislavery origins and some racial tensions that had infiltrated the institution, consult Du Bois's study, published the very year Roe Cloud attended Oberlin: The College-Bred Negro American (1911), 1–104, see 41–45, reprinted in The Atlanta University Publications (New York: Arno Press and the New York Times, 1968).

108 McNickle, "The Indian as viewed by the Indian Education Service in 1898" (n.d.) in JC, reel 15, 250.

109 See "Application for a Tuition Scholarship," 1909, in Roe Cloud's Yale alumni file. Mary Roe's diaries discuss Roe Cloud's brother (perhaps brother-in-law) Anson (Oct. 17, 1908, RFPD), his "grandfather" Husky (Sept. 3, 1913, RFPD), and his guardian Mrs. Nunn (July 22, 1907, RFPD), all of whom lived on the Winnebago reservation.

110 I am grateful to the Yale Registrar's office for providing me with Roe Cloud's transcript. It is university policy to allow transcripts to be made public seventy-five years after a student has graduated. Tetzloff estimates that Roe Cloud achieved an average of 78, "a respectable average" for that time ("To Do Some Good among the Indians," 22). On Phi Beta Kappa, see Roe Cloud

to Walter Roe, April 4, 1910, RFP, and Walter Roe to Roe Cloud, April 9, 1910. Roe Cloud must have been doing well enough to think that his election to Phi Beta Kappa was possible to this point late in his senior year. Dr. Roe urged him not to give up. Trying to put this effort in perspective, he also reminded Roe Cloud that there would be more important challenges and achievements ahead of him.

111 Du Bois, *Dusk of Dawn*, 36, 37–38. *Blacks at Harvard*, eds. Sollors, Titcomb, and Underwood, 81; on his estrangement from students, see 74.

112 Tetzloff offers another explanation for the move to Auburn: its location in the east, where most of Roe Cloud's speaking engagements took place ("To Do Some Good among the Indians," 28).

113 Adams, *The Education of Henry Adams* (New York: Modern Library, 1931 [1918]), 69.

114 Again, see Tetzloff, "To Do Some Good among the Indians," 26, on Roe Cloud's use of his Yale affiliation.

115 There were five second-place prizes awarded that year. See "Ten Eyck Prize Awarded," *YDN* (April 24, 1909): 1. It was described as, "One of the most interesting contests in years" (1).

116 Washington, *Up From Slavery*, 240.

117 Du Bois, *Dusk of Dawn*, 36–37.

118 Adams, *Education of Henry Adams*, 68–69.

119 Joseph Roe to Mary Roe, Nov. 4, 1909, RFP.

120 Radin, *Winnebago Tribe*, 156, 315.

121 See Minutes of the Elihu Club, Manuscripts and Archives, Yale University Library. Also see Dan A. Oren, *Joining the Club: A History of Jews and Yale* (New Haven: Yale University Press, 1985), 17–37.

122 Standing Bear, *My People The Sioux*, 147.

123 See Dr. Carlos Montezuma's conception of himself as a warrior in Ellinghaus, *Taking Assimilation to Heart*, 66.

124 Du Bois, *Dusk of Dawn*, 18, 25, 32, 40–41, 47, 41, 25; Marable, *W. E. B. Du Bois*, 12. On Marx, see W. E. B. Du Bois, *The Autobiography of W. E. B. Du Bois: A Soliloquy on Viewing My Life from the Last Decade of Its First Century* (n.p.: International Publishers, 1968), 133. David Levering Lewis, quoting Du Bois, attributes to Du Bois–the-college-student an exclusion-focused politics: " 'What the white world was doing, its goals and ideals,' he criticized as deficient only in the degree to which they excluded people like himself" (*W. E. B. Du Bois*, 86). Adams, *Education of Henry Adams*, 60.

125 Memmi, *The Colonizer and the Colonized*, 121, x, 127.

126 Roe Cloud to Mary Roe, March 19, 1910, RFP.

127 Roe Cloud to Mary Roe, July 5, 1909, RFP.

128 Roe Cloud to Mary Roe, Jan. 3, 1912, RFP, and Roe Cloud to Mary Roe, June 2, 1912, RFP.

129 Roe Cloud to Dr. and Mary Roe, May 29, 1911, RFP.

130 W. McD. Tait, "Indian Dances," *Red Man* 8 (January 1916): 178–82, see 182 (reprinted from *The Overland Monthly*). Roe Cloud to Mary Roe, May 5, 1908, RFP.

131 Roe Cloud to Mary Roe, Dec. 2, 1907, RFP.

132 Thus the Commissioner of Indian Affairs Robert Valentine, who was wary of overdeveloped individualism and self-interest in tribes, asked Roe Cloud to Washington, all expenses paid, to talk to him. Writing to Dr. Roe, Roe Cloud confided that he would try to influence Valentine to oppose the enactment of Sun Dances (Roe Cloud to Dr. Roe, c. 1910, RFP).

133 Roe Cloud to Dr. Roe, April 4, 1910.

134 Roe Cloud to Mary Roe, April 7, 1910, RFP.

135 Roe Cloud to Mary Roe, April 5, 1909, RFP.

136 Roe Cloud, "Missions to the American Indians," *The Yale Courant* 45 (May 1909): 520–23: page numbers will appear in parentheses after the quotation.

137 This question was taken up again in another piece Roe Cloud wrote for a Yale publication during college: "Indian Education," *The Yale Courant* 46 (April 1910): 400–402. What Roe Cloud learned from Yale was not only the importance of producing and disseminating higher knowledge, but also the institutional effectiveness of educating and inciting the emotions. His claim, in defiance of the latest anthropological theorizing, would no doubt have been taken as self-reflexive: "Wherever an Indian has been shown the boundlessness of knowledge and his ambition stirred to search for it, that Indian has emerged from barbarism and has taken a place beside the thinking men of our country" (401).

138 Roe Cloud, "Education of the American Indian," 10.

139 Roe Cloud to Mary Roe, May 24, 1907, RFP. Roe Cloud–the-evangelist had certainly learned in churches, halls, and parlors what the literary theorist Mette Hjort, almost a century later, has argued: "Emotions may either themselves be strategic or may play a strategic role in interaction" (*The Strategy of Letters* [Cambridge, Mass.: Harvard University Press, 1993], 10).

140 Roe Cloud to Mary Roe, Nov. 30, 1909, RFP.

141 Stewart to Dr. Roe, n.d. (c. 1912), RFP.

142 Roe Cloud to Mary Roe, Jan. 7, 1908, RFP.

143 Mary Roe to Roe Cloud, Oct. 1, 1909, RFP. See Philip J. Deloria, *Playing Indian* (New Haven: Yale University Press, 1998), and Leah Dilworth, *Imagining Indians in the Southwest: Persistent Visions of a Primitive Past* (Washington, D.C.: Smithsonian Institution Press, 1996).

144 Page to Roe Cloud, July 29, 1909, RFP. Bessie Page's performative interest was by no means atypical. Maddox relates white interest in performing in a pageant written by Charles Eastman, "The Conspiracy of Pontiac": "Eastman and his wife, Elaine Goodale Eastman, were . . . running an Indian-themed

summer camp for young women in New Hampshire. The Pontiac pageant was developed and first performed at the camp, with the campers—students from Wellesley, Vassar, and Smith—taking the roles" (*Citizen Indian*, 51).

145   Sometimes the educated Indian risked being responded to as both fetish and freak. One young woman wrote Montezuma: "All my friends are getting pictures of Indians and I thought to have yours would be best of all. An *educated* Indian Dr!! I will have your picture *framed* and hang it up" (quoted in Ellinghaus, *Taking Assimilation to Heart*, 52, and on the Eastmans' camp, see 66).

146   Mary Roe, a purveyor of Indian goods, was a founder and director of The Mohonk Lodge in Oklahoma. Its letterhead lists it as selling moccasins, belts, peace pipes, war bonnets, shields, spears, and other Indian curios (Dec. 10, 1934, RFP).

147   Mary Roe to Roe Cloud, Nov. 1909, RFP.

148   Washington, *Up From Slavery*, 223, 311. Tetzloff discusses Roe Cloud's fascinating efforts to cultivate a relationship with Wanamaker and his publicity expert and pseudo-preservationist, Joseph Kossuth Dixon, and his attempts to raise money from the millionaire (46–49) and other wealthy men and women, including Cyrus McCormick and his wife, for the American Indian Institute (102, 109). See "Christian Motive Power in History," in Newman Smyth, *Christian Ethic* (New York: Scribner's, 1892).

149   Roe Cloud to Rodman Wanamaker, 1914, RFP.

150   Roe Cloud to Mary Roe, May 28, 1914, RFP.

151   Roe Cloud to Mary Roe, Nov. 23, 1913, RFP.

152   Roe Cloud to Mary Roe, Nov. 8, 1907, RFP.

153   Roe Cloud to Mary Roe, Aug. 6, 1916, RFP.

154   Washington, *Up From Slavery*, 106.

155   Roe Cloud, "Missions to the Indians," 523. See his account of the raucous Yale freshman march through the streets of New Haven: "It was a great moment to me, when, marching through the streets, I joined with several thousand students for the first time in the cry of Aristophanes' frogs" ("From Wigwam to Pulpit," 13). Also see Earl T. Williams's reminiscence of this in his essay "Freshman Year" in *History of the Class of 1910, Yale College*, vol. 1, ed. Robert Dudley French (New Haven: Yale University, 1910), 9–18. The march was led by the seniors, who held "flaring torches. . . . Suddenly there burst forth the first strains of 'March, March on Down the Field.' Unconsciously we drew in a deep breath, and the next minute we were whirling down the street, utterly content as we skipped to and fro in the gyrations of the snake dance" (9).

156   I thank Chris McNeil for this insight into Yale's tribalism.

157   See *History of the Class of 1910 Yale College Volume IV Twenty-fifth Year Record*, ed. Carl A. Lohmann (New Haven: Class Secretaries Bureau, 1935), 55. On Mar-

ion, see Florence Dannals, "Mrs. Roe Cloud, Oregon Mother of '50," *Oregon Journal* (April 5, 1950), two unnumbered pages collected in Manuscripts and Archives, Yale University.

158   See Lohmann's letter of February 2, 1926, in Roe Cloud's Yale alumni file. Another document in the file titled "Yale University Secretary's Office Notes for Alumni Records" records that Roe Cloud "spoke on 'The Yale Spirit in Indian Education' at the second regular dinner of the Yale Club of Boston, held at the Yale Club, 1/12/24." There is also a clipping of brief comments on the talk: "Speaks at Yale Club on Indian Education," *Boston Globe* (Jan. 11, 1924).

159   See Lohmann's letter of February 23, 1926, in Roe Cloud's Yale alumni file.

160   See Lohmann's letter of October 3, 1934, in Roe Cloud's Yale alumni file.

161   See the anonymous letter (probably from Carl Lohmann) of May 24, 1935, in Roe Cloud's Yale alumni file. Beinecke Rare Book and Manuscript Library at Yale does have many issues of *The Indian Outlook*.

162   Mary Roe to Roe Cloud, May 15, 1910, RFP.

163   Mary Roe to Roe Cloud, April 30, 1911, RFP.

164   On Lake Mohonk's significance in the context of other white reform groups, see Francis Paul Prucha, *American Indian Policy in Crisis: Christian Reformers and the Indian, 1865–1900* (Norman: University of Oklahoma Press, 1976), 132–68, and *Americanizing the American Indian*, ed. Prucha, 5–6, 207. Also see Tetzloff, "To Do Some Good among the Indians," 33–36.

165   See letterhead (Roe Cloud was one of four vice-presidents and chairman of membership), Roe Cloud to Dr. Roe, April 20, 1912, RFP. For an excellent history of the Society of American Indians, see Hertzberg, *Search for an American Indian Identity*. Tetzloff reports that Roe Cloud served as vice-president of membership from 1911 to 1913, vice-president for education in 1916 and 1918, and a member of the editorial board of the society's journal—he was a superb editor—from 1915 to 1917, although Arthur Parker held sway in editorial matters ("To Do Some Good among the Indians," 40–42).

166   Du Bois, *Souls of Black Folk*, 87, 88, 81 88, 94.

167   Ibid., 89, 93, 87.

168   Du Bois, "The Talented Tenth," 60, 54, and Washington, "Industrial Education for the Negro," 9–29, see 17, 22, 16, in Washington et al., *The Negro Problem*. Also see Du Bois, *The Education of Black People*, ed. Aptheker.

169   Maddox, *Citizen Indian*, 11. Hertzberg, *Search for an American Indian Identity*, 47, 48.

170   Montezuma to Pratt, April 7, 1904, RHPP.

171   Montezuma to Pratt, July 11, 1917, RHPP. Montezuma had some similar class-based criticisms of Arthur Parker, but was far more censorious. He suggests that Parker's efforts to associate himself with universities and with white luminaries such as Fayette McKenzie and Pratt were opportunistic (11–12).

172   Montezuma to Pratt, July 11, 1917, RHPP. Pratt was proud of Carlisle students

who obtained the supplementary high school education after Carlisle that permitted them to go to college, but he did little in terms of educational policy to facilitate this. See Pfister, *Individuality Incorporated*, 33–95, especially 45 (Howard Gansworth, then at Princeton, returns to speak at Carlisle); 54 (praise for Hampton student Susan La Flesche [Ponca and Omaha] bound for the Women's Medical College of Pennsylvania); 55 (encourages students to excel and win Rhodes Scholarships); 55 (article on George W. Ferris, who intends to study at Stanford); 81 (Pratt's interest in enabling Carlisle to defeat college teams in sports); 82 (Pratt rejects the idea that Carlisle be expanded as a college); 94 (Pratt's commitment to training students as skilled and semi-skilled manual laborers).

173 Pratt wrote Montezuma: "Of course I do not like Parker's idea of an Indian University, because all Universities are open to Indians and it is so much better [for them] to enter our schools and universities for then they would have to size up the situation." Dennison Wheelock was an Oneida who had studied at Carlisle, then had served as the school's bandleader (gaining international fame), had become a lawyer, and later aspired to become the Indian Bureau's commissioner. He published a response to Parker's article in the *Quarterly Journal* and took a position that resonates both with Pratt's reasoning and Roe Cloud's approach: "If it is a good thing for the white man's children to attend Yale, Harvard, and other famous institutions of learning, why would it not be a good thing for the Indians to be permitted to attend those institutions also? . . . I am opposed to any scheme or policy which has for its object the separation of the Indian and white race" (Maddox, *Citizen Indian*, 100, 101). See Pfister, *Individuality Incorporated*, on Wheelock's career (79–80, 122–23) and Pratt's response to the notion that Carlisle embrace higher education (82–83).

174 Mooney to Arthur Parker, the president of the Society of American Indians, Oct. 31, 1918 (Gertrude Bonnin—Zitkala-Ša—appended a copy of Mooney's letter to her letter to Pratt, Jan. 29, 1919, RHPP). Mooney, asked to address the Society of American Indians by Secretary Marie L. Baldwin (Chippewa) in 1914, responded: "Your organization seems to hold the promise of good for the Indian if it can secure the cooperation of the intelligent full-blood leadership" (quoted in L. G. Moses, *The Indian Man: A Biography of James Mooney* [Urbana: University of Illinois Press, 1984], 181).

175 On Bonnin, see Maddox, *Citizen Indian*, 102; also see 103–5 (Parker is quoted on 104 and 105).

176 The comments of Joseph Griffis (Tahan), originally published in the second issue of the Society of American Indians' *Quarterly Journal* (1913), are quoted in Hertzberg, *Search for an American Indian Identity*, 88. See Griffis, *Tahan: Out of Savagery into Civilization: An Autobiography* (New York: George H. Doran, 1915). A photograph of Tahan opposite the title page—something like an advertisement—represents him in his chief's traditional costume, which, according to

the caption, he dons for professional purposes (passing as a certain kind of Indian): "Tahan in the costume of an Indian chief as he appears on the lecture platform today." His dedication embraces the "modern" and inevitability discourse: "To the Red Heroes and Patriots of America who fought to the last gasp for their rights and suffered defeat without self-pity, and to those who with resolution are struggling to adjust themselves to the trend of modern progress" (5). On Griffis-performing-Tahan, also consult Maddox, *Citizen Indian*, 30–32.

177 Porter, *To Be Indian*, 99, 106, 92, 108 and 121; also see 93, 97, 100, 101, 103, 107, 110, 111, 121, 122, 141. Maddox, *Citizen Indian*, 106, 32. Du Bois, "The Talented Tenth," 45.

178 On Eastman leaving the society, see Porter, *To Be Indian*, 110.

179 Eastman, *Indian Heroes and Great Chieftains*, 102, 1–2, 53.

180 Wheelock to Pratt, Oct. 14, 1914, RHPP.

181 Parker to Pratt, April 23, 1915, RHPP. See Hazel W. Hertzberg, "Arthur C. Parker, Seneca, 1881–1955," in *American Indian Intellectuals*, ed. Margot Liberty (St. Paul, Minn.: West, 1978), 129–38.

182 Parker to Pratt, April 4, 1916, RHPP.

183 Parker to Pratt, April 23, 1915, RHPP.

184 Gansworth to Pratt, Jan. 16, 1922, RHPP.

185 On Indianism, see Parker to Pratt, September 10, 1915, RHPP; on American Indian Day, see Parker to Pratt, Nov. 3, 1915, RHPP; and on the official proclamation of American Indian Day in New York State, see Parker to Pratt, May 12, 1916, RHPP.

186 Sloan to Pratt, June 5, 1920, RHPP. On Parker's role in redesigning the society's journal as a magazine, see Porter, *To Be Indian*, 124. Theodore Roosevelt, *The Winning of the West*, vols. 1–6 (New York: G. P. Putnam's Sons, 1900 [1885–94]). On Roosevelt's *The Winning of the West*, see Slotkin, *Gunfighter Nation*, 29–62.

187 See Dennison Wheelock to Richard Henry Pratt, Oct. 14, 1914, RHPP. Also see Arthur Parker to Richard Henry Pratt, Oct. 26, 1915, RHPP. Parker wrote Pratt about the disagreements rampant at the Society of American Indians conference in Lawrence, Kansas. Tetzloff discusses Roe Cloud's opposition to the peyote cult on the Winnebago reservation during his Yale and seminary years ("To Do Some Good among the Indians," 53). Hertzberg writes about Roe Cloud's position on peyote: "Perhaps the fact that in his tribe the peyote religion attracted the best-educated and ablest men accounts for his somewhat tolerant and understanding attitude toward it, in contrast to many other SAI leaders. Personally, however, he was strongly opposed to the use of peyote." Quoting Dr. Walter Roe, Hertzberg notes that he believed " 'one of the worst results of its [peyote's] use is that it creates a very strong barrier in the way of the presentation of the Christian religion to any tribe that has adopted its use, and is an attempt on the part of the more enlightened of the

Indians to establish a racial and tribal religion as against what they call the white man's religion' " (*Search for an American Indian Identity*, 47, 252).

188 Roe Cloud to Dr. Roe, May 1, 1912, RFP. Tetzloff notes that Roe Cloud and Parker withdrew from the Society of American Indians in the early 1920s when extremists (in their view), such as Sloan and Montezuma, gained control. The extremists wanted to politicize their organization's stand on citizenship (pressing for it) and the Bureau of Indian Affairs (lobbying against it). He also observes that Roe Cloud used the society effectively to establish contacts with influential Bureau of Indian Affairs officials and to win support for his American Indian Institute ("To Do Some Good among the Indians," 40–44, 57, 61).

189 Roe Cloud to Dr. Roe, July 11, 1912, RFP.

TWO   SENTIMENTALIZED EDUCATION

1 On Protestant reformers, Maddox writes: "Some evidence of the extent of the Protestant influence on the work of Indian reform is found in the (often overlapping) membership lists of the Lake Mohonk Conference and the Society of American Indians." She also observes: "The political reform of Indian policy was, for [Dr. Lyman] Abbott and others at Lake Mohonk, undeniably a Christianizing project" (*Citizen Indian*, 78, 79; also see 80). Roe Cloud, "An Appeal to the Christian People of America," *Word Carrier of Santee Normal Training School* 39 (November–December 1910): 21.

2 See Edmunds, "Introduction," in *New Warriors*, ed. Edmunds, 3.

3 Presbyterian missionaries saw spiritual transformation and emotional transformation as symbiotic. As Sue McBeth, a Presbyterian missionary to the Indians, put it in 1871: "I think that there is no sweeter, purer pleasure, outside of the love of Christ in our own souls, than comes into the heart at such a moment as that" (Coleman, *Presbyterian Missionary Attitudes toward American Indians*, 24).

4 Jane Hunter, *The Gospel of Gentility: American Women Missionaries in Turn-of-the-Century China* (New Haven: Yale University Press, 1984), 182. She adds: "Male preachers assembled congregations to hear the Word, while women were more likely to 'look love'" (182).

5 See Ann Douglas, *The Feminization of American Culture* (New York: Avon, 1978 [1977]).

6 For a fascinating analysis of nineteenth-century debates about what biography should stress as the true self—the public person or the private "inner" person—see Scott E. Casper, *Constructing American Lives: Biography and Culture in Nineteenth-Century America* (Chapel Hill: University of North Carolina Press, 1999).

7 Pratt, "Official Report of the Nineteenth Annual Conference of Charities and Correction" (1892) in *Americanizing the American Indians*, ed. Prucha, 260–71,

see 268. On the "outing program," see Pratt's 1923 unpublished memoir, *Battlefield and Classroom: Four Decades with the American Indian, 1867–1904*, ed. Robert M. Utley (New Haven: Yale University Press, 1964), 311–15; Bell, "Telling Tales Out of School," 165–208; Adams, *Education for Extinction*, 155–63.

8 See Demos, "Oedipus and America: Historical Perspectives on the Reception of Psychoanalysis in the United States," in *Inventing the Psychological*, ed. Pfister and Schnog, 63–78, especially 71–74. On the social conditions of privatization that produce oedipal relations, also see Mark Poster, *Critical Theory of the Family* (New York: Seabury, 1980), especially 21, 14, 19. Also see *An Emotional History of the United States*, ed. Peter N. Stearns and Jan Lewis (New York: New York University Press, 1998); George Levine, ed., *Constructions of the Self* (New Brunswick, N.J.: Rutgers University Press, 1992); Elaine Tyler May, "Myths and Realities of the American Family," in *A History of Private Life*. Volume 5: *Riddles of Identity in Modern Times*, ed. Antoine Prost and Gérard Vincent (Cambridge, Mass.: Harvard University Press, 1991), 539–91.

9 For a fuller explanation of this historical approach, see Pfister, "On Conceptualizing the Cultural History of Emotional and Psychological Life in America," in *Inventing the Psychological*, ed. Pfister and Schnog, 17–59. For a smart and useful survey of shifts in selfhood models, see Merle Curti, *Human Nature in American Thought: A History* (Madison: University of Wisconsin Press, 1980).

10 Quoted in Ellinghaus, *Taking Assimilation to Heart*, 71.

11 Their letters include neither the Winnebago direct address (Na'ni) nor indirect address (Hi-u-ni) for "mother" (Radin, *Winnebago Tribe*, 83).

12 Jackson, *Bits of Talk About Home Matters* (Boston: Roberts Brothers, 1873), 76. Yet Jackson also stresses how crucial it is to nurture a child's independence (79, 81).

13 Demos, "Oedipus and America," in *Inventing the Psychological*, ed. Pfister and Schnog, 72, 71, 74. See Melville, *Pierre; Or, the Ambiguities* (1852).

14 Harold E. Driver, *Indians of North America* (Chicago: University of Chicago Press, 1969), 454. It is particularly significant that Driver makes this generalization, since his own approach, one that sometimes can be problematically ahistorical in my view, is disposed to making use of psychological categories to describe and explain Indian lives and subjectivities. For a revealing example of scholarship of the 1950s that tries to insert Indians into psychological categories typically used by the white professional and managerial class to portray (sometimes to mystify) itself to itself, see George D. Spindler and Louise S. Spindler, "American Indian Personality Types and Their Sociocultural Roots," *The Annals of the American Academy of Political and Social Science* 311 (May 1957): 147–57. Frederick E. Hoxie writes about the Crows: "The kinship terms Crows used to describe one another . . . made it clear that their ideas of family membership were far more extensive than those held by Europeans. Individuals did not think of themselves as members of a nuclear

unit. . . . Because Crow society was perceived as an amalgam of clans, marriages were more significant as unions of individuals. For Crow men and women the formation of a household brought together several generations and a large network of kin. When consolidated into an extended family containing children, this marriage created a complex web of social loyalties and social obligations" (*Parading through History: The Making of the Crow Nation in America, 1805–1935* [New York: Cambridge University Press, 1995], 171, 189). Also consult James Welch's (Blackfeet and Gros Ventre) novel *Fools Crow* (New York: Penguin, 1986). The story is about life in the mid-nineteenth-century Pikuni tribe in what is now Montana. Two sons of a man with three wives desire their father's youngest wife—she is not their biological mother—and one commits adultery with her. But it is crucial to note that the three Pikunis are in their late teens. Recently, Philip J. Deloria gave a lecture at Wesleyan University, "Crossing the (Indian) Color Line: A Family Memoir." He analyzed aspects of the 58-year marriage between his Sioux grandfather, Vine, and his white grandmother, Barbara. In their socially symbolic union, two histories and different emotional structures sometimes clashed. He mentioned the Oedipal tensions—which could be traced back a few generations—that shaped competitive relations among the *men* in his family. Driver's assertion, even if generally valid, merits reconsideration, especially in *modern* times. For thoughts on conceptualizing the self as being comprised of biological and psychological *potentials*, see Leonore Tiefer, *Sex Is Not a Natural Act and Other Essays* (Boulder: Westview Press, 1995), 1–3, 37, 185, 195, and Demos, "Oedipus and America," in *Inventing the Psychological*, ed. Pfister and Schnog, 74.

15 Frantz Fanon also recognized the social specificity of the Oedipus complex. In 1952 Fanon, trained in psychiatry, reflected on how his native Antilleans were living contradictions of what had become widespread "psychological" truisms. It made sociological sense that Sigmund Freud, Alfred Adler, and Carl Jung had ignored blacks, he maintained, for this group had failed to conform to (and confirm) the supposed "universality" of Oedipal crises. He made no apologies for this ostensible psychological superficiality: "It would be relatively easy for me to show that in the French Antilles 97 percent of the families cannot produce one Oedipal neurosis. This incapacity is one on which we heartily congratulate ourselves." Nevertheless, he recognized that gradually his fellow Antilleans were being psychologized, subjectively and affectively racialized, by colonial culture and mass culture. "Every neurosis, every abnormal manifestation, every affective erethism in an Antillean is the product of his cultural situation." He stressed that "books, newspapers, schools and their texts, advertisements, films, radio" were restructuring Antillean behaviors, self-understandings, and group identities (*Black Skin, White Masks*, trans. Charles Lam Markmann [New York: Grove Weidenfeld, 1967], 151–52).

16 Radin, *Winnebago Tribe*, 118. Lurie, "Winnebago," in *Handbook*, ed. Trigger, 694–95.

17 For instance, pregnant women and females experiencing the menarche retired to a menstrual lodge. A man could not joke with certain relatives but should endeavor to joke with others. The clan name could be conferred on a child only when the parents held a feast. There had once been rules that forbade a man to communicate with his mother-in-law or father-in-law. Males should regard "women as sacred," but also not be "slaves of women." See Radin, *Winnebago Tribe*, 126, 88–89, 85–86, 80, 122, 127.

18 Radin, *Winnebago Tribe*, 91. Lurie, Preface, in Mountain Wolf Woman, *Mountain Wolf Woman*, ed. Lurie, xi–xii. On the Roes' interest in tribal customs, see Stark and Ducharme, "Roe Family Papers," 18–19. Also see Jean Sanders, "Henry Roe Cloud: Pioneering Native American Educator," published by the Nebraska State Education Association (http://www.nsea.org/news/RoeCloud Profile.htm). Sanders notes: "According to Winnebago tradition, a mother whose child has died may adopt another child who is a family friend whether or not that child's parents are still living. Both families agree, but waive legal proceedings." When Roe Cloud's son died from pneumonia, she observes, "Elizabeth Cloud adopted Jay Hunter."

19 Hunter writes: "When [the missionary Gertrude] Howe accompanied K'ang Cheng and Shih Mei-yu, known as Mary Stone, to the United States and enrolled, coached, and cooked for them through two years of medical school at the University of Michigan, she assured their prominence in the mission church as examples of a new kind of woman" (*Gospel of Gentility*, 191, 192, 194, 196).

20 Consult Coleman, *Presbyterian Missionary Attitudes toward American Indians*, 159, also see 25.

21 Tetzloff, "To Do Some Good among the Indians," 25.

22 On cultural form, see Raymond Williams, *The Sociology of Culture* (New York: Schocken, 1981), 148–80.

23 I have found two books on melodrama and race especially useful: Linda Williams, *Playing the Race Card: Melodramas of Black and White from Uncle Tom to O. J. Simpson* (Princeton: Princeton University Press, 2001), and Susan Gillman, *Blood Talk: American Race Melodrama and the Culture of the Occult* (Chicago: University of Chicago Press, 2003), as well as Gillman's essay, "The Mulatto, Tragic or Triumphant? The Nineteenth-Century American Race Melodrama," 221–43 (particularly 223–25), in *The Culture of Sentiment: Race, Gender, and Sentimentality in Nineteenth-Century America*, ed. Shirley Samuels (New York: Oxford University Press, 1992). On bourgeois domestic melodrama, see Arnold Hauser, *The Social History of Art: Rococo, Classicism, Romanticism*, Volume 3, trans. Stanley Godman (New York: Vintage, 1960 [1958]), 84–99, and Chuck Kleinhans, "Notes on Melodrama and the Family under Capitalism," in *Imitations of Life: A Reader on Film and Television Melodrama*, ed. Marcia Landy (Detroit: Wayne

State University Press, 1991), 197–204. Also see Peter Brooks's classic, *The Melodramatic Imagination: Balzac, Henry James, and the Mode of Excess* (New Haven: Yale University Press, 1976); David Grimsted, *Melodrama Unveiled: American Theatre and Culture, 1800–1850* (Berkeley: University of California Press, 1987 [1968]); Bruce McConachie, *Melodramatic Formations: American Theatre and Society, 1820–1870* (Iowa City: University of Iowa Press, 1992); Jeffrey D. Mason, *Melodrama and the Myth of America* (Bloomington: Indiana University Press, 1993); Elaine Hadley, *Melodramatic Tactics: Theatricalized Dissent in the English Marketplace, 1800–1885* (Stanford, Calif.: Stanford University Press, 1995); Jacky Bratton, Jim Cook, and Christine Gledhill, ed., *Melodrama: Stage, Picture, Screen* (London: British Film Institute, 1994); Michael Hays and Anastasia Nikolopoulou, ed., *Melodrama: The Cultural Emergence of a Genre* (London: Macmillan, 1999).

24 Crane, *Maggie: A Girl of the Streets*, in Stephen Crane, *The Portable Stephen Crane*, ed. Joseph Katz (New York: Penguin, 1980), 35.

25 Henry James, *The Turn of the Screw*, in Henry James, *The Turn of the Screw and Other Short Fiction* (New York: Bantam, 1981), 33.

26 Deloria, *Indians in Unexpected Places*, 83–85, 96–100.

27 On the theme of female self-sacrifice in bourgeois domestic melodrama, see Kleinhans, "Notes on Melodrama and the Family under Capitalism," in *Imitations of Life*, ed. Landy, 201. Kleinhans argues that the "bourgeois melodrama" tends to situate social "problems in the area of the family, precisely where many of the issues raised cannot ever be solved" (203). On the politics of race melodrama, see Gillman, *Blood Talk*, 5, 4. In formulating my ideas about uplift melodrama, I have been influenced by Micki McGee, *Self-Help, Inc.: Makeover Culture in American Life* (New York: Oxford University Press, 2005). McGee's analysis of the self-help industry ranges from Benjamin Franklin to the present, though her focus is on self-help and mind-power discourses from the 1970s to the present. In sundry ways—from mind management to psychology to New Age spiritualism—many of the books she studies more or less instill melodramatic struggles in readers. Many popular nineteenth-century novels —for example, Horatio Alger's *Ragged Dick; Or, Street Life in New York* (1868) and Louisa May Alcott's *Little Women, or, Meg, Jo, Beth and Amy* (1868–69)—provide varied examples of melodramatic efforts to control, improve, and "uplift" the self.

28 Prucha, *American Indian Policy in Crisis*, 25–26.

29 Jackson, *Century of Dishonor*, 29–30. In his preface to Jackson's book, Bishop H. B. Whipple attested: "I cannot refuse the request of one whose woman's heart has pleaded so eloquently for the poor Red men" (Preface, v–x, see v). Prucha calls Jackson's *Century of Dishonor* "a sentimental overdramatization of a complex problem" and assesses the influence of the book as a catalyst for reform in *American Indian Policy in Crisis*, 161–64, especially 163.

30 See Stephanie Coontz's *The Social Origins of Private Life: A History of American Families, 1600–1900* (London: Verso, 1988), *The Way We Never Were: American Families and the Nostalgia Trap* (New York: Basic, 1992), and *The Way We Really Are: Coming to Terms with America's Changing Families* (New York: Basic, 1997); Eli Zaretsky, *Capitalism, the Family, and Personal Life* (New York: Harper Colophon, 1979); and Pfister, *Production of Personal Life*.

31 Mary Roe to Roe Cloud, April 30, 1911, RFP. For sweeping historical perspectives on these conventions and their implications, see Christopher Lasch, *Haven in a Heartless World: The Family Besieged* (New York: Basic, 1977) and his *Culture of Narcissism*; and on the nineteenth century see Mary P. Ryan, *The Cradle of the Middle Class: The Family in Oneida County, New York, 1700–1865* (Cambridge: Cambridge University Press, 1981) and Stuart Blumin, *The Emergence of the Middle Class: Social Experience in the American City, 1760–1900* (Cambridge: Cambridge University Press, 1989); June Howard, *Publishing the Family* (Durham: Duke University Press, 2001) and her brief overview "Sentiment," in *Keywords for American Cultural Studies*, ed. Bruce Burgett and Glenn Hendler (New York: New York University Press, 2007), 213–17; Glenn Hendler, *Public Sentiments: Structures of Feeling in Nineteenth-Century American Literature* (Chapel Hill: University of North Carolina Press, 2001); and Michael McKeon's magisterial *The Secret History of Domesticity: Public, Private, and the Division of Knowledge* (Baltimore: Johns Hopkins University Press, 2005). The sheer conventionality of Mary's sentiments along these lines must be appreciated. The Reverend E. H. Chapin sketched sentimental domesticity and motherhood as therapeutic antidotes to America's "bitter world" of competition in which the male worker, fighting for the family in the marketplace, is "driven . . . back on himself." This capitalist warrior, without the humanizing touch of mother and wife, may suffer "anger, scorn, or calumny," and be pushed and shoved into "madness." The enormous sentimental expectation placed on women, Chapin and so many other advice book authors underscored, was to create home as a zone of order, stability, sanity, and purity (*Duties of Young Women* [Boston: George W. Briggs, 1851], 15). John Ruskin purveyed many of these conventions in his 1864 transatlantic classic of domestic sentimentality, "Of Queen's Gardens" (in *Sesame and Lilies* [New York: John Wiley, 1865]). Ruskin rhapsodized about the sentimental power of the "angel in the house," the hearthside "queen." Her home had to be "the place of Peace; the shelter, not only from injury, but from all terror, doubt and division." This therapeutic home is "wherever she is" (91). The world beyond these edenic, sentimental gardens is "torn up by the agony of men, and beat level by the drift of their life-blood" (115). In 1842, shortly after marrying Sophia Peabody and moving to the Old Manse near Concord, Nathaniel Hawthorne gushed in his notebooks: "The fight with the world,—the struggle of man among men,—the agony of the universal effort to wrench the means of life from a host of greedy

competitors,—all this seems like a dream to me" (quoted in Pfister, *Production of Personal Life*, 16). Mary's use of sentimental clichés makes her thinking and feeling no less sincere. But it does highlight in part how history, the emotional needs and roles created by American capitalism, were working through her—her language, self-understanding, self-expectations, practices, needs—and her relation to Henry Roe Cloud. On the ideological capacity of nineteenth-century middle-class gender discourse to form class identity even as it supplanted class discourse, see Nancy F. Cott, *The Bonds of Womanhood: "Woman's Sphere" in New England, 1780–1835* (New Haven: Yale University Press, 1977), 69, 98; Mary P. Ryan, "Femininity and Capitalism in Antebellum America," in *Capitalist Patriarchy and the Case for Socialist Feminism*, ed. Zillah R. Eisenstein (New York: Monthly Review Press, 1979), 151–68; Amy Schrager Lang, *The Syntax of Class: Writing Inequality in Nineteenth-Century America* (Princeton: Princeton University Press, 2003), particularly 14–41. "The vocabulary of gender," Lang argues, "is structurally able to displace that of class because the attributes—racial, sexual, spiritual, occupational, temperamental—that define class position are rendered either so intrinsic or so transcendent that they pass below or above history" (23).

32 Roe Cloud to Mary Roe, February, 1909, RFP.

33 Abraham Lincoln fit this pattern when he acknowledged: "All that I am or hope to be I owe to my angel mother." Sentimental family roles are very much alive and marketable in this century. For the Lincoln quote, see Bradley Trevor Greive, *Dear Mom: Thank You for Everything* (Kansas City, Mo.: Andrews McMeel, 2001), n.p.

34 For some remarks about the relationship between Manifest Destiny and forms of imperial "individuality," see Arnold Krupat, *For Those Who Come After: A Study of Native American Autobiography* (Berkeley: University of California Press, 1985), 40, and Pfister, *Individuality Incorporated*, 100. Sentimentalism, Wexler argues, "aimed at the subjection of different classes and even races who were compelled to play not the leading roles but the human scenery before which the melodrama of middle-class redemption could be enacted, for the enlightenment of an audience that was not even themselves." Wexler calls this subjection "tender violence" ("Tender Violence: Literary Eavesdropping, Domestic Fiction, and Educational Reform," in *Culture of Sentiment*, ed. Samuels, 9–37, see 15; for an elaboration of this thesis, see Laura Wexler, *Tender Violence: Domestic Visions in an Age of U. S. Imperialism* [Chapel Hill: University of North Carolina Press, 2000]). Kaplan terms this sentimental domination "imperial domesticity." Their point is that the snug "empire of the mother," empire of the sentimental angel in the house, was complicitous. It could encourage white families to ignore or sanction the ruthless empire building of the United States, confidently and piously scorning ways of organizing family life, economic value, and love unlike their own as insufficiently

"humanized." Kaplan connects America's middle-class domesticity project ("Manifest Domesticity") to America's empire ("Manifest Destiny"). She notes that in *Cherokee Nation v. the State of Georgia* (1831) the Supreme Court classified Indians as forming "domestic dependent nations" within the larger American homeland. Manifest Destiny, Wexler and Kaplan both note, gained ideological strength by tapping into the middle-class preoccupation with the idea of self-conquest. "Domesticity not only monitors the borders between the civilized and the savage," Kaplan writes, "but also regulates traces of the savage within itself." Inner selfhood ideologies (harnessing the savage in the self) and imperial ideologies (harnessing the savage in the nation) were fused. In the antebellum period, Kaplan observes, sometimes even "unmarried women" were permitted to adopt Indian children so as to enact their own as well as their charges' regeneration through domesticity. "Mother" acted as a colonial governor of sorts, ruling herself and the "souls" in her keeping through the rhetoric and emotional bonds of domesticity. See Kaplan, "Manifest Domesticity," in *No More Separate Spheres!*, ed. Cathy N. Davidson and Jessamya Hatcher (Durham: Duke University Press, 2002), 183–207, see 184, 186, 188, 184, 191. Also see Kaplan, *The Anarchy of Empire in the Making of U.S. Culture* (Cambridge, Mass.: Harvard University Press, 2002). Sentimentally dictated self-government was productive. Indian boarding schools run by missionaries or the government made the link between an education in self-regimentation and the molding of Indian workers blatant. Frances Sparhawk wrote a thinly disguised novel about Carlisle in 1890. She portrays sentimental femininity as a force in orchestrating a "well-dressed" spiritual and emotional conquest of Indian boarding school students. If the Indian school was like a "mill" engineered to "grind out the American, and leave the Indian by the way," then sentiment helped power its reconstitutive machinery (*A Chronicle of Conquest* [Boston: D. Lothrop, 1890], 30, 212, and also Pfister, *Individuality Incorporated*, 64–65). Other important works include Mary P. Ryan, *The Empire of the Mother: American Writing about Domesticity*, a Special Issue of *Women and History* 2/3 (Summer/Fall 1982); Robert F. Berkhofer Jr., *Salvation and the Savage: An Analysis of Protestant Missions and American Indian Response, 1787–1862* (New York: Atheneum, 1976); Lora Romero, *Home Fronts: Domesticity and Its Critics in the Antebellum United States* (Durham: Duke University Press, 1997); and Lori Melish, *Sentimental Materialism: Gender, Commodity Culture, and Nineteenth-Century American Literature* (Durham: Duke University Press, 2000).

35 My own thinking about capitalism as an emotional system, or system of emotion making, has been enhanced by Eva Illouz's provocative *Cold Intimacies: The Making of Emotional Capitalism* (Malden, Mass.: Polity, 2007). Two suggestive historical reassessments of the role that productions of emotional life and subjectivity have played in the development of a not-simply-"rational" capitalism, what might be termed *subjectivity capitalism*, are Colin Campbell,

The Romantic Ethic and the Spirit of Modern Consumerism (Oxford: Basil Blackwell, 1987), and Eli Zaretsky, Secrets of the Soul: A Social and Cultural History of Psycho-analysis (New York: Vintage, 2005 [2004]). Also see Pfister, "Getting Personal and Getting Personnel: U.S. Capitalism as a System of Emotional Reproduc-tion" (American Quarterly 60 [December 2008], 1135–42).

36 Melville, Typee: A Peep at Polynesian Life (New York: Penguin, 1996 [1846]), 194–95. Roe Cloud to Mary Roe, Feb. 9, 1915, RFP.

37 See Pfister, "Glamorizing the Psychological," in Inventing the Psychological, ed. Pfister and Schnog, 181–82, and Pfister, Individuality Incorporated, 135–41. On the intertwined emotional and industrial revolutions, see Philippe Ariès's Centuries of Childhood: A Social History of Family Life, trans. Robert Baldick (New York: Village, 1962 [1960]), especially 40, and also 386, 413, and his "The Family and the City in the Old World and the New," in Changing Images of the Family, ed. Virginia Tufte and Barbara Myerhoff (New Haven: Yale University Press, 1979), 29–41, 32. Zaretsky, Capitalism, the Family, and Personal Life, 76, and also see 120.

38 Hoxie, Parading, 190, 171. For a broad overview of aspects of the history of romantic love see Edward Shorter, The Making of the Modern Family (New York: Basic, 1975).

39 Coontz, Social Origins of Private Life, 1.

40 Schurz, "Present Aspects of the Indian Problem," 13–26, see 20, and Gates, "Land and Law as Agents in Educating Indians," 45–56, see 51–52, reprinted in Americanizing the American Indians, ed. Prucha. Also see Pfister, Individuality Incorporated, 31–94, especially 49–65. Consult William Scott, In Pursuit of Hap-piness: American Conceptions of Property from the Seventeenth to the Twentieth Century (Bloomington: Indiana University Press, 1977).

41 Rosaldo, "Toward an Anthropology of Self and Feeling," in Culture Theory: Essays on Mind, Self, and Emotion, ed. Richard A. Shweder and Robert A. LeVine (Cambridge: Cambridge University Press, 1984), 137–57, see 149, 141, 142, 148.

42 Lutz and Needham are quoted in Pfister, "On Conceptualizing the Cultural History of Emotional and Psychological Life in America," in Inventing the Psychological, ed. Pfister and Schnog, 22. Also see Pfister, Individuality Incorpo-rated, 16–17. See Lila Abu-Lughod and Catherine Lutz, "Introduction: Emo-tion, Discourse, and the Politics of Everyday Life," in Language and the Politics of Emotion, ed. Catherine Lutz and Lila Abu-Lughod (Cambridge: Cambridge University Press; Paris: Editions de la Maison des Sciences de l'Homme, 1990); Catherine Lutz, Unnatural Emotions: Everyday Sentiments on a Micronesian Atoll and their Challenge to Western Theory (Chicago: University of Chicago Press, 1988); Paul Heelas, "Emotion Talk across Cultures," in The Social Construction of Emotions, ed. Rom Harré (Oxford: Basil Blackwell, 1986); Indigenous Psychol-ogies: The Anthropology of the Self, ed. Paul Heelas and Andrew Lock (London:

Academic Press, 1981); Richard A. Shweder, *Thinking Through Cultures: Expeditions in Cultural Psychology* (Cambridge, Mass.: Harvard University Press, 1991); Elizabeth Povinelli, *The Empire of Love: Toward a Theory of Intimacy, Genealogy, and Carnality* (Durham: Duke University Press, 2006), 193. For a good brief overview see Christopher Castiglia, "Interiority," in *Keywords for American Cultural Studies*, ed. Burgett and Hendler, 135–37.

43 Quoted in Adams, *Education for Extinction*, 168–69.

44 Quoted in Calvin Luther Martin, *In the Spirit of the Earth*, 3. Silko, *Ceremony* (New York: Penguin, 1986 [1977]), 68.

45 Krupat, *Ethnocriticism*, 209–10, and Weaver, *That the People Might Live*, 39.

46 Roe Cloud entered what Rosaldo calls a "motivation system of the self" (*Knowledge and Passion: Ilongot Notions of Self and Social Life* [Cambridge: Cambridge University Press, 1980], 225, 223).

47 On Pratt's 1890 letter to Montezuma and O'Malley's "The Descent of Man," see Ellinghaus, *Taking Assimilation to Heart*, 50, 43.

48 Quoted in Pfister, *Staging Depth*, 133.

49 Nineteenth-century Presbyterian missionaries, Coleman writes, were troubled by the "ever-present fear that hard-won converts might 'backslide' into the abyss of heathenism" (*Presbyterian Missionary Attitudes toward American Indians*, 87).

50 Coleman generalizes that nineteenth-century Presbyterian missionaries believed that all humans were "by nature totally depraved" and that the Indians' "sexual morality," polygamy, and (in contemporary terms) easy divorce "appalled" them (*Presbyterian Missionary Attitudes toward American Indians*, 35, 85–86).

51 On nineteenth-century sentiment and reformism, see Barbara Berg, *The Remembered Gate: Origins of American Feminism: The Woman and the City, 1800–1860* (New York: Oxford University Press, 1978) and Valerie Sherer Mathes, "Nineteenth-Century Women and Reform: The Women's National Indian Association," *American Indian Quarterly* 14 (Winter 1990): 1–18.

52 The historical sociologist Niklas Luhmann holds that "we love and suffer according to cultural imperatives," and has analyzed aspects of the history of European "love codes" to explore this. He has also urged historical scholars to conceptualize modern European intimacy not only as a psychologizing system but an individualizing system (*Love as Passion: The Codification of Intimacy*, trans. Jeremy Gaines and Doris L. Jones [Stanford: Stanford University Press, 1998 (1982)], 4, 160, 16). The Roe Cloud–Roe correspondence makes visible the lineaments and processes of parts of the early-twentieth-century upper-middle-class American intimacy system. See Howard Gadlin's classic overview, "Private Lives and Public Order: A Critical View of the History of Intimate Relations in the United States," in *Close Relationships: Perspectives on the Meaning of Intimacy*, ed. George Levinger and Harold Rausch (Amherst: University of Massachusetts Press, 1977). Also consult Anthony Giddens, *The*

Transformation of Intimacy: Sexuality, Love and Eroticism in Modern Societies (Stanford: Stanford University Press, 1992). Although Mary's diaries contain entries that record the intensity of her bond with Henry, including some references to quarrels and misunderstandings, she preferred to inscribe these investments and tensions in her letters (see RFPD: Nov. 24, 1908; Oct. 2, 1913; Oct. 7, 1914; June 6, 1916; 1916 end of year Memoranda; Feb. 25, 1921).

53 Roe Cloud, "The Winnebago Situation," 13. On their efforts to provide religious and financial counsel to the Winnebago, see Mary Roe's diaries, RFPD: Oct. 18, 1908; Jan. 8, 1909; March 1, 1912.

54 Mary Roe to Roe Cloud, Feb. 22, 1913, RFP.

55 Mary Roe to Roe Cloud, Dec. 31, 1912, RFP.

56 Mary Roe to Roe Cloud, Nov. 18, 1909, RFP.

57 Mary Roe to Roe Cloud, Dec. 16, 1909.

58 Mary Roe to Roe Cloud, Jan. 5, 1910, RFP.

59 Mary Roe to Roe Cloud, Feb. 22, 1913. Walter Roe's diaries are full of references to his headaches, sicknesses, and debilities, for instance; see RFPD. Many of Mary Roe's diary entries confirm how devastated she was by her husband's passing, even many years after the event. For example, see her closing Memoranda for 1913, the year he died. She praises Henry's support, but even that cannot assuage the sting and loneliness of her mourning. Thus she places her trust in God (RFPD).

60 Hall, "Commentary," in *Haunted by Empire: Geographies of Intimacy in North American History*, ed. Ann Stoler (Durham: Duke University Press, 2006), 452–68, see 462–63.

61 Kovel, *Age of Desire*, 119. On the history of pressures on twentieth-century mothers, see *"Bad" Mothers: The Politics of Blame in Twentieth-Century America*, ed. Molly Ladd-Taylor and Lauri Umansky (New York: New York University Press, 1998), especially Molly Ladd-Taylor and Lauri Umansky, Introduction, 1–26, specifically 10–12, and Sharon Hays, *The Cultural Contradictions of Motherhood* (New Haven: Yale University Press, 1996), particularly 19–50.

62 Mary Roe to Roe Cloud, Dec. 17, 1912, RFP.

63 Mary Roe to Roe Cloud, Nov. 5, 1912, RFP. Mary and Walter were first cousins and felt some hesitation about marrying because of this blood relation. On their relationship as first cousins, see Stark and Ducharme, "Roe Family Papers," 12, and on Walter's illnesses and the move to Texas, see 3, 12.

64 Walter Roe to Roe Cloud, April 9, 1910.

65 Roe Cloud to Mary Roe, July, 1907, RFP. Roe Cloud to Mary Roe, Jan. 6, 1909, RFP.

66 On endearments, see Mary Roe to Roe Cloud, letters written in 1907, RFP, and Mary Roe to Roe Cloud, Dec. 17, 1908, RFP.

67 See Mary Roe to Roe Cloud, June 15, 1914, RFP, and Mary Roe to Roe Cloud, June 24, 1914, RFP.

68 Mary Roe to Roe Cloud, Nov. 1909, RFP.

69 See Mary Roe to Roe Cloud, April 14, 1910; Mary Roe to Roe Cloud, July 24, 1914, RFP; Mary Roe to Roe Cloud, May 4, 1915.

70 Mary Roe to Roe Cloud, March, 1910, RFP.

71 Mary Roe to Roe Cloud, Feb. 22, 1913.

72 See Walter Roe diaries, RFPD.

73 For historical background, see Carroll Smith-Rosenberg, "Sex as Symbol and Victorian Purity: An Ethnohistorical Analysis of Jacksonian America," *American Journal of Sociology* 84 (Special Summer Supplement, 1978): 212–47; G. J. Barker-Benfield, *The Horrors of the Half-Known Life: Male Attitudes toward Women and Sexuality in Nineteenth-Century America* (New York: Harper Colophon, 1977), and his classic essay, "The Spermatic Economy: A Nineteenth-Century View of Sexuality," in *The American Family in Social-Historical Perspective*, ed. Michael Gordon (New York: St. Martin's Press, 1973), 336–72. Also see John D'Emilio and Estelle B. Freedman, *Intimate Matters: A History of Sexuality in America* (New York: Harper & Row, 1988). More generally, see Philippe Ariès and André Béjin, eds., *Western Sexuality: Practice and Precept in Past and Present Times* (Oxford: Basil Blackwell, 1985 [1982]).

74 Mary Roe to Roe Cloud, March 21, 1909, RFP.

75 Demos, "Oedipus and America," in *Inventing the Psychological*, ed. Pfister and Demos, 73. Also see Richard H. Brodhead, "Sparing the Rod: Discipline and Fiction in Antebellum America," in his *Cultures of Letters: Scenes of Reading and Writing in Nineteenth-Century America* (Chicago: University of Chicago Press, 1993), 13–47.

76 Mary Roe to Roe Cloud, Dec. 17, 1912.

77 Mary Roe to Roe Cloud, March 23, 1909, RFP.

78 Demos, "Oedipus and America," in *Inventing the Psychological*, ed. Pfister and Schnog, 71. Also see Bruce Robbins, *Upward Mobility and the Common Good: Toward a Literary History of the Welfare State* (Princeton: Princeton University Press, 2007), 24. In his early chapters Robbins studies the intense affective sentimentalized bonds between older female guides and young men that structured the men's incentive and social sympathy.

79 Jackson, *Ramona: A Story* (Boston: Roberts Brothers, 1887 [1884]), 10, 14.

80 Mary Roe to Roe Cloud, Dec. 16, 1909.

81 Hall, "Commentary," in *Haunted by Empire*, ed. Stoler, 463.

82 Mary Roe to Roe Cloud, May 9, 1907, RFP.

83 Roe Cloud to Mary Roe, Jan. 10, 1911, RFP.

84 Hall, "Commentary," in *Haunted by Empire*, ed. Stoler. 464. Stoler, *Carnal Knowledge and Imperial Power: Race and the Intimate in Colonial Rule* (Berkeley: University of California Press, 2002), 110. Stoler, "Tense and Tender Ties: The Politics of Comparison in North American History and (Post) Colonial Studies," in *Haunted by Empire*, ed. Stoler, 23–67, see 37, 57.

85 Mary Roe to Roe Cloud, (probably August) 1911, RFP.

86 Mary Roe to Roe Cloud, Sept. 3, 1911, RFP.

87 Roe Cloud to Mary Roe, Feb. 24, 1910, RFP.

88 Roe Cloud to Mary Roe, April 26, 1912, RFP.

89 Roe Cloud to Mary Roe, Dec. 5, 1909, RFP.

90 Roe Cloud to Mary Roe, March 26, 1910, RFP.

91 Coleman, Presbyterian Missionary Attitudes toward American Indians, 157–58.

92 See Ellinghaus, Taking Assimilation to Heart, 38 (also see 220), 86, 98, 48–49, 54, 34, 2. Anti-miscegenation laws against Indian-white marriages existed only in twelve states (xxii). Ellinghaus concludes: "It was much more likely for a Native American man's civilization to be assured in the minds of reformers thanks to his marriage to a white woman" (34). And: "For the humanitarian reformers who believed in assimilation, there was no better demonstration of their goals than an educated, civilized Native American who had been born into traditional society and then, through education, had acquired the trappings of middle-class America" (41).

93 Ellinghaus, for example, considers the ideological variety of possible responses at Carlisle: "Depending on the circumstances, Carlisle might celebrate the interracial relationship of one of its students, bemoan them, or punish them, and these reactions are revealing of the intricacies of what assimilation meant during this period" (ibid., 40).

94 Jackson, Ramona, 156, 247, 248. Grey, The Vanishing American (New York: Grosset and Dunlap, 1925), 139, 205–6.

95 Gregory Jay, " 'White Man's Book No Good': D. W. Griffith and the American Indian," Cinema Journal 39 (Summer 2000): 3–26, quotes are on 11 and 10.

96 Mathews, Sundown, 129–30, 160, 148, 141, 142.

97 Quoted in Ellinghaus, Taking Assimilation to Heart, 72, 73, 84.

98 Philip J. Deloria, Indians in Unexpected Places, 83–103, especially 96 for the analysis quoted. Also consult Jay's analyses of Griffith's Indian films in " 'White Man's Book No Good,' " and see the "Carlisle College" description and the quote from the protagonist on 10; Andrew Brodie Smith's chapter on Young Deer and Red Wing in his Shooting Cowboys and Indians: Silent Western Films, American Culture, and the Birth of Hollywood (Boulder: University Press of Colorado, 2003) 71–103; and Christina Berndt, "Voices in the Era of Silents: An American Indian Aesthetic in Early Silent Film," Native Studies Review 16 (2005): 39–76, especially see 46–48. I thank Berndt for discussing some of the film plots that she has analyzed with me and for giving me copies of some key Moving Picture World plot summaries. Among Montezuma's papers, Ellinghaus found "A Caricature on 'Strongheart,' " but did not make the connection with the film. "The sketch shows a white woman walking away from a Native American Man with her nose and chin raised firmly in the air while the man walks dejectedly back to a teepee in the background. On the ground between them lies a broken heart" (Taking Assimilation to Heart, 73).

99 Radin, *Winnebago Tribe*, 90.

100 Mary Roe to Roe Cloud, Dec. 20, 1912, RFP.

101 Mary Roe to Roe Cloud, March 22, 1909, RFP.

102 Mary Roe to Roe Cloud, March 21, 1909.

103 Roe Cloud to Mary Roe, Nov. 13, 1916, RFP.

104 Roe Cloud to Mary Roe, May 4, 1909, RFP.

105 Roe Cloud to Mary Roe, Jan. 16, 1909, RFP.

106 Roe Cloud to Mary Roe, Sept. 11, 1911, RFP.

107 Roe Cloud to Mary Roe, Sept. 26, 1912, RFP.

108 Roe Cloud to Mary Roe, Jan. 9, 1913, RFP.

109 Roe Cloud to Mary Roe, Nov. 4, 1912, RFP.

110 Smiles, the Victorian propagandist of character, distrusted the romantics' reimagining of individuality as conflicted psychological inwardness, "the 'tendency towards discontent, unhappiness, inaction and reverie' which in England has been called Byronism, and in Germany Wertherism" (Briggs, "Self-Help," in Smiles, *Self-Help*, 26). Yet, as the historian Asa Briggs notes, ideologies of literary and psychological inwardness would become increasingly accepted in the middle and upper classes (whose interests eventually extended beyond books like *Self-Help* to encompass the early-twentieth-century translations and pop versions of Sigmund Freud's works).

111 Roe Cloud to Mary Roe, May 22, 1910, RFP.

112 Lutz, *American Nervousness, 1903: An Anecdotal History* (Ithaca: Cornell University Press, 1991), see 6, also see 15, 26, and on race, 269. On Henry Adams, William James, and the internationalization of this bourgeois ailment, see Tom Lutz, *Doing Nothing: A History of Loafers, Loungers, Slackers, and Bums in America* (New York: Farrar, Straus and Giroux, 2006), 143.

113 Roe Cloud to Mary Roe, (probably April or May) 1910, RFP. On the socially grounded "hysterization" of the body, see Michel Foucault, *The History of Sexuality. Volume 1: An Introduction* (New York: Vintage, 1980 [1976]), 104.

114 Pfister, *Individuality Incorporated*, 135–83.

115 Roe Cloud to Mary Roe, Dec. 9, 1912, RFP. For some astute philosophical and generally historical reflections on the sociality of the passions see Robert C. Solomon, *The Passions* (Garden City, N.Y.: Anchor Press, 1976), especially Solomon's remarks on the erroneous dichotomization of "inner" and "outer" (57).

116 Fanon, *Black Skin, White Masks*, 192, 197.

117 Mary Roe, June 17, 1917, RFPD.

118 See the brief biographical entry for Elizabeth G. Bender in Littlefield and Parins, *Biobibliography of Native American Writers 1772–1924*, 174. Consult Jack Newcombe, *The Best of Athletic Boys: The White Man's Impact on Jim Thorpe* (New York: Doubleday, 1975). On the Carlisle scandals, see Bell, "Telling Tales Out of School," 88–97.

119 Bender, "Training Indian Girls for Efficient Home Makers," *Red Man* 8 (January 1916): 154–56, see 155. Roe Cloud spoke at Carlisle a couple of months before marrying Bender; Mary Roe, April 1, 1916, and April 9, 1916, RFPD.

120 Bender to Mary Roe, Nov. 22, 1915, RFP.

121 Roe Cloud to Mary Roe, Dec. 23, 1915, RFP.

122 See Dannals, "Mrs. Roe Cloud, Oregon Mother of '50."

123 See Roe Cloud to Mary Roe, March 20, 1915, RFP. For other polyvalent associations, consult Roe Cloud to Mary Roe, Dec. 17, 1914, RFP.

124 Roe Cloud to Mary Roe, June 24, 1916, RFP. Ann Stoler's observation that "white women" in other colonial settings in this period were "charged with maintaining racial prestige, while women of different hue were seen as a threat to it," may help explain the mix of racial prestige and class prestige binds that complicated Mary's and Henry's emotional responses ("Tense and Tender Ties," in *Haunted by Empire*, ed. Stoler, 36). "Racial thinking was not subsequent to the bourgeois order but constitutive of it," Stoler notes. "Few have sought to ask whether a language of race developed out of the language of class (as nineteenth-century racial discourse suggests) rather than the other way around" (*Carnal Knowledge and Imperial Power*, 144, 158).

125 Ellinghaus writes that highly educated Indian men "occupied such an unstable position between two cultures that not many women existed who were suitable partners—that is, similar in terms of class, education, and ethnic background. While there were white woman who had received an equivalent education and expected a middle-class future, most of these would not be willing to cross the barrier of race. Although there were a small number of highly educated Native American women, the majority were hardly likely to have received an education that would equip them for entrance to the middle class" (*Taking Assimilation to Heart*, 67). On Wisconsin, see chap. 1, n. 153.

126 Elizabeth is first mentioned, without comment, in Mary's diary, Nov. 27, 1915, RFPD. Wedding day diary entry, June 12, 1916, RFPD. In fact their chapter continued immediately, for Henry and Elizabeth welcomed Mary in their hotel during the first days of their honeymoon in New York City (June 16, 1916, RFPD).

127 Hall, "Commentary," in *Haunted by Empire*, ed. Stoler, 466.

128 See the following diary entries, RFPD: Nov. 12, 1916; Nov. 19, 1916; Nov. 20, 1916; Nov. 25, 1916; Nov. 26, 1916; Dec. 12, 1916; Memoranda for 1916. It is important to appreciate that Roe was very pious and, especially after her husband's death, often lonely. This put pressure on Henry. A week and a half after Roe Cloud got married, Roe wrote in her diary that she constantly yearns for her deceased spouse (June 28, 1916, RFPD). Her Memoranda of 1915 links Roe Cloud's nuptials, her longing for her husband, and her losing battle against loneliness (Dec. 18, 1915, RFPD). A couple of years later she wrote again of the relation between loneliness and her loss of Henry to marriage

(June 20, 1917, RFPD). Roe was lonely in spite of the fact that she kept herself busy traveling (often staying with friends) throughout America. To be sure, one can be lonely even in the presence of others.

129 Ian Tyrrell, a historian of temperance missionaries, stresses what was never acknowledged in official reports, sermons, or obituaries: missionaries' "careers concerned the reality of loneliness, doubt, and failure in the face of monumental obstacles" (*Woman's World/Woman's Empire: The Woman's Christian Temperance Union in Its International Perspective, 1880–1930* [Chapel Hill: University of North Carolina Press, 1991], 82).

130 Elizabeth Bender Cloud, editorial, *IO* (September–November 1931): 6. Hertzberg, *Search for an American Indian Identity*, 48.

131 See *Indians of Today*, ed. Marion E. Gridley (Chicago: n.p., 1936), 5, 34, and 15.

132 Dannals, "Mrs. Henry Roe Cloud."

133 Mrs. Henry Roe Cloud, "Mother of the Year Finds Responsibilities of Motherhood Balance Its Privileges," *New Haven Register* (May 14, 1950). Collected in the Henry Roe Cloud Yale alumni file.

134 White women long held special maternal significance as colonial civilizers of "heathens" in the thinking of missionaries, as this statement, published in 1822 by the directors of the Episcopal Domestic Missionary Society, suggests: women are essential "in the forming of the personal characters of all the individuals of a community. . . . It is in a great measure, the line of discrimination between civilized society and barbarism" (quoted in Berkhofer, *Salvation and the Savage*, 76). Berkhofer also notes that women contributed "a great deal of financial support for missionary societies" (76).

135 Susan Thorne calls "missions . . . a feminized variant of the social imperial agenda" (*Congregational Missions and the Making of an Imperial Culture in Nineteenth-Century England* [Stanford, Calif.: Stanford University Press, 1999], 123). And Ann Stoler studies missionaries as "agents of empire" ("Tense and Tender Ties," in *Haunted by Empire*, ed. Stoler, 45).

136 Wilson, *Ohiyesa*, 192; also see 164. Some of Eastman's relatives suggested that his wife was "overbearing" and that he had " 'an eye for the ladies' " (164). He published little after they separated, apparently because he had become reliant on her editing skills (164; also see 191). Wilson suggests poignantly that he was racked with self-doubt: "Eastman wanted to be the winner [Ohiyesa, his Sioux name, means winner], to win the race, and be judged a champion, and to a great extent he was a winner, yet he kept casting himself as a loser" (192). In 1935 Elaine Goodale Eastman wrote against Collier's emerging protomulticultural modernizing and may well have had in mind the famous husband from whom she had been separated for fifteen years when broaching this astonishing query: "Can two mental patterns ["primitive" and "modern"], two sets of habits, two fundamentally antagonistic attitudes exist side by side in the same individual?" (*Pratt*, 193). On women as symbols of class and racial order, see Hunter, *Gospel of Gentility*, 153.

137   Ellinghaus, *Taking Assimilation to Heart*, 236.

138   Memmi, *The Colonizer and the Colonized*, vii.

139   For perspectives on the positioning of women, see Mary P. Ryan's *Womanhood in America: From Colonial Times to the Present* (New York: New Viewpoints, 1979), 98–203 (especially 98–101), and her "Gender and Public Access: Women's Politics in Nineteenth-Century America," in *Habermas and the Public Sphere*, ed. Craig Calhoun (Cambridge, Mass.: MIT Press, 1992), 259–88, as well as Nancy F. Cott, *The Grounding of Modern Feminism* (New Haven: Yale University Press, 1987). Profiling wives of nineteenth-century Presbyterian missionaries to the Indians, Coleman writes: "As a teacher, a missionary wife, or even a missionary herself, she could participate in the great work of carrying the Gospel to the world. But she must shun public performance and preaching; her contribution would generally be through influence in the home, rather than from the pulpit, or from 'the polls and the rostrum' " (*Presbyterian Missionary Attitudes toward American Indians*, 94). Yet Coleman also notes that the much respected Presbyterian missionary Sue McBeth—who "served among the Choctaws from 1860 to 1861, and began her service to the Nez Perces in 1873" (23) till she died in 1893—"would never have been allowed to instruct male seminary students on the home front" (25) but was permitted to do so on the reservation. By 1896 the Presbyterians advocated higher education for women, yet would not support the ordination of women for decades. See Lois A. Boyd and R. Douglas Brackenridge, *Presbyterian Women in America: Two Centuries of a Quest for Status* (Westport, Conn.: Greenwood Press, 1996), 73 on education (also see 72, 74–76) and 100–10 on struggles and debates surrounding ordination. Boyd and Brackenridge point out that Louisa L. Woolsey was ordained by her presbytery in 1889, but this was invalidated in 1894 and reauthorized in 1911 (104–6). Presbyterians had differing views of women's rights agitation (Elizabeth Cady Stanton spearheaded the compilation of the *Woman's Bible* in 1894), but generally were conservative on this matter (105–6). Boyd and Brackenridge conclude: "Between 1880 and 1920 efforts made by several Protestant denominations to widen women's sphere met limited success. Women's de facto if not de jure status as teachers, speakers, missionaries, and deacons raised sporadic but not serious controversy" (109–10). In addition, see two earlier articles by Lois A. Boyd: "Presbyterian Ministers' Wives: A Nineteenth-Century Portrait," *Journal of Presbyterian History* 59 (Spring 1981): 3–17, and "Shall Women Speak? Confrontation in the Church 1876," *Journal of Presbyterian History* 56 (Winter 1978): 281–94.

140   It is likely that Mary Roe delivered an address that was printed (without the author's name indicated) in *The Indian Outlook*. Internal evidence (her references to Roe Cloud and first encounters with him) and a note handwritten in the Yale University Beinecke Rare Book and Manuscript Library copy ("Address delivered by Mrs. Walter C. Roe, East Northfield, Mass. Missionary Conference July 8, 1929") suggest her authorship. The author was filling in

for Roe Cloud, who could not attend. If Roe did give this address, her speech exhibits a fine example of her rousing oratorical ability and suggests that she was successful with both whites and Indians in part because she sold an idea of *power*, God's power. One of the great appeals of Indian spirituality is its pragmatic slant—spirituality is geared around gaining access to spiritual power. See "The American Indian—In Two Continents," *10* (November 1929): 1–3, see 2. Roe was equally at home in New York City, Chicago, Washington, D. C., and Oklahoma. She also took trips to South America, Central America, and Europe. Her diaries demonstrate how alert she was to many social matters, such as the predicament of Chinese laborers in the West and the development of the Western tourism industry (March 21, 1907, RFPD).

141 Hill, *The World Their Household: The American Women's Foreign Mission Movement and Cultural Transformation, 1870–1920* (Ann Arbor: University of Michigan Press, 1985), 8–22. The "golden age of missionary expansion" was from 1880 to 1920. By the 1920s the career opportunities open to an increasing number of college-educated women helped erode the appeal of missionary work for women. Women in missionary societies, like Mary Roe, played key roles in lending feminine ideological authority to the spiritualizing and moralizing of the cultural and economic colonization-assimilation of Indians. Roe exulted in her speaking tours, crowds, and status. On her oratorical achievements see Mary Roe to Roe Cloud, June 24, 1914. On travel and adventures, see Tyrrell, *Woman's World/Woman's Empire*, 82, 89–90.

142 Smith-Rosenberg, "Sex as Symbol," 245, 243, 220, 228, 220, and 244; Nissenbaum, *Sex, Diet, and Debility in Jacksonian America: Sylvester Graham and Health Reform* (Westport, Conn.: Greenwood, 1980); Kasson, *Rudeness and Civility: Manners in Nineteenth-Century Urban America* (New York: Hill and Wang, 1990). Also see Carroll Smith-Rosenberg, "Davy Crockett as Trickster: Pornography, Liminality, and Symbolic Inversion in Victorian America," 90–108, in her *Disorderly Conduct: Visions of Gender in Victorian America* (New York: Oxford, 1985): "Especially when the social fabric is rent in fundamental ways, bodily and familial imagery will assume ascendency. . . . When all the world spins out of control, the last intuitive resource of any individual is her or his own body, and especially its sexual impulses. That, at least, one can control and manipulate. Thus sexuality and the family . . . serve as reservoirs of physical imagery through which individuals seek to express and rationalize their experience of social change" (90). Smith-Rosenberg's work draws on Mary Douglas's brilliant analyses of taboo and the body-as-image-of-society in *Purity and Danger: An Analysis of Concepts of Pollution and Taboo* (London: Routledge and Kegan Paul, 1979), see especially 98–99. For some thoughts on connections between the ideological making of "therapeutic" Indians—the instinctualizaton of Indians—and the politics of bohemian libido revolution in the twentieth cen-

tury, see Pfister, *Individuality Incorporated*, 135–227. And for a discussion of the control model—control implies something that exists in need of control—see Pfister, "On Conceptualizing the Cultural History of Emotional and Psychological Life in America," in *Inventing the Psychological*, ed. Pfister and Schnog, 25–34.

143 Michel Foucault theorizes the cultural and discursive "incitement" of what we take to be "inner" or "deep" selves in *The History of Sexuality*, 12–13. Nancy Armstrong and Leonard Tennenhouse elaborate this idea of culture's generative or productive power: "In placing prohibitions on human nature, culture calls a whole new form of nature into existence, a nature that requires precisely such regulations" (*The Imaginary Puritan: Literature, Intellectual Labor, and the Origins of Personal Life* [Berkeley: University of California Press, 1992], 166). Thinking about the cultural fabrication of what may appear to be human essences, James Averill writes: "If we admit that some of the rules of emotion are also constitutive, then the role of society becomes constructive as well as regulative" ("The Acquisition of Emotions during Adulthood," in *The Social Construction of Emotions*, ed. Harré, 113).

144 Kaplan, "Manifest Domesticity," 202, in Davidson and Hatcher, ed., *No More Separate Spheres!* Sparhawk, *Chronicle of Conquest*, 57, 197, and see Pfister, *Individuality Incorporated*, 65. On "I-am-We," see Krupat, *Ethnocriticism*, 209–10, and Weaver, *That the People Might Live*, 43, 39.

145 See Ellinghaus, *Taking Assimilation to Heart*, 1–104.

146 Philip J. Deloria, *Indians in Unexpected Places*, 96.

147 Berkhofer discusses basically the same tale (the Indian is not designated as a Crow) as one current among the Ottawas and Ojibwas decades before Roe Cloud heard its Crow version from his grandmother, *Salvation and the Savage*, 124.

148 Roe Cloud, "From Wigwam to Pulpit," 10. Philip J. Deloria briefly discusses the film *Lone Star* (1916) in which "an Indian man becomes a famous surgeon . . . but is rejected by whites for being Indian and by Indians for going white" (*Indians in Unexpected Places*, 90).

149 Fanon, *Black Skin, White Masks*, 215, 44, 51, 8. Fanon suggests that black colonial officials are particularly prone to experience these anxieties (68).

150 Roe Cloud to Mary Roe, May 10, 1939, RFP.

151 See the "1949–50" biographical sheet in Roe Cloud's Yale alumni file. Also consult Stark and Ducharme, "Roe Family Papers," 14, 21. On "I-am-We," see Krupat, *Ethnocriticism*, 209–10, and Weaver, *That the People Might Live*, 43, 39.

152 I thank Tom Hampson for broaching this difference in mission and similarity of language and framework.

153 The idea that highly educated Indians could serve as missionaries to the middle and upper classes was not unique to Roe Cloud. Carlos Montezuma actually referred to himself as "a missionary to the whites." And in 1901

Zitkala-Ša criticized Montezuma: "Is there no reason that would make you think it by far a grander thing to live among the Indians, to give a little cheer to the fast dying old people than to be a missionary among the whites?" (quoted in Ellinghaus, *Taking Assimilation to Heart*, 51, 70).

154 Parker is quoted in Maddox, *Citizen Indian*, 32.

THREE   CULTURAL INCENTIVE-AND-ACTIVISM EDUCATION

1 Quoted in Adams, *Education for Extinction*, 152. Zitkala-Ša (later Gertrude Bonnin) offered several critiques of Carlisle and in a 1901 letter to Carlos Montezuma objected: "To be compelled to work when you do not wish is drudgery" (quoted in Ellinghaus, *Taking Assimilation to Heart*, 69).

2 See Mihesuah, *Cultivating the Rosebuds*. Mihesuah gives details of debates within the National Council of Cherokees about the Cherokee Seminary (1851–1909), regarding education for Cherokee boys and girls: "The seminary and its students were labeled as elitist, and intratribal debates raged over the practicality of a curriculum that included Latin and English literature instead of farming" (3). She adds that only about 3,550 out of 25,438 Cherokees pursued agricultural work (62): "Because most of the councilmen's children attended the seminaries and they had no intention of becoming laborers or farmers, exclusively, the seminaries never became manual labor or industrial schools" (63). The "progressives" who championed liberal arts "civilizing" were members of the more powerful classes within the Cherokee Nation and "viewed their fellow Cherokees as their inferiors and as impediments to achieving their goal of a new, 'enlightened' Cherokee Nation that would be comprised of the best elements of White society" (84).

3 Roe Cloud, "From Wigwam to Pulpit," 15.

4 Roe Cloud, "Some Social and Economic Aspects of the Reservation," written for the Society of the American Indians, Columbus, Ohio, October 1912, typescript, Manuscript and Archives, Yale University Library, 8, 9, 3.

5 On the managerial development of personnel departments in the 1920s and 1930s, see Elton Mayo, *The Problems of an Industrial Civilization* (Salem, N. H.: Ayer, 1992 [1933]), and Loren Baritz, *The Servants of Power: A History of the Use of Social Science in American Industry* (Westport, Conn.: Greenwood Press, 1977).

6 Roe Cloud to Dr. Roe, April 4, 1910. Dr. Roe responded on April 9, 1910. He counseled Roe Cloud to take a balanced view of Carlisle's achievements as well as its drawbacks.

7 Roe Cloud to Mary Roe, May 31, 1910, RFP.

8 Roe Cloud to Mary Roe, Feb. 9, 1915. See Mary Roe's diary on Henry and Mary's battle with Pratt, a dispute that dated back to a conflict between Walter Roe and Pratt (Jan. 6, 1915, Feb. 11, 1915, end of year Memoranda for 1915, RFPD).

9 Roe Cloud to Professor Henry B. Wright, Aug. 23, 1909, RFP.

10 Mary Roe to Roe Cloud, Nov. 18, 1909, RFP.

11 Nancy E. Chapman with Jessica C. Plumb, The Yale-in-China Association: A Centennial History (Hong Kong: Chinese University Press, 2002), 14–15. Also see Reuben Holden, Yale in China: The Mainland 1901–1951 (New Haven: Yale in China Association, 1964), 41–82.

12 Roe Cloud wrote this to Mary Roe on May 5, 1908, quoted by Tetzloff, "To Do Some Good among the Indians," 96.

13 See Tetzloff, "To Do Some Good among the Indians," 90.

14 Hofstadter, The Age of Reform (New York: Vintage, 1955) 148.

15 See Tetzloff, "To Do Some Good among the Indians," 99 (on Pratt's comment), 95 (on Roe Cloud's concept of the Institute in relation to Mount Hermon), and 92, 95, 104, 118 (on nonacademic training and labor at the school). Tetzloff explains that the trustees elected to change the name from Roe to American Indian Institute because they wanted to win more interdenominational backing as well as support from patriotic groups like the Daughters of the American Revolution. Mary Roe agreed and did not think that her husband would have wanted the school to be identified with one man (106).

16 Thompson, "From Wigwam to Mr. Bigwig."

17 See, for example, Williams, "Freshman Year," in History of the Class of 1910, vol. I, ed. French. Williams begins his chronicle by noting that the convention of class histories is to brag about how exceptional the author's class is: "To greet 1910 in a similar way, however, would be not only conventional but also bromidic. Too many have already sung its praises to add unnecessary comment" (9). Also see Merrell Clement's essay "Senior Year," 33–43, in which he writes: "Perhaps a little catalogue . . . half in earnest, half in jest, of what we have done, may serve to recall and freshen memories that will grow dim as we become engrossed in selling bonds or buying Spencerville apples" (33).

18 History of the Class of 1910 Yale College Volume III, ed. Lohmann, 108–9. For a discussion of Roe Cloud's astute analysis of the social production of race inertia—which entails his critique of the reservation system—see Hertzberg, Search for an American Indian Identity, 88–90.

19 Roe Cloud, "Some Social and Economic Aspects of the Reservation," 3.

20 See Crum, "Henry Roe Cloud," 173–74, and Tetzloff, "To Do Some Good among the Indians," 103 (for more details of Roe Cloud's fundraising challenges and frustrations, see 109–13).

21 On the transfer of the school's property, see trustee William Bancroft Hill to Roe Cloud, June 1, 1939, RFP. On the worth of the Institute and for more details about the takeover, see Tetzloff, "To Do Some Good among the Indians," 114, 124–26.

22 For early twentieth-century proposals that an Indian college be established, put forth by August Breuninger (Menominee), Arthur Parker, and other In-

dians, see Steven Crum, "The Idea of an Indian College or University in Twentieth-Century America before the Formation of the Navajo Community College in 1968," *Tribal College: Journal of American Indian Higher Education* 1 (Summer 1989): 20–23, see 20–21.

23 "Progress at the Roe Indian Institute," n.p.

24 Washington, *Up from Slavery*, 129, also see 79. Washington says next to nothing in his autobiography about the intellectual content of Tuskegee's offerings. Although at one point he notes, "even at that early period in my life, [I felt] that there was something to be done to prepare the way for successful lawyers, Congressmen, and music teachers" (97).

25 See William R. Moody, *The Life of Dwight L. Moody* (New York: Fleming H. Revell, 1900), 327–37; Thomas Coyle, *The Story of Mount Hermon* (Mount Hermon, Mass.: Mount Hermon Alumni Association, 1906); Findlay, *Dwight L. Moody*, 308–20, 395–96. See also Fahnestock and Sorci, "Henry Roe Cloud," 86, and Thomas Sorci, "Latter Day Father of the Indian Nations," *News, Northfield Mount Hermon Magazine* (Summer 1988): 17–19.

26 Pratt, from the "Official Report of the Nineteenth Annual Conference of Charities and Corrections," in *Americanizing the American Indians*, ed. Prucha, 261. "The Strategic School for the Native American," 1, 2.

27 "Why Should I Help the American Indian Institute?," 5.

28 "The Strategic School for the Native American," 3.

29 "Progress at the Roe Indian Institute," n.p.

30 "The Strategic School for the Native American," 3.

31 Du Bois, "The Talented Tenth," 74–75, 62.

32 "Why Should I Help the American Indian Institute?," 3, 5.

33 Crum, "Henry Roe Cloud," 174. Five to seven students graduated each year (Tetzloff, "To Do Some Good among the Indians," 128).

34 See Bryan Jay Wolf, *Romantic Re-Vision: Culture and Consciousness in Nineteenth-Century American Art and Literature* (Chicago: University of Chicago Press, 1982).

35 "The Earth How She Goes," *School News* 3 (April 1883): n.p. Ralph I. E. Feather, "Dear Father," *Eadle Keahtah Toh* 2 (February 1882): 6. Also consider Charles Eastman's multifaceted responses to Chicago and Boston in *From Deep Woods to Civilization: Chapters in the Autobiography of an Indian* (Lincoln: University of Nebraska Press, 1977 [1916]), 62, 72, 64–65.

36 For example, see Roe Cloud, "The Greater Challenge," *10* (May 17, 1929): 6–7; Roe Cloud, "Keeping the End in View," *10* (Nov. 1, 1923): 2; Roe Cloud, "First Settlers Become Citizens," *10* (March–April 1929): 2–3.

37 Roe Cloud, "The Greater Challenge," 6.

38 Roe Cloud, "Keeping the End in View," 2.

39 Roe Cloud, "Saving America through the Boys and Girls," *10* (Dec. 10, 1923): 2, 6, see 6.

40 Roe Cloud,"Saving America through the Boys and Girls," 2.

41 On Pratt, see Pfister, *Individuality Incorporated*, 78–85.

42 Crum, "Henry Roe Cloud," 174. Tetzloff adds that Roe Cloud "frequently appeared in Indian dress and often spoke with pride about being able to converse in Winnebago and some Sioux dialects." Curiously, Tetzloff observes, Roe Cloud had spoken against the toleration of some Indian dances in his early Lake Mohonk speeches. By the late 1920s he encouraged dancing at the Institute. Moreover, he permitted students to call themselves by their Indian as well as Christian names. I concur with Tetzloff's characterization of Roe Cloud's policy at the school as a "limited" cultural pluralism ("To Do Some Good among the Indians," 118–19). After Pratt was fired in 1904, Carlisle moved closer toward a cultural pluralism that respected, and even taught, aspects of Indian culture (especially arts and crafts that could be commodified). Yet this incipient cultural-pluralism regime, like Pratt's earlier regime, was dead set on producing compliant skilled and semiskilled manual laborers. On the implications of this partial cultural relativism, see Pfister, *Individuality Incorporated*, 85–95, 226.

43 Roe Cloud, "Saving America through the Boys and Girls," 2.

44 My thinking in this section has been influenced by Michel Foucault's concept of "governmentalizing"—putting the strategies of "governmentality" into practice ("Technologies of the Self," in *Technologies of the Self: A Seminar with Michel Foucault*, ed. Luther H. Martin, Huck Gutman, Patrick H. Hutton [Amherst: University of Massachusetts Press, 1988], 16–49). Foucault conceptualizes governmentality as the "contact between the technologies of domination and those of the self." These cultural and institutional technologies attempt to govern "how an individual acts upon himself"—how he or she imagines, monitors, motivates, relates to, and individualizes himself or herself (19). For historical perspectives on why Foucault developed this concept, which he never fully explicated, consult Foucault's "Governmentality," *Ideology of Consciousness* 6 (Autumn 1979): 5–21. Here Foucault draws connections between the governmentalizing of the state and the governmentalizing of "individuals" (in part through expanded state powers and interventionist institutions). Also see Graham Burchell, Colin Gordon, and Peter Miller, eds., *The Foucault Effect: Studies in Governmentality* (Chicago: University of Chicago Press, 1991). Since the late nineteenth century, reservations, federal boarding schools, and the Bureau of Indian Affairs have flagrantly subjected Indians to governmental authority. This has included bureaucratic and institutional efforts to shape Indian consciousness, value, and incentive. The Meriam Report advised the government to update the psychological and sociological ways in which Indians were governmentalized, while the Indian New Deal initiated protomulticultural forms of governmentalizing (and so-called self-government) that in some respects and instances were as invasively managerial as the forms of governmentalizing carried out by previous regimes. The

Bureau of Indian Affairs, before and during the Indian New Deal, had been particularly dedicated to governmentalizing skilled and semiskilled compliant workers. For more details on shifts in the style, strategies, and implementation of governmentalizing from the 1870s to 1940s, see Pfister, *Individuality Incorporated*.

45 Roe Cloud, "Education of the American Indian," 16. For a general overview of this modern system, see James S. Olson and Raymond Wilson, *Native Americans in the Twentieth Century* (Urbana: University of Illinois Press, 1986 [1984]).

46 Crum, "Henry Roe Cloud," 175. On the Coolidge administration's reformist Committee of One Hundred (on which John Collier, Charles Eastman, Thomas Sloan, and Arthur Parker served), see Vine Deloria Jr. (Dakota Sioux) and Clifford M. Lytle, *The Nations Within: The Past and Future of American Indian Sovereignty* (New York: Pantheon, 1984), 41. They proposed, Deloria and Lytle relate, "that the government support better-quality education for Indians, assist young Indians with federal scholarships for college and vocational training, seek the admission of Indians to public schools, and secure more adequate health and sanitation programs on the reservations" (42). Writing about the 1920s, Margaret Szasz observes: "Few federal boarding schools had a high school curriculum, and none of those that did compared favorably in quality to the public schools. Vocational training in Bureau schools remained inferior" (*Education and the American Indian: The Road to Self-Determination, 1928–1973* [Albuquerque: University of New Mexico Press, 1974], 15). Tetzloff gives details of the conservative bent of many committee members. The committee parroted many Bureau of Indian Affairs positions against dancing on reservations and against giving Indians full citizenship. Although Roe Cloud's input is difficult to discern, he strategically took a less conservative position. John Collier, a radical member of the group, protested the committee's ideological subservience to official government Indian policy. This public shift in viewpoint "increased his status" and "further[ed] his career." In 1929 Roe Cloud participated in another Institute for Government Research report conducted by Meriam on law and order on Indian reservations ("To Do Some Good among the Indians," 62–64, 79).

47 Crum, "Henry Roe Cloud," 175–79. On the development of federal Indian high schools in the late 1920s, see Adams, *Education for Extinction*, 63.

48 Fahnestock and Sorci, "Henry Roe Cloud," 86. The 872-page *The Problem of Indian Administration* offered not just detailed analyses but "Recommendations for Immediate Action," 52–55.

49 On McKenzie, see Maddox, *Citizen Indian*, 116.

50 See Tetzloff on Roe Cloud's role in "To Do Some Good among the Indians," 69–77. Tetzloff points out that Roe Cloud's work on the Meriam team, like his service on the Committee of One Hundred, enhanced his "national stature and exposure" and enabled him to establish himself as one of the country's "Indian expert[s]" (77).

51 Will Carson Ryan Jr., who became the Bureau of Indian Affairs director of education under John Collier's New Deal reorganization of government-Indian relations, was the key contributor to the chapter on education. Authors of individual chapters are not specified.

52 Zitkala-Ša, *American Indian Stories*, 67. The Indian narrator calls her school a "civilizing machine," an "iron routine" regulated by bells.

53 Richard Henry Pratt, "The Indian No Problem," *Red Man and Helper* 5 (June 24 and July 1, 1904): 7–8, see 8. See "Indian Asks for Better Education for His Race," *New York Herald* (Nov. 18, 1913), a clipping in Roe Cloud's Yale alumni file.

54 Roe Cloud, "Education of the American Indian," 16.

55 Quoted in Berkhofer, *White Man's Indian*, 181.

56 See *The Red Man* 9 (February 1889): 4. Also see Pfister, *Individuality Incorporated*, 45–46.

57 See "As An Indian Sees It—Address Delivered at the National Conference for Social Work, July 3, 1929," *IO* (Nov. 1929): 4–6, quoted and discussed in Tetzloff, "To Do Some Good among the Indians," 86–87.

58 Pfister, *Individuality Incorporated*, 182, 186–87, 200.

59 See Porter, *To Be Indian*, 139–40.

60 Quoted ibid., 142.

61 See Crum, "Henry Roe Cloud," 180–82.

62 Roe Cloud is quoted ibid., 182. Joseph Eagle Hawk (Sioux), of Pine Ridge, accused Roe Cloud of serving as the steer in the stockyards who is trained to lead the other steers to their demise. Roe Cloud, by contrast, said that he intended to help conduct the Indians to safety (quoted in Tetzloff, "To Do Some Good among the Indians," 160). Philip J. Deloria, "Vine V. Deloria Sr.," in *New Warriors*, ed. Edmunds, 89.

63 Roe Cloud to John Collier, Nov. 14, 1934, JC reel 16, 319.

64 Writing about Roe Cloud in 1927, Fahnestock and Sorci observe: "He aspired then and later to be commissioner of Indian affairs but was not appointed." They note one difference between Roe Cloud and Collier (this is suggested by the letter I refer to): "Cloud was at odds with Collier's hopes of restoring traditional ways, because Indian religions and cultures were based on hunting and gathering of resources that were now insufficient" ("Henry Roe Cloud," 86). Roe Cloud to Bessie Page, Nov. 14, 1945, RFP.

65 Collier to Lewis Meriam, July 3, 1930; Collier to Meriam, June 3, 1931; Meriam to Collier, June 8, 1931; and Meriam to Collier, Sept. 14, 1931, all JC reel 3, 102. On Collier's use of Roe Cloud to persuade Indians to vote for Indian New Deal legislation, see Tetzloff, "To Do Some Good among the Indians," 152. In 1932 Gertrude Bonnin and Raymond T. Bonnin (Dakota Sioux) accused Collier of manipulating Indians to make it seem like they supported his proposals and implied that he adhered to a racial hierarchy that subordinated Indians in his campaign for Indians (Pfister, *Individuality Incorporated*, 203).

66 See Graham D. Taylor, *The New Deal and American Indian Tribalism: The Administration of the Indian Reorganization Act, 1934–45* (Lincoln: University of Nebraska Press, 1980), xii (for a summary of Taylor's thesis), and especially 31–91. On Indian factionalism, also see Vine Deloria Jr. and Clifford M. Lytle, *Nations Within*, 169–70.

67 By contrast, Collier and the novelist and anthropologist D'Arcy McNickle, one of his Bureau assistants, seem to have gotten along well with one another (consult Dorothy R. Parker, *Singing an Indian Song: A Biography of D'Arcy McNickle* [Lincoln: University of Nebraska Press, 1992], especially 62–64, 92–94). For McNickle's laudatory appraisal of Collier, see his *Indian Man: A Life of Oliver La Farge* (Bloomington: Indiana University Press, 1971), 120. And for evidence of Collier's attitude toward higher education for Indians, consult Collier, untitled address to the National Conference of Social Work, typescript, June 13, 1933, 1–13, see 5, JC reel 32, 617. In this address Collier admits that the government has not provided Indians with the chance to pursue higher education and professional training (5). Also see Collier, "Memorandum, Talk by the Commissioner of Indian Affairs, John Collier, to the Returned Students of the Navajos at Program of the Returned Students, Fort Wingate, New Mexico," typescript, July 7 1933, 1–3, JC reel 32, 632, in which he discusses education with the Navajo students, but omits reference to higher education.

68 Vine Deloria Jr. and Clifford M. Lytle, *Nations Within*, 153.

69 Collier, "Indian Education Should Be Practical," *IW* (Sept. 15, 1934): 13–14.

70 Vine Deloria Jr. and Clifford M. Lytle, *Nations Within*, 102.

71 For some historical perspectives on Haskell, see Brenda J. Child (Red Lake Ojibwe), *Boarding School Seasons: American Indian Families, 1900–1940* (Lincoln: University of Nebraska Press, 1998), 4, 76, 37, 75, 96–97, 7, 55, 83–85, 93–94, 40. Also on Haskell's stadium and sports profile, see Philip J. Deloria, " 'I Am of the Body,' " 331. On the brief existence of Haskell's junior college program, see Crum, "The Idea of an Indian College or University," 21–22.

72 See Szasz, *Education and the American Indian*, 31–32, 64, 65. On the departing staff members, consult "Changes in Roster of Employees," *IL* 37 (Sept. 8, 1933): 2–3, see 2. Donal F. Lindsey notes Haskell's status as the only boarding school high school (*Indians at Hampton Institute, 1877–1923* [Urbana: University of Illinois Press, 1995], 13). K. Tsianina Lomawaima gives some useful background about Ryan: "[He] had to postpone his vision of the demise of boarding schools. He wrote to C. E. Correll [superintendent of Chilocco] that high unemployment levels necessitated the removal of as many older students as possible from competition with adults in the labor force." She quotes Ryan: " 'We must be surer than ever that we give these young men and women training that will really fit them for their future needs as workers. . . . The risk

of inculcating dependence—always a serious one in Indian work—is especially bad under present conditions, and every experiment in developing responsibility for earning and spending wisely will be vigorously encouraged' " (*They Called It Prairie Light*, 40). Consult Tetzloff, "To Do Some Good among the Indians," 138–40 and 144, 131–32, 145.

73 Collier, "Letter to a Highly Valued Superintendent," *IL* 38 (May 3, 1935): 1, 5, see 1.

74 Collier, "Haskell Needed for Future Work," *IL* 38 (Nov. 23, 1934): 17–18, see 18. Nonetheless, in their discussion of Collier's campaigns for the Indian Reorganization Act, Vine Deloria Jr. and Clifford M. Lytle recount the role Roe Cloud played in Collier's visit to Anadarko, Oklahoma: "Roe Cloud's presence lent a good deal of prestige to the bill's proponents, and even though in his role as moderator he was supposed to be neutral, it was abundantly clear that he was a great admirer not only of John Collier but of the bill as well" (*Nations Within*, 112–13). Roe Cloud was only in full-time residence at Haskell for about six months. He officially left the post in 1936 and then became Collier's Supervisor of Indian Education (Tetzloff, "To Do Some Good among the Indians," 148, 163–64).

75 "Henry Roe Cloud New Superintendent of Haskell Institute," *IL* 37 (Sept. 8, 1933): 6.

76 As Lomawaima observes, "Activists and social scientists like Jane Addams and John Dewey saw in vocational education an opportunity to fit industry to the needs of the workers." Yet, "industrialists and corporate planners saw an opportunity to construct workers according to a blue-print of production requirements." She also notes that "[Will Carson] Ryan replaced the obsolete 'Uniform Course of Study' with a program oriented to practical and vocational education, at the same time reducing the amount of menial labor, such as scrubbing floors, that previously had passed as vocational training" (*Prairie Light*, 65, 8). Also see Harvey Kantor and David Tynack, eds., *Work, Youth, and Schooling: Historical Perspectives on Vocationalism in American Education* (Stanford, Calif.: Stanford University Press, 1982).

77 Lingelbach, "Indian Leadership: Reading Past History," *IL* 37 (Nov. 17, 1933): 9–10, see 9. On using music to win adherents see Linglebach, "Indian Leadership: Indian Music," *IL* 37 (Dec. 22, 1933): 5–6, see 6. Lingelbach included her Iowa address after each installment so that students could correspond with her. A blurb explains that she writes articles for *The Etude Music* and poetry for *The Blue Moon* and that she is secretary-treasurer of the National League of American Pen Women: see "Talks on Indian Leadership," *IL* 37 (March 2, 1934): 4.

78 Lingelbach, "Indian Leadership: Reading Past History," 10.

79 Lingelbach, "Indian Leadership: Tribal Prominence," *IL* 37 (Dec. 8, 1933): 7–8, see 7 and 8.

80 Lingelbach, "Indian Leadership: The Beauty of Verse," *IL* 37 (Jan. 15, 1934): 7–8, see 7.

81 Lingelbach, "Indian Leadership: Book Reviews," *IL* 37 (Dec. 29, 1933): 1–3, see 3.

82 Lingelbach, "Indian Leadership: Characteristics," *IL* 37 (Feb. 2, 1934): 9. On Hine, see Alan Trachtenberg's "Ever—The Human Document," in *America and Lewis Hine Photographs 1904–1940* (Millerton, N.Y.: Aperture, 1977), and *Reading American Photographs: Images as History, Mathew Brady to Walker Evans* (New York: Hill and Wang, 1989), 164–230.

83 Parker, untitled, *IL* 37 (Dec. 8, 1933): 8.

84 Lipps, "The Indian's Future Hope," *IL* 37 (Dec. 1, 1933): 1.

85 Marie Martinez, "Indian Master-Potter," *IL* 37 (Sept. 29, 1933): 1–2, see 1.

86 On the politics of the commercial tourist development of the Indian industry in the southwest, see Dilworth, *Imagining Indians in the Southwest*.

87 Parsons, "What White Man Has Done, Indian Can Do," *IL* 37 (June 8, 1934): 9–13. Henceforth, all quotations from this essay will be followed by page numbers in parenthesis in the text.

88 On the Society of American Indians' use of the discourse of race, see Maddox, *Citizen Indian*, 62. Maddox notes: "In 1916, the society began placing the phrase 'A Journal of Race Ideas' beneath the title of its journal, changing that to 'A Journal of Race Progress' the following year" (62). Interestingly, Patricia Sullivan's *Days of Hope: Race and Democracy in the New Deal Era* (Chapel Hill: University of North Carolina Press, 1996) neither investigates the implications of subsuming Indians within the category of "race" nor discusses the Indian New Deal.

89 Roe Cloud, "Haskell and Her New Frontiers," *IL* 37 (June 8, 1934): 14–17, see 17.

90 Roe Cloud, "Value of Mythology to a Race of People," *IL* 37 (March 2, 1934): 1, 8, see 1. Similarly, Eastman contended that America needed Indian qualities to be a better place: "We must keep our . . . characteristics that we have contributed to the country—those characteristics that have been put into the Constitution of the United States itself" (quoted in Ellinghaus, *Taking Assimilation to Heart*, 60).

91 Roe Cloud, "Haskell and Her New Frontiers," 16.

92 Ibid., 14.

93 Roe Cloud, "Supt. Roe Cloud's Address to the Sioux," *IL* 37 (May 4, 1934): 1–5, see 4. One of the earliest pieces that Roe Cloud published—five years before he entered Yale, in Santee's school newspaper—was about Europe: "Growth of Church Architecture in Europe," *Word Carrier* 30 (April 1901): 12.

94 Roe Cloud, "Haskell and Her New Frontiers," 14, 17.

95 Roe Cloud, "Supt. Roe Cloud's Address to the Sioux," 3.

96 Roe Cloud, "Haskell and Her New Frontiers," 15.

97 Ibid., 14, 15.
98 Roe Cloud, "Supt. Roe Cloud's Address to the Sioux," 1. Walter Benn Michaels holds that nativist modernism categorizes "modernization" as "racial betrayal" (*Our America: Nativism, Modernism, and Pluralism* [Durham: Duke University Press, 1995], 113). Roe Cloud, on the contrary, endeavored to devise a critical modernism that viewed modernization as one path to racial enfranchisement.
99 Roe Cloud, "Haskell and Her New Frontiers," 14, 15, 14, 16.
100 On these innovations, and objections to them made by alumni and alumnae and reservation superintendents, see Tetzloff, "To Do Some Good among the Indians," 146–47.
101 "Indian Architecture and the New Indian Day Schools," *IL* 37 (March 16, 1934): 1.
102 See Avery Gordon, "The Work of Corporate Culture: Diversity Management," *Social Text* 13 (Fall/Winter 1995): 3–30, see especially 6, 12, 18.
103 Eastman, *Indian To-day*, 130.
104 Collier, "Address of Hon. John Collier," *IL* 37 (Feb. 2, 1934): 1–2, see 1.
105 Ibid., 2. Radical Indian critics have also criticized the act on different grounds. Ward Churchill, for instance, regards Collier's administration as exemplifying "the methodology of colonialist rule" ("Marxism and the Native American," 183–203, see 191).
106 "Tips from the Irish," *IL* 38 (May 10, 1935): 1.
107 Collier, "Letter to a Highly Valued Superintendent," 1.
108 See K. Tsianina Lomawaima, "American Indian Education by Indians versus for Indians," in *Companion to American Indian History*, ed. [Philip J.] Deloria and Salisbury, 422–40.
109 Roe Cloud, "Supt. Roe Cloud's Address to the Sioux," 1.
110 "The Wheeler-Howard Act," *IL* 38 (Oct. 26, 1934): 1–3, see 2–3. Roe Cloud addressed five of the ten Indian congresses that Collier organized to discuss the proposed legislation. It is ironic that in these intertribal meetings Roe Cloud had to defend the legislation's proposals for education, proposals that he must have believed did not go far enough to meet the Indians' needs. For details, see Tetzloff, "To Do Some Good among the Indians," 151–53. Tetzloff writes that at the Plains Congress Roe Cloud argued that the legislation would provide for the education of new Indian leaders who would serve as "lawyers, foresters, doctors, and teachers" for their tribes (153). Put in different terms, Roe Cloud contended that the legislation would aid the formation of a professional and managerial class of Indians that would stress service. But would it—compared to what Roe Cloud must have wanted? Also see Laurence M. Hauptman, "The Indian Reorganization Act," in *The Aggressions of Civilization: Federal Indian Policy since the 1880s*, ed. Sandra L. Cadwalader and Vine Deloria Jr. (Philadelphia: Temple University Press, 1984), 131–48.

111   See Vine Deloria Jr. and Clifford M. Lytle, *Nations Within*, 72, 145.

112   Crum, "Crow Warrior," 21–22. "Collier wanted Sherman to be left primarily a high school," Steven Crum observes, "emphasizing vocational training rather than converting it into a boarding place for college-bound natives" (22). Crum notes that when Collier was forced to resign as Bureau commissioner in 1945, Yellowtail lobbied to take his place and made Indian higher education a key issue in his campaign (22). Clearly, Indian higher education was on neither the New Deal nor the post–New Deal (later misnamed the Fair Deal) agendas for Indians.

113   On rural Indians, see Carey McWilliams, *Brothers under the Skin* (Boston: Little, Brown, 1943), 69–70. On the clothing request, see Szasz, *Education and the American Indian*, 103.

114   Roe Cloud tried to develop individual incentive through group incentive, whereas Pratt attempted to cultivate group incentive through individual incentive (ideally dissolving the group into the "American" mainstream).

115   Mary Roe to Elmer [G. Elmer Lindquist?], Nov. 9, 1935, RFP. For a description and assessment of Elaine Goodale Eastman's published and private debates with Collier, see Ellinghaus, *Taking Assimilation to Heart*, 92–95, 100–01.

116   G. E. E. Lindquist, "Missionary at Large, Society for Propagating the Gospel Among Indians," reprinted from *The Missionary Review of the World* (ca. 1935), RFP.

117   No author or date indicated, typescript, "Some Items on the Proposed Collier Policies with Special Reference to H. R. 7902 and S. 2755," RFP.

118   Lindquist, "Missionary at Large."

119   Seymour, "Federal Favor for Fetishism: The American Government and the American Indian," reprinted from *The Missionary Review of the World* (September 1935): 1–4, see 2, RFP. Seymour, like many missionaries, was perturbed because Collier required that missionaries obtain the concurrence of the parents of Indian children on reservations before administering religious instruction (2). Mary Roe's interest in Indian culture also extended to the production and sale of Indians curios, for she was the founder and president of The Mohonk Lodge in Oklahoma. Reese Kincaide managed this enterprise and was unhappy with Collier's position, as his letter to Roe attests. He criticized the New Deal's impact on the Indian arts and crafts industry (March 11, 1935, RFPD). Henry and Elizabeth served on The Mohonk Lodge's Board of Directors.

120   Anna [?] to Mary Roe, March 19, 1934, RFP (also see the Ohlerking statement here).

121   Mary Roe to Elmer [Lindquist?], Nov. 9, 1935.

122   Chris McNeil noted in conversation with me (April 2005) that some Tribal Councils had tried to draft Roe Cloud as a candidate for commissioner before Collier was first appointed in 1933. Fahnestock and Sorci allude to tensions

between Roe Cloud and Collier: "[Roe Cloud] wanted tribal traditions preserved while assimilation progressed, and he saw the school's [Haskell's] vocational curriculum as hobbling to students. Changes he instituted and sought were unpopular with the old guard there and in the Indian Service, although Collier called him the 'most important living Indian.' . . . [Roe Cloud] continued to annoy the Indian Affairs bureaucracy [in the late 1930s]" ("Henry Roe Cloud," 86).

123 Margaret Connell Szasz, "The Path to Self-Determination: American Indian Education, 1940–1990," in Sally Hyer, One House, One Voice, One Heart: Native American Education at the Santa Fe Indian School (Santa Fe: Museum of New Mexico Press, 1990), 95–98, see 97. Haskell is now considered one of the finest Indian-run colleges (Hilden, When Nickels Were Indians, 243). For some background on developments at Haskell since the 1900s, consult Norman T. Oppelt, The Tribally Controlled Indian College: The Beginnings of Self Determination in American Indian Education (Tsaile, Ariz.: Navajo Community College Press, 1990), 94–96. For some historical perspectives on Haskell, see Child, Boarding School Seasons, 8.

124 Tetzloff, "To Do Some Good among the Indians," 81, 130, 136, 148, 163, 167, 189–191, 193 (Roe Cloud's pattern as an administrator), and 166 (Roe Cloud's letter to Collier about his memo leading to the conceptualization of the Indian New Deal). Unfortunately, Tetzloff did not find the memo where it should have been in Collier's files (166). Tetzloff quotes a note from Williard Thompson Beatty, director of Indian Education, to Secretary of the Interior Harold Ickes, probably written around June 1936. Roe Cloud, he avowed, did not have the managerial expertise requisite to run Haskell (149). Tetzloff also quotes Collier in 1939 writing to Roe Cloud, who wanted his job at Haskell back, that even if Haskell were in great need of a superintendent, Roe Cloud would never be given the job (166). On Roe Cloud's challenges as the Umatilla superintendent and, in his last two years, as regional representative in Portland, also see Tetzloff, "To Do Some Good among the Indians," 171–96. Tetzloff cites a 1940 estimate that Bureau superintendents had to write approximately 593 reports a year (193). Roe Cloud laid low, writing "virtually nothing for a national audience during the last ten years of his life and spoke only rarely on matters beyond his official duties" (194). Pratt is quoted in Pfister, Individuality Incorporated, 80.

CODA

1 See "Mollie Spotted Elk," Indians of Today, 111. Also see Bunny McBride, Molly Spotted Elk: A Penobscot in Paris (Norman: University of Oklahoma Press, 1995), 56–64. Hazel Hertzberg notes that the mostly Chicago-based Pan-Indian Grand Council Fire altered its name to Indian Council Fire in 1932 and that it

placed "more emphasis on fraternal and educational matters than on reform issues" and was "national in character" (*Search for an American Indian Identity*, 233). For an important chapter on the history of Indians and higher education, see Steven Crum, "The Choctaw Nation: Changing the Appearance of American Higher Education, 1830–1907," *History of Education Quarterly* 47 (February 2007): 49–68.

2 The secretary of the Indian Council Fire is quoted in Goodale Eastman, *Pratt*, 202; for general background about this organization, see 110.

3 His entry "Arthur C. Parker" in *Indians of Today* has him receiving an M.S. degree from the University of Rochester (95). Littlefield Jr.'s and Parins's biographical sketch says that he "attended Harvard and the University of Rochester" (*Biobibliography of Native American Writers*, 263). Parker actually graduated from high school and studied at, but did not graduate from, Dickinson Seminary. Hertzberg writes: "He considered but ultimately rejected Franz Boas' suggestion of becoming an anthropologist through the academic route at Columbia College and Boas' seminar. . . . Because Parker rejected the academic route which his contemporaries took his credentials were bound to be considered not quite right. He felt this keenly and compensated for it by claiming some which he had not earned, but for which he invented equivalents" ("Arthur C. Parker, Seneca, 1881–1955," in *American Indian Intellectuals*, ed. Liberty, 131, 133).

4 See Porter, *To Be Indian*, 103, also 111, and Maddox, *Citizen Indian*, 99–100. Dannals, "Mrs. Henry Roe Cloud."

5 Lipsitz, *American Studies in a Moment of Danger* (Minneapolis: University of Minnesota Press, 2001), 43.

6 Bell, "Telling Tales out of School," 199–202.

7 Thompson describes the role Elizabeth and her fellow club members played in the Pendleton Roundup in "From Wigwam to Mr. Bigwig."

8 Booker T. Washington also recognized the roles that higher education and what is termed "high culture" have played in constructing a sense of individual and class potency and legitimacy: "There was a feeling that a knowledge, however little, of the Greek and Latin languages would make one a very superior being, something bordering almost on the supernatural. I remember that the first coloured man whom I saw who knew something about foreign language impressed me at that time as being a man of all others to be envied" (*Up from Slavery*, 85). But Washington, unlike Roe Cloud, did not seek to develop this social insight into an intellectual program and institutional strategy for racial "uplift." Fanon observes the compensatory cultural route that some Antilleans had taken in response to the pressures of French colonialism: "There are many people in Martinique who at the age of twenty or thirty begin to steep themselves in Montesquieu or Claudel for the sole purpose of being able to quote them. That is because, through their knowledge

of these writers, they expect their color to be forgotten" (*Black Skin, White Masks*, 193).

9 I thank Tom Hampson for this speculation, based on his own long experience working on the Umatilla Reservation.

10 Memmi, *The Colonizer and the Colonized*, 124. Standing Bear, *My People the Sioux*, 142–44. For critical perspectives on performances of Indianness, consult Philip J. Deloria, *Playing Indian*; Winfried Fluck, "Playing Indian: Media Reception as Transfer," *Figurationen* 2 (2007): 67–86, see 72–84; and Pfister, *Individuality Incorporated*, 120–32.

11 Gilroy, *Against Race: Imagining Political Culture beyond the Color Line* (Cambridge, Mass.: Harvard University Press, 2000), 276.

12 Fanon, *Black Skin, White Masks*, 117, He continues: "Insofar as he conceives of European culture as a means of stripping himself from his race, he becomes alienated" (224). Henry Louis Gates Jr. suggests that the magnificently self-reflexive Fanon be viewed historically, ideologically, and emotionally as "a battlefield in himself" ("Critical Fanonism," 470).

13 Memmi, *The Colonizer and the Colonized*, 9.

14 James, *American Civilization* (Cambridge, Mass.: Blackwell, 1993), 206. James wrote his book draft, originally titled "Notes on American Civilization," in 1950; it was not published in his lifetime.

15 On the goals and dangers associated with performing the role of early-twentieth-century Indian bicultural "bridge" figures (Eastman, Parker, Ella Deloria [Sioux]), see Philip J. Deloria, *Playing Indian*, 122–26. Interestingly, Roe Cloud, Eastman, Parker, and Ella Deloria all worked with youth during phases of their careers (122). For an important historical investigation of this theme, surveying the late seventeenth century through the twentieth, see Margaret Connell Szasz, ed., *Between Indian and White Worlds: The Cultural Broker* (Norman: University of Oklahoma Press, 1994). Mihesuah's analyses of the Cherokee Female Seminary's nineteenth- and early-twentieth-century tendency to espouse race loyalty (and middle-class loyalty), as opposed to loyalty to traditional Indian cultures, and of the Cherokees' wish to keep education in Indian hands (even when that schooling trained students in ways similar to those of white schools) help me appreciate the complexity of Roe Cloud's ideological and strategic orientation early in his career (*Cultivating the Rosebuds*, 5, 110). Indian cultural traditions could still be and no doubt were learned outside school. On race, class, and corporate relations in the 1990s, consult Gordon, "Work of Corporate Culture," 22. She notes: "The racialized dimensions of the 'disuniting of America' are so fraught with fear and loathing that corporatism could be ready to abandon white purity for class cohesion" (22).

16 See Robert Coles, *The Call of Service: A Witness to Idealism* (Boston: Houghton Mifflin, 1993), especially "Religious Sanctioned Action," 56–62.

17 Maddox points out that Arthur Parker framed the concern in those very words: "How the Indian is to deal with the 'white problem' " (*Citizen Indian*, 87).

18 Crum, "Crow Warrior," 19.

19 See "Robert Yellowtail," *Indians of Today*, 128. Hoxie and Bernardis write: "Yellowtail's critics charged him with being ill-tempered, a bully, and of working primarily for his own interests, but his lifelong, consistently self-stated goals were for human rights, self-determination, tribal autonomy, and economic rehabilitation of his people" ("Robert Yellowtail/Crow," 58, in Edmunds, ed., *New Warriors*).

20 Krupat, *Ethnocriticism*, 209–10, and Weaver, *That the People Might Live*, 43, 39.

21 Du Bois, *Dusk of Dawn*, vii–viii.

22 This "modern" strategic Indianizing was something like a protomulticultural revision of the ideology that informed some students at the Cherokee Female Seminary around the turn of the century, who, proud to be Cherokee and proud of their heritage, nonetheless were neither "culturally ambivalent" about, nor "bicultural" in, their education and lifeways: "They promoted a 'new Indianness,' " writes Mihesuah in *Cultivating the Rosebuds*, within which they envisioned themselves as "people who would manage their own affairs according to the ways of the white, not traditional, Cherokee society" (107–8). Mihesuah observes that the school's ideology and instruction were effective in achieving some goals (goals that Roe Cloud advocated). It helped those "who went on to colleges and universities. The training offered by the school was invaluable to the acculturated girls' success in business and in social circles within and outside the Cherokee Nation. It was unquestionably the catalyst for the prosperity of many Cherokee women and their families" (112).

23 Szasz, *Education and the American Indian*, 202.

24 Peltier, *Prison Writings*, 67.

25 Silko, *Storyteller* (New York: Arcade, 1981), 192.

26 Lomawaima, *They Called It Prairie Light*, 170. African Americans also have negotiated similar restrictions outside and inside the academy. In Lansing, Michigan, Malcolm X was "one of [his] school's top students." In the eighth grade, looking ahead to high school, he was pleased when one of his favorite teachers asked him about his career aspirations. He responded that he dreamed of attending law school. His teacher counseled him instead to consider carpentry because of his excellence in the carpentry shop. "A lawyer—that's no realistic goal for a nigger. You need to think about something you *can* be." This contrasted with his advice to promising though less successful white students, whom he guided toward the professions. Malcolm X's exchange with his teacher proved to be the start of his radical education and the beginning of his skepticism about conventional education as racially rigged. "It was then that I began to change—inside. I drew away from white peo-

ple. . . . Where 'nigger' had slipped off my back before, wherever I heard it now, I stopped and looked at whoever said it. And they looked surprised that I did" (The Autobiography of Malcolm X [New York: One World, 1999 (1965)], 41–42). I thank Lisa Wyant for pointing out this passage.

27 See Szasz, Education and the American Indian, 98.

28 Garrod and Larimore, "Introduction," in First Person, First Peoples, ed. Garrod and Larimore, 2. Arnold Krupat reports on the challenges that remained at the close of the century in which Roe Cloud waged his battles: "In 1986 . . . minorities accounted for 22.4 percent of American high school graduates; of these 0.7 percent were American Indian. American Indian and Alaskan Natives in 1986 received only 0.4 percent of bachelor's degrees in all fields, by far the lowest percentage of all minority groups." Moreover, he notes, in 1991 about 0.2 percent of full professors in higher education were American Indian (The Turn to the Native: Studies in Criticism and Culture [Lincoln: University of Nebraska Press, 1996], 7, 8).

29 Alexie, The Lone Ranger and Tonto Fistfight in Heaven (New York: Atlantic Monthly Press, 1993), 188.

30 Peltier, Prison Writings, 37.

31 Philip J. Deloria, "Vine V. Deloria Sr./Dakota," in New Warriors, ed. Edmunds, 92. Similarly, Dr. Carlos Montezuma, explaining why he wanted to become a physician, affirmed: "I wished to share with my people whatever I might attain" (quoted in Ellinghaus, Taking Assimilation to Heart, 57).

32 Erdrich, "Foreword," x–xi, in First Person, First Peoples, ed. Garrod and Larimore.

33 See Alvord, "Full Circle," ibid., 212–29, see 226, 228. Garrod, a professor of education at Dartmouth, and Larrimore, formerly director of the Native American Program at Dartmouth, write: "Young Native American professionals are using Western economics, politics, law, medicine, anthropology, and even education to try to regain this basic right of self-determination for their tribes" ("Introduction," ibid., 16). Guchxweina (also called Ricardo Worl) (Tlingit), another Dartmouth contributor of an autobiographical essay to First Person, First Peoples, is now a loan officer and corporate relations officer for the National Bank of Alaska. He concludes: "Utilizing elements of Western society to cultivate and protect Native American culture is not naive. In fact, Tlingits, like other Native American tribes, have a history of cultural adaptation. . . . I still believe there is merit in the thesis that economic assimilation can occur without jeopardizing traditional values and ancestral lands. . . . Our ancestors spent a thousand years structuring the tribe to ensure our survival" ("A Tlingit Brother of Alpha Chi," ibid., 64–79, see 78). Of course, forces within multicultural capitalism may be willing to countenance and even promote the perpetuation of ethnoracial identities to ensure "economic assimilation." On this topic, see Pfister, Individuality Incorporated, 234–

45, especially 243–45; Martin J. Matustík, "Ludic, Corporate, and Imperial Multiculturalism," in *Theorizing Multiculturalism: A Guide to the Current Debate*, ed. Cynthia Walker (Malden, Mass.: Blackwell, 1998), 100–17, see especially 102–4; Henry Giroux, *Disturbing Pleasures: Learning Popular Culture* (New York: Routledge, 1994), 4, 14; and Gilroy, *Against Race*, 254, 264. One thing that is striking about the thirteen Dartmouth Indian autobiographers who contributed essays to *First Person, First People* is the value they place on their families and tribes not only as centers of affection, but as educators in ways of life, feeling, and thought. These contributors entered Dartmouth with highly developed educations—in group cooperation, family value, and humility—that differed from some of what they found in college. See Tyler Hill, "Deloria '64 Champions Native American Rights," *YDN* (Nov. 10, 2005), 1, 4, and "Native Americans Mark a Centennial," *Yale Alumni Magazine* 69 (January–February 2006), 14. For postmodern reflections on the strategies and dimensions of Indian surviving and thriving, see Gerald Vizenor, *Manifest Manners: Narratives on Postindian Survivance* (Lincoln: University of Nebraska Press, 1999 [1994]).

34 Judy Wang, "Students Stand up for Heritage," *YDN* (April 2, 2007): 1, 4, see 4 (Yale stereotyping); Christine Graef, "At Yale, She's Telling the American Indian Story to an Eager Audience," *New York Times* (February 25, 2007): 5 (support system, future leaders); Kara Arsenault, "Native Americans Mark a Centennial," in the "Light and Verity" column in *Yale Alumni Magazine* (January/February 2006): 14 (returning to tribe); Alex Hemmer, "Cloud's Legacy Inspires Continued Native American Spirit," *Yale Herald* 46 (April 4, 2008): 5 (Roe Cloud as public intellectual); Neena Satija, "Yale Lags Behind Peers in Native American Outreach," *Yale Herald* (April 4, 2008): 5 (Yale third in Ivy League in number of American Indian students). In Satija's article Yale's American Indian students point out that many Yale Indians come from cities rather than reservations because of the arduous social contradictions that shape education, life, and aspiration on many reservations. Consequently, extensive outreach by the admissions office, institutional supports from deans and counselors, the hiring of Indian faculty to teach Native American studies courses, and the allocation of space for Indian cultural and educational activities are imperative. Efforts to recruit and retain more American Indian faculty can be challenging. "Judith Chevalier, the William S. Beinecke Professor of Economics and Deputy Provost for Faculty Development, noted, 'The Ph.D. pool is not enormous.' However, she explained that 'hopefully, the scholarly community [at Yale] interested in Native American history and culture will be a draw' in the recruitment of Native American faculty members." Several of these articles praise the fairly recent appointment of Alyssa Mt. Pleasant (Tuscarora), who received her Ph.D. in history and American Indian studies at Cornell and is now an assistant professor of history and American studies at Yale.

35 In 1942 the great African American author and anthropologist Zora Neale

Hurston warned: "Bitterness is the under-arm odor of wishful weakness. It is the graceless acknowledgment of defeat" (*Dust Tracks on a Road* [1942] in *Zora Neale Hurston: Folklore, Memoirs, and Other Writings* [New York: Library of America, 1995], 765). Thinking about "racial understanding," she writes, perhaps a bit optimistically: "I found out . . . that you are bound to be jostled in the 'crowded street of life.' That in itself need not be dangerous unless you have the open razors of personal vanity in your pants pocket. The passers-by don't hurt you, but if you go around like that, they make you hurt yourself" (664). Hurston, who studied at Howard and Barnard, and who did graduate work in anthropology with Franz Boas and Ruth Benedict at Columbia, was, like Roe Cloud, appreciative of her studies and attuned to the uses of educational prestige, and the class prestige associated with it, in improving race relations (see 673–74, 684–85, 687–88, 719–20, 721, 726, 733).

36 Hilden, *When Nickels Were Indians*, 114.
37 Radin, *Winnebago Tribe*, 123.

APPENDIX

1 On November 2, 2005, in an e-mail to some of Roe Cloud's descendants, I suggested that a portrait of Roe Cloud be painted and hung in that space in Sterling Memorial Library. I hope this comes about. On the African American college-graduate ethos of service in Bouchet's era, see Du Bois, "The Talented Tenth," 50–51, 55.

and, 183 n. 31; class- and race-based
attitudes on, 26–28, 163–73, 236
n. 8, 237 n. 15; cross-cultural brokering by Indians and, 13; cultural
determinism and, 46; cultural pluralism and Indian education and,
227 n. 42; family dynamics and, 85–
93; forms, genres, and conventions
of, that shape subjectivities, 90;
Foucault's governmentalizing concept and, 227 n. 44; historical
change and, 16–17, 183 n. 71;
incentive-and-activism education
and, 127–60; Indian-white romance
and, 108–10; Roe Cloud's cultural
activism and, 15, 146–52; in Roe
Cloud's life, xi, 9; of Winnebago,
15–17. *See also* cross-cultural brokering; tribal culture
Curtis, Charles (Senator), 6, 27

Dakota culture, religion in, 31–32
Dartmouth College, Indians and, 26–
27, 131, 161, 170–72, 186 n. 9, 193
n. 69, 195 n. 88, 239 n. 33
Daughters of the American Revolution
(DAR), 132, 225 n. 15
debating: Roe Cloud's participation in,
24, 47, 59, 73, 195 n. 90, 205 n. 6; at
Yale, 34–35, 38, 44, 48, 59–60
Deloria, Ella, 237 n. 15
Deloria, Philip J., xi, 9, 19–21, 180
n. 10, 184 n. 44; on bicultural bridg-
ing, 237 n. 15; on Christianity, 31–
32; Indian ethos of service and,
170–71; on Indian New Deal, 142–
43; on Indian-white melodrama in
popular culture, 91; on interracial
romances and Indian films, 109–10,
122–23, 217 n. 98, 223 n. 148; on
Oedipal relations and Indians, 206
n. 14, 207 n. 14

Deloria, Sam, 171
Deloria, Vine, Jr., 145–46, 228 n. 46,
230 n. 66, 231 n. 74
Deloria, Vine, Sr., 9, 21, 55–56, 170,
207 n. 14
democracy: Du Bois on, 64; Roe Cloud
on, 136, 153; Yale concept of, 39
Demos, John, 86–89, 103–4
Denning, Michael, 185 n. 45
Descent of Man, The (O'Malley painting),
98
discrimination, Roe Cloud's awareness
of, 71–73, 171
diversity: Collier's views on, 155; cultural diversity, 150–51; Roe Cloud on
benefits of, 11, 24, 144, 155; tribal,
139
diversity capitalism, 183 n. 26
diversity management, 154, 166
Dixon, Joseph Kossuth, 201 n. 148
domesticity: imperial sentiment and,
93–94, 122, 211 n. 34; sentimentalization of, 85–93, 210 n. 31
Douglas, Mary, 222 n. 142
Douglass, Frederick, 91
Driver, Harold E., 206–7 n. 14
Du Bois, W. E. B., xvi; academic ambitions of, 56–58; class and race
awareness of, 64–65, 168, 199
n. 124; on racial discrimination, 52–
55, 58, 134; Roe Cloud compared
with, 11–12, 74–75, 132; Society of
American Indians and, 79; "Talented Tenth" paradigm and, 3, 79,
134; Washington and, 75–76
Duncan, William Young, 59
Durham, Jimmie, 177

Eagle Hawk, Joseph, 229 n. 62
Eagleton, Terry, 183 n. 31
Eastman, Charles (Dr.), xvi, 3, 124, 179
n. 9; at Dartmouth, 47–48, 66, 195

inner self: cross-cultural perspectives
on, 97–99; cultural incitement of,
121–22, 223 n. 143; sentimentalization of, 94–96, 209 n. 27
Institute for Government Research
(Brookings Institute), 138, 141
interracial romance and marriage: assimilation and, 119–24; film images of,
109–10; latency production and, 103–
10; politicization of, 105; Roe Cloud's
experiences with, 100–101, 105–11
intimacy, sentimental conventions of,
99–103, 214 n. 52

Jackson, Helen Hunt, xvi, 29, 87, 91,
104, 108, 209 n. 29
Jacobs, Harriet, 91
James, C. L. R., 166
James, Henry, 90
James, William, xvi, 37, 57
Jay, Gregory, 108, 217 n. 98
Johnson, Owen, 38–39
Jones, William, 26–27, 122
Jones, William A. (BIA head), 24, 185
n. 3
Jung, Carl, 207 n. 15

Kabotie, Fred, 161
Kaplan, Amy, 93, 122, 211 n. 34
Kasson, John, 120–21
Kearney Military Academy, 55
Keasby, Lindley, 45
kinship relations: ethos of service and,
18–19, 167–73; in Indian cultures,
88–93, 110, 206 n. 14, 208 n. 17; in-
ner self and, 97–99, 112–14, 121–24
Kovel, Joel, 101–2
Krupat, Arnold, xi, 97, 168, 239 n. 28

La Flesche Picotte, Susan, 26–27
Lake Mohonk Conference of Friends of
the Indian, 26, 74, 83, 96, 128

Lake Mohonk Fund, 26
Lamere, Oliver, 17–18
Lang, Amy Schrager, 210 n. 31
Larrimore, Colleen, 187 n. 9
Last of the Mohicans, The (Cooper), 196
n. 97
latency, cultural production and con-
trol of, 103–10
Lawrence, D. H., 192 n. 66
leadership development for Indian stu-
dents, cultural activism and, 149–
52, 156 57
Leupp, Francis E. (BIA head), 25, 45–
46, 145
Lewis, David Levering, 199 n. 124
Linder, Louis, 48
Lindquist, G. E. E. (Elmer), 157
Lingelbach, Annette M., 148–49, 231
n. 77
Lipps, Oscar H., 150–52
Lipsitz, George, 162–63
literature, class and racial issues in,
36–40, 51–52, 90, 106–10, 192
n. 65, 196 n. 97
Little Crow, 16, 79
Lohmann, Carl, 73
Lomawaima, K. Tsianina, 5, 169–70
Lone Star (film), 223 n. 148
Luhan, Mabel Dodge, 141
Luhan, Tony, 141
Luhmann, Niklas, 214 n. 52
Lummis, Charles, 45
Lurie, Nancy Oestereich, 188 n. 18, 189
n. 31
Luther, Martin, 65
Lutz, Catherine, 97
Lutz, Tom, 112
Lytle, Clifford M., 146, 228 n. 46, 231
n. 74

Maddox, Lucy, 8, 182 n. 19, 182 n. 23, 195
n. 82, 200 n. 144, 205 n. 1, 232 n. 88

Parker and, 202 n. 171; on tribal culture, 80, 98, 201 n. 145

Moody, Dwight, 131

Mooney, George, 78, 82, 203 n. 174

Moor's Charity School, 186 n. 9

Morgan, Clement, 53–54

Morgan, Thomas Jefferson (BIA head), 24–25, 185 n. 3

Mory's Restaurant, 48

motherhood, historical sentimentalization of, 86–93

Mountain Wolf Woman, 180 n. 31

Mount Hermon Club at Yale, 59

Mount Hermon School, Roe Cloud at, 2, 23, 32, 54, 57, 59–60, 127–28, 131, 133, 190 n. 39

multiculturalism. See cross-cultural brokering; protomulticulturalism

nation, concept of: cult of domesticity and, 115; justification for injustice against Indians and, 91–92; missionary race and class management and, 105

National Congress of American Indians American Indian Development self-help program, 118

Native American studies, American studies and, xi–xii, xv–xvi

Nebraska Winnebago Reservation, 29–30

Needham, Rodney, 97

Negro Problem, The, 75

neurasthenia, Roe Cloud and the discourse of, 112–14

New Haven, Connecticut, Indian population in, 53, 196 n. 99

New Warriors: Native American Leaders since 1900, The (Edmunds), 6

New York Indian Welfare Society, 80–81

Nez Perce tribe, 89

Nissenbaum, Stephen, 120–21

"noble savage" stereotype, interracial marriage and, 108

nonconformity, at Yale, 35, 38–40

North, Anne Woesha Cloud, xv, 43, 162, 194 n. 75

Oberlin Seminary College, 2, 23, 57, 106, 157, 198 n. 107

Occum, Samuel, 186 n. 9

Oedipus complex, 86–89, 95, 206 n. 14, 207 n. 15

Oklahoma Indian territory, 28, 53, 108–9, 131, 161

O'Malley, Power, 98

oratory: Harvard contests in, 54; Indian tradition of, 47, 149; of Elizabeth Bender Roe Cloud, 118; of Mary Roe, 120; Roe Cloud's success in, 24, 58–59

Oregon Trail Women's Club, 163

Osage tribe, 19, 28, 45, 107, 119

outing programs for Indians, 85, 138, 146

Owens, Louis, xi

Page, Bessie, 70, 200 n. 144

Painter, Charles C., 56, 141, 198 n. 106

parental control, Roe Cloud and, 103–10

Parker, Arthur C., 1; academic training of, 162, 236 n. 3; assimilationism and, 12; Bureau of Indian Affairs and, 3, 205 n. 188; class issues and, 7; on Committee of One Hundred, 228 n. 46; on cultural pluralism, 142, 237 n. 15; on higher education for Indians, 203 n. 173, 203 n. 174, 225 n. 22; on Indian education, 77–82; on Indian performances, 182 n. 19; Montezuma and, 202 n. 171; peyote cult and, 204 n. 187

Parker, Ely, 122

Parker, Gabe E., 150–52
Parsons, David, 151–52
Peltier, Leonard, 1, 169–70
Pendleton Roundup, 163–64
performances by Indians: as cross-
    cultural brokering, 70–71, 200
    n. 144, 201 n. 145; Roe Cloud's Elihu
    Club speech as, 63–64; Roe Cloud's
    rejection of stereotypical, 12; for
    whites, 8, 181 n. 17, 182 n. 19
peyote cult: Indian divisions over, 81–
    82, 204 n. 187; Winnebago practice
    of, 17–18, 30, 78, 184 n. 38
Phelps, William Lyon, 43–44, 46, 194
    nn. 76–77
Phi Beta Kappa society, 57, 198 n. 110
Pierson, George Wilson, 34, 40, 191
    n. 47, 191 n. 48, 192 n. 65
pluralism: at American Indian In-
    stitute, 137–46; cultural, 139–41,
    227 n. 42; New Deal bureaucracy
    and, xv–xvi; racial pride and, 114
Pontiac (Chief), 47
Porter, Joy, 6
power dynamics: culture and, 16–17,
    183 n. 35; Du Bois–Washington dis-
    agreements over, 75–76; Indian cos-
    mopolitanism and, 153–57; in Roe
    Cloud–Roe correspondence, 100–103
Pratt, Richard Henry (General): Bureau
    of Indian Affairs criticized by, 136;
    Carlisle Industrial School and, 10,
    19–20; firing of, from Carlisle, 227
    n. 42; on Indian education, 63, 76–
    78, 129, 131, 133, 139, 151, 234
    n. 114; on Indian higher education,
    202–3 nn. 172–73; on interracial
    marriage, 107; Parker and, 202
    n. 171; sentimentalization of depen-
    dency by, 85; Society of American
    Indians and, 204 n. 187; on tribal
    culture, 80–81, 98, 153–54

Presbyterian missions, 41–42, 83–84,
    193 n. 71, 205 n. 3, 214 n. 50; Ameri-
    can Indian Institute and, 132; silence
    on interracial marriage of, 106–7;
    women and, 120–21, 221 n. 139
primitivist ideology: class issues and,
    43–46; Indian-white melodrama in
    popular culture and, 91; interracial
    romances and, 109–10; sentimental-
    ization of self-management and,
    105–10
private property, Indian cultures and
    the ideology of, 96
Problem of Indian Administration, The, 2,
    138, 179 n. 3; Meriam Report, 2, 96,
    137–48, 227 n. 44, 228 n. 50
professional and managerial class: Af-
    rican American integration into, 76,
    98–99; Fanon's discussion of, 123–
    24; Indian integration into, xiii, xvi,
    5, 9, 27–28, 42–43, 77, 79–80, 98,
    110–15; Roe Cloud and, 4–5, 8–9,
    27–28, 66, 129, 161–73; Yale as
    training ground for, 34, 39–40, 60
Progressive Era, 67; Indian class his-
    tory and, 6–7
property losses of Winnebago, 29–32
Protestantism: capitalism and, 10;
    family structure of Indians assaulted
    by, 95–96; Indian reform movement
    and, 29, 83, 91–93, 205 n. 1; interra-
    cial romance and marriage and,
    120–24; peyote cult and, 184 n. 38;
    reaction to Meriam Report and,
    140–41; sentimentalization through,
    83–84; women's rights and, 221
    n. 139; at Yale, 33–36. See also Pres-
    byterian missions
protomulticulturalism: assimilation
    and, 12, 183 n. 26; Haskell Institute
    activism and vocationalism and,
    146–52, 168–69, 238 n. 22; Roe

JOEL PFISTER recently served as chair of American studies and currently is chair of English at Wesleyan University. He is the author of four books, including *Critique for What? Cultural Studies, American Studies, Left Studies* (2006) and *Individuality Incorporated: Indians and the Multicultural Modern* (2004), and is a co-editor of *Inventing the Psychological: Toward a Cultural History of Emotional Life in America* (1997).

Library of Congress Cataloging-in-Publication Data

Pfister, Joel.
The Yale Indian : the education of Henry Roe Cloud /
Joel Pfister.
p. cm. — (New Americanists)
Includes bibliographical references and index.
ISBN 978-0-8223-4402-5 (cloth : alk. paper)
ISBN 978-0-8223-4421-6 (pbk. : alk. paper)
1. Cloud, Henry Roe, 1885–1950.
2. Indians of North America—Biography.
3. Yale University—Students—Biography.
4. Indians of North America—Education—
United States—History—20th century.
I. Title.
II. Series: New Americanists.
E90.C48P45 2009
371.829′97073—dc22
2009003272